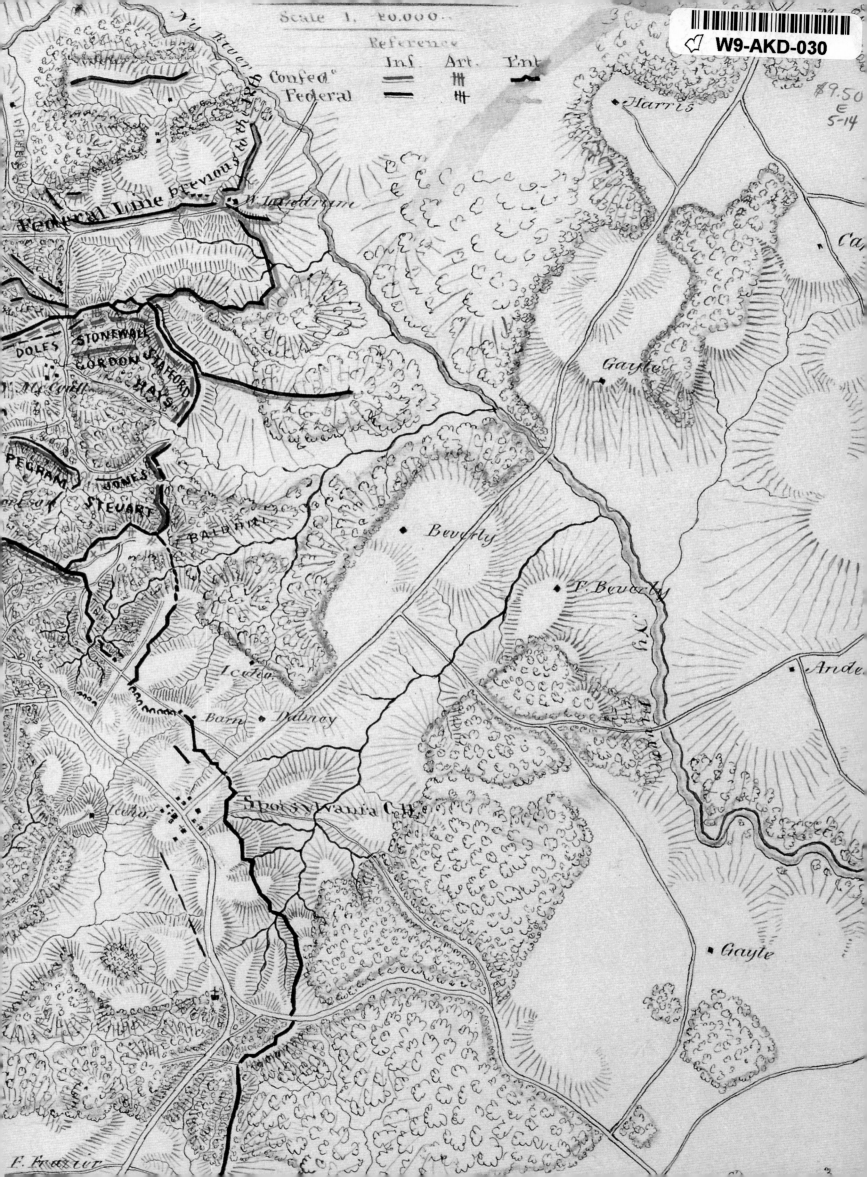

Maps of the Civil War

The Roads They Took

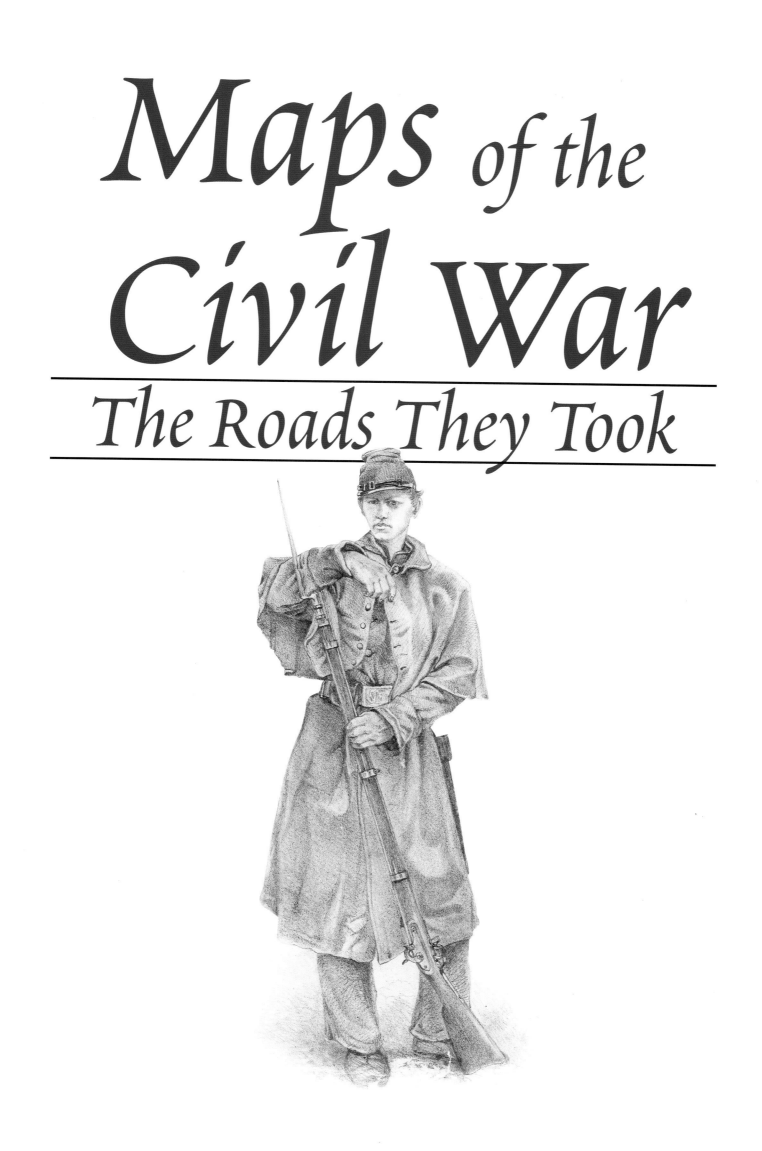

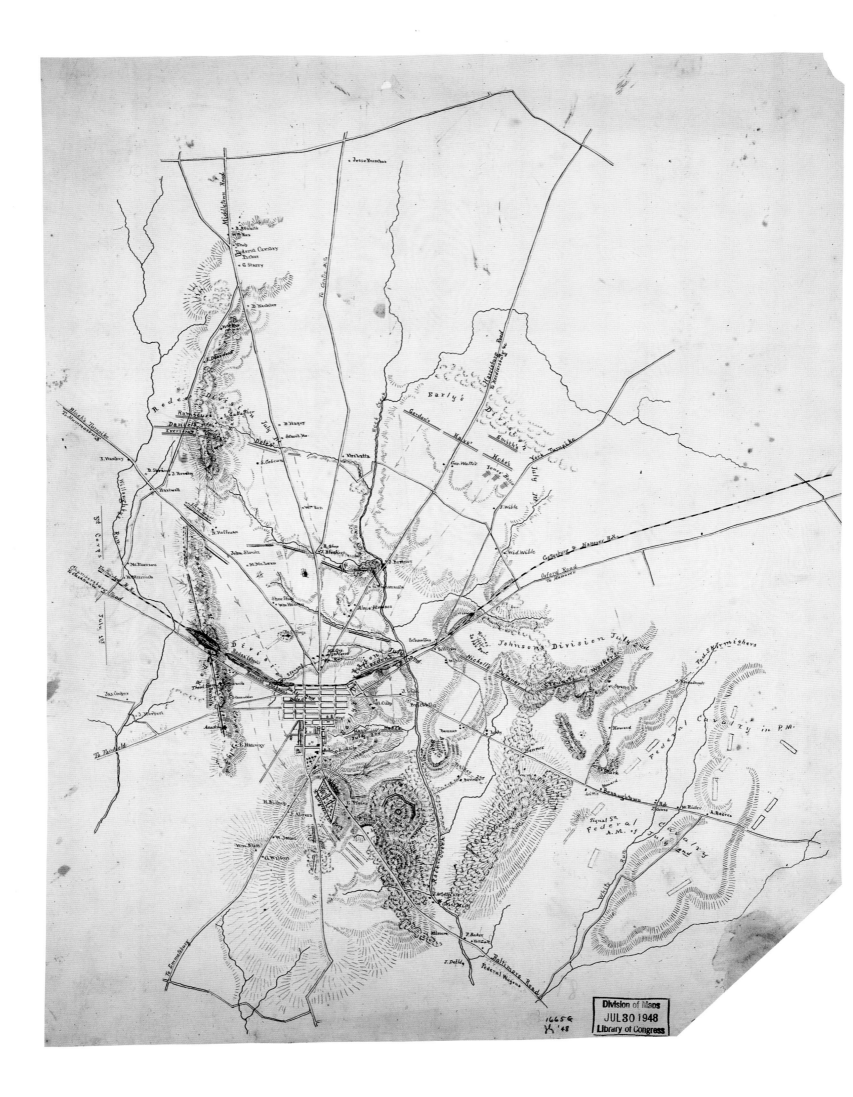

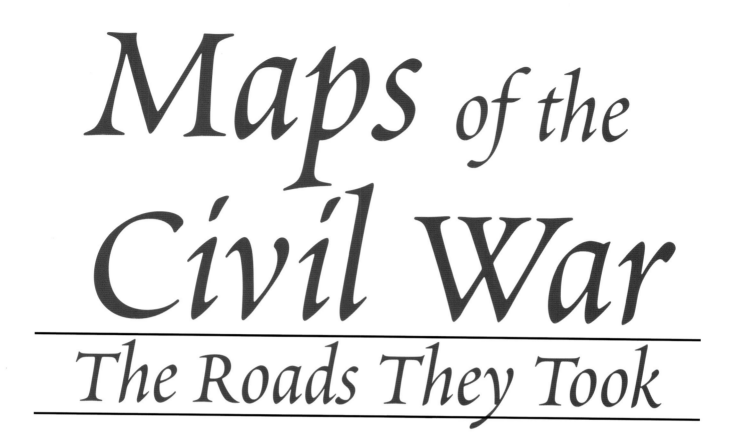

Maps *of the* Civil War

The Roads They Took

DAVID PHILLIPS

BARNES & NOBLE BOOKS

NEW YORK

A BARNES & NOBLE BOOK

©2005, 1998 by Barnes & Noble Publishing, Inc.

ISBN 0-7607-6878-1

Color separations by Radstock Repro
Printed and bound in China by SNP Leefung Printers Limited

1 3 5 7 9 10 8 6 4 2

CONTENTS PAGE: *In 1864, as part of his plan to wear down the Confederacy and prevent access to the north by denying southern armies the fertile Shenandoah Valley, Grant sent in an invading force under General Franz Sigel, who was promptly defeated by a ragtag army led by Confederate General John Breckinridge at New Market, Virginia. Lee was forced to recall Breckinridge, so the Federals reentered the valley; in response, Lee once again sent a force, under Jubal Early, to chase the northerners out. On this expedition, Early nearly captured Washington, D.C., but was repulsed at the capital's gates by a delaying action by General Lew Wallace. Retreating southwest through the valley, Early was pursued by the extremely capable General Philip Sheridan, whose orders were to take the valley once and for all. The campaign would come to an end in the battle of Cedar Creek in mid-October. On October 6, just to the west of New Market and to the north of Bridgewater, at Brock's Gap, cavalry under Confederate Brigadier General Thomas Rosser skirmished with the cavalry division commanded by Union General George A. Custer. Although the Confederate cavalry won some initial gains by raiding Union supply convoys, the northern cavalry at this point was too strong, well-equipped, and confident for the southern cavalry to handle. This superb map is from a pamphlet prepared by topographical engineer Jedidiah Hotchkiss called "Report of the camps, marches, and engagements, of the Second Corps, A.N.V."*

Dedication

To my wonderful wife, Sue Ann Phillips, whose support, hard work, and patience made this book possible.

Acknowledgments

Maps of the Civil War: The Roads They Took is the culmination of the hard work of a great number of people, all of whom deserve credit for their contributions.

This book would not have been possible without the original work of the great Civil War cartographers, who tirelessly documented each battlefield and significant raid, frequently preparing maps for the commanders before the campaigns were undertaken. Respect must also be paid to the pioneering photographers whose art has preserved the unforgettable drama of the Civil War. And, of course, credit must go to the amazing archives of the Library of Congress (and to the men and women who tend to this national treasure), where the majority of the materials in this book were found.

This book is graced with the outstanding work of several modern artists whose careful research and remarkable talents bring the war to life, including Keith Rocco, John Paul Strain, and Don Troiani.

A good portion of the research that went into locating the maps was done by the hard-working team of Nathaniel Marunas, Kevin Ullrich, and Bob Keene, who spent long hours with me at the Library of Congress. Special credit is due to editor Nathaniel Marunas, whose tireless efforts resulted in an outstanding text; designer Kevin Ullrich, who made the book a graphic marvel; and Civil War historian Phillip Tucker, whose profound knowledge of this grand conflict ensured the accuracy of this atlas.

A modern cartographer with skills rapidly approaching those possessed by the original Civil War mapmakers, Bob Keene worked diligently to see this project completed. His original maps illustrate the unique challenges posed by the terrain over which many Civil War battles were fought. Deservedly, his talents are becoming widely recognized.

Contents

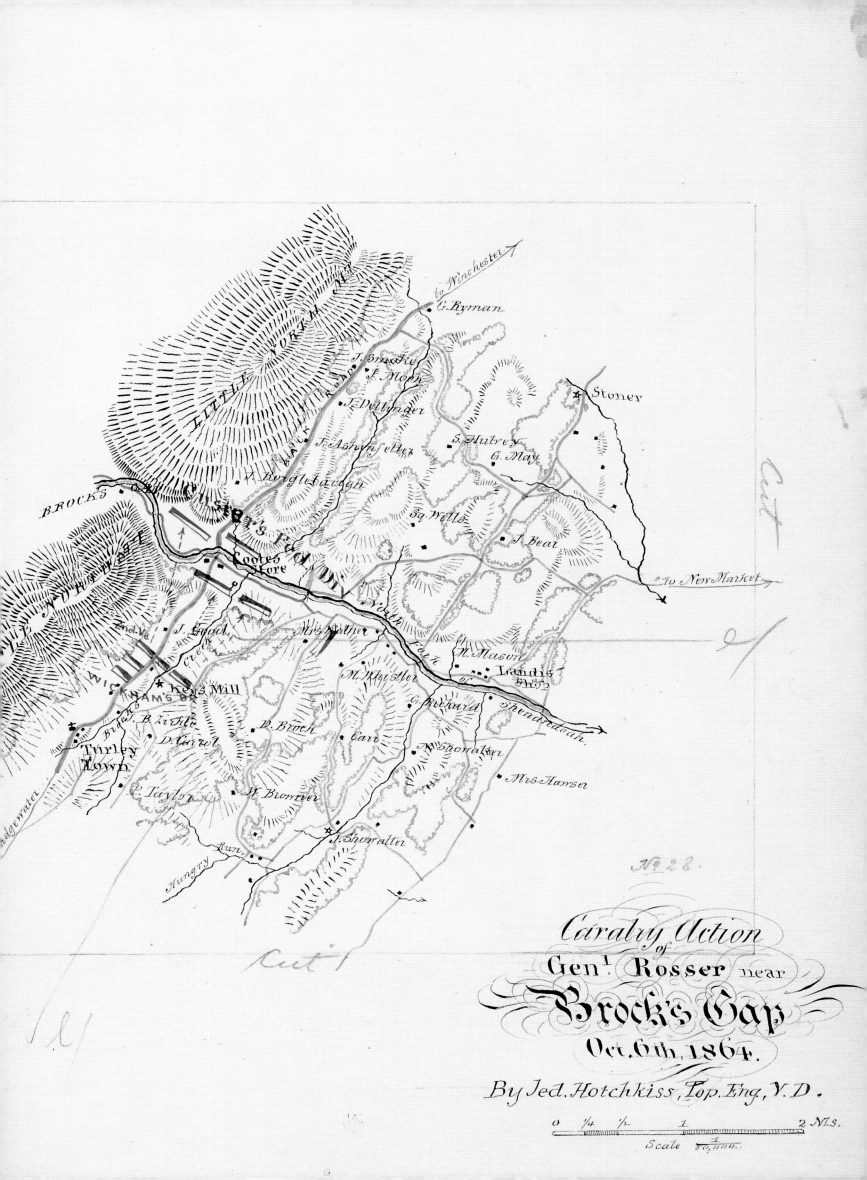

to Winchester

G. Ryman

LITTLE FORK MT.

J. Brodie

J. Moch

J. Dellinger

Stoner

J. Ashenfelter

S. Hutrey

G. May

J. Ronglebaugh

BROCKS GAP

Sq. Wills

J. Bear

Cootes Store

to New Market

North Fork

NORTH MT.

End. Va.

J. Good

Creek

Mrs Walker

M. Mason

M. Kleistler

Landis Shop

Keys Mill

G. Richard

Shenandoah

HAM'S BR.

J. Zirkle

D. Brock

Carr

M. Showalter

Turley Town

D. Carrol

Mrs Hanser

Bridgewater

P. Taylor

W. Bowman

Run

Hungry

J. Showalter

Nº 28.

Cavalry Action of Genl. Rosser near Brock's Gap Oct. 6th. 1864.

By Jed. Hotchkiss, Top. Eng. V. D.

0   ¼   ½   1   2 Mls.

Scale $\frac{1}{80,000}$

Introduction

A complex series of political events began to develop within the rapidly expanding United States of America in the aftermath of the war with Mexico. The two fundamentally different sections (North and South) of the nation began to drift further apart as each began to worry that the other might gain control of the new region captured from Mexico. Their fears stemmed from the fact that such control in turn might lead to political supremacy and influence over the socioeconomic and cultural life of the country as a whole. Specifically, what concerned both sides was the issue of whether or not slavery would be allowed to spread to the new territories.

The southern states felt particularly vulnerable when their assets were compared to those of their northern neighbors. The North had decisive advantages in industrial capacity, manpower, and agricultural potential. As a result, the South began to fear that political domination might be asserted by the North through the Federal government, particularly through congressional legislation pertaining to slavery.

Moderate politicians within the U.S. Congress crafted compromise after compromise as they sought to maintain a balance of political power between the slave-holding states and the "free" states. But the divisive forces at work around the country were reflected by changes taking place in the nation's political parties. The old Whig party had begun to divide: southern Whigs, who had been viewed as moderates, began to shift their loyalties to the Democratic party while in the North, abolitionist Whigs began to unite with the "Free Soilers," forming the nucleus of what would soon become the Republican party. Southern radicals, called "Fire Eaters," and the northern radical abolitionists began to level increasingly antagonistic rhetoric toward one another. The nation began to feel the strain.

In order to survive as a political force, the northern Democrats had to deal with their rivals, the antislavery Whigs and "Free Soilers," just as their moderate allies in the South, the southern Democrats, were forced to cope with the increasingly hostile activities of the radical "Fire Eaters." The nation's moderates continued to lose ground and supporters at a time when the nation's political leadership was especially weak.

The Democratic Convention of 1852 had remained deadlocked with regard to the nomination of a candidate for the presidency through nearly fifty ballots when finally the delegates turned in desperation to a northerner who would be acceptable to the southerners: Franklin Pierce. After defeating Winfield Scott in the national election, President Pierce moved into the White House. Unfortunately, he had just lost his son in a railroad accident. His wife was overcome with grief and Pierce, in an effort to find companionship, turned to his southern friends for support, especially the Secretary of War, Jefferson Davis, recently the senator from Mississippi. This special relationship

ABOVE: *Approximately ten million African slaves were brought to the New World—both North and South America—from the 1500s through the mid-1800s. As the institution of slavery began to come under direct attack by abolitionists, southern leaders began to react aggressively to protect the institution they felt was the underpinning of their society. For a while they managed to maintain a balance of power within the national government, but there were increasingly strident calls from reactionary southerners for the creation of a new country where slavery would be protected from any outside interference. As the radicals on each side of the issue began to gain control over national politics, an internecine war became all but inevitable. A young Abraham Lincoln stands on the left in this illustration showing a slave auction.*

OPPOSITE: *The representatives of the six states originally adopting the Ordinance of Secession met in Montgomery, Alabama, on February 14, 1861, to form a new nation. They quickly adopted a new constitution based on the original document prepared by the nation's founding fathers, designed a new flag, and chose a new president. Jefferson Davis, born in Kentucky, had relocated to Mississippi and served his adopted state as an officer in the Mexican War, in congress, in the senate, and in the president's cabinet as Secretary of War. He was well prepared by his governmental experience to attempt to guide the new nation through its birth pains, but no one contemplated the degree of difficulty Davis would face over the next four years.*

with President Pierce gave Davis opportunities to advance his agenda in the political maneuvering in Washington, D.C.

Davis had political ambitions of his own, and in an attempt to become a nationally recognized political figure, championed the effort to build the transcontinental railroad, which would connect California with the nation's eastern seaboard. Davis supported a southern route for the railroad; this would eventually enrich the southern cities along the route, which would benefit from trade with California. But he faced powerful competition for the new railroad, which would bring prosperity to whatever land it crossed.

Illinois' senator, Stephen Douglas, wanted the new railroad to follow a northerly route that would connect with Chicago. The challenge he faced was to generate sufficient support from southern congressmen to bring the railroad through an area where slavery had been forbidden by the Missouri Compromise of 1820. The compromise, Henry Clay's great accomplishment, permitted the entry of Missouri as a slave state provided that no additional slave states be allowed into the Union if they were above 30 degrees, 30 minutes latitude (the southern boundary of Missouri). At the same time, Maine entered the Union as a free state, maintaining the national balance—eleven free and eleven slave states.

Determined to secure the railroad for Illinois, Douglas designed a concession package that more or less guaranteed the support of most southern political figures for his efforts. He designed a bill organizing a new pair of territories—areas that would eventually enter the Union as states—with a provision repealing the portion of the Missouri Compromise that prevented slavery at that latitude. Southern congressmen did not hesitate to support this bill, which would open a large region—the future states of Kansas and Nebraska—to the expansion of slavery, where such a practice had been forbidden for thirty years.

Douglas, like Jefferson Davis, had national ambitions of his own and he skillfully maneuvered himself into a position where he felt he had gained the support of both northern and southern Democrats. After all, Douglas had suc-

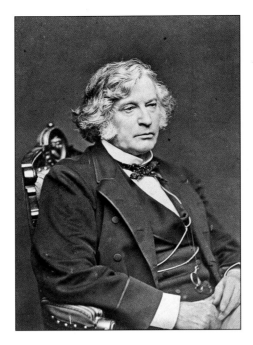

ABOVE: *Massachusetts' senator Charles Sumner was a prominent supporter of the northern abolitionists during a period when the spirit of compromise had vanished from the U.S. government. Sumner made a speech on the floor of the Senate on May 22, 1856, in which he ridiculed a senator from South Carolina, Andrew Butler. Soon afterward, Sumner was brutally attacked with a cane by Butler's nephew, a congressman from South Carolina. This unprovoked attack was widely reported in newspapers and the story was to have a profound impact on a reader in Kansas: John Brown.*

cessfully lobbied for the northern route of the transcontinental railroad while at the same time opening Kansas up for colonization by slave owners.

As the Kansas-Nebraska Act was cleared through Congress, the Whig party began to collapse. The southern Whigs voted with southern Democrats on the new act as they separated from the northern wing, which was joining the "Free Soilers" as the new Republican party was forming.

Outraged by the Kansas-Nebraska Act of 1854, many northerners began to rally to the new political party, the Republicans, as a form of protest as they demanded the legislation's repeal. Northern sentiment can be measured by the fact that the newly formed Republican party gained control of the House of Representatives in the midterm elections of 1854. The sudden shift of political power was clearly a reaction to the legislation.

Northern Whigs, many of them accomplished politicians, had become abolitionists while others were content to tolerate slavery in the South (though they were unwilling to allow it to spread). Slavery had been dying out gradually in many areas of the North, and the gradual extinction of slavery was the goal of the northern moderates. Not long after, these moderates, as Republicans, were able to neutralize Douglas' railroad ambitions by gaining support of the central route. They gained additional support for their new party through the proposal of the Homestead Act. They also created high protective tariffs to protect the nation's developing industry, gaining the support of industrialists as they also supported liberal immigration policies that would facilitate the arrival of inexpensive labor to the country. The new Republicans rapidly became a viable political party, although as yet they lacked widespread national appeal.

Skilled political strategists within the Republican party began to plan for election wins in all of the free states to secure control of the House of Representatives, and then add to their strength by gaining the presidency. Their skilled maneuvering eventually proved successful, and a Republican government formed (after experiencing only a single loss in a presidential election) that represented only the interests of the North. The monolithic Republican tenure would come to pose a major threat to the rest of the country.

The United States was entering the most volatile period in its short history, and strong leadership was needed to guide the young nation through these difficult times. The country could have used a skillful leader along the lines of George Washington, who would have possessed sufficient prestige to be respected by both sides. Unfortunately, the Whig party was actively unraveling and the Democrats—in order to win the White House—had to nominate a northern Democrat who was acceptable to the southern wing of their party. Equally unfortunate for the endangered country, Washingtons and Jeffersons were in short supply at a time when they were badly needed. Setting the stage for the calamitous events that led to the Civil War, the Democrats nominated James Buchanan.

The election of 1856 may have sealed the fate of the country. Buchanan carried the Democratic party's banner while the Republicans fielded the young, dynamic, and nationally known John C. Fremont. Former president Millard Filmore led a third-party challenge as the "Know Nothing" candidate and probably unwittingly sabotaged Fremont's bid by taking away sufficient Republican votes to allow Buchanan to win. Unfortunately, Buchanan possessed neither the charisma nor the strength necessary to guide the national vessel through the treacherous waters that lay ahead.

The deadly combination of the election of Buchanan and the extremely serious political events that unfolded shortly thereafter swiftly endangered the unity of the nation. Within days of Buchanan's inauguration, the Supreme Court decided the landmark Dred Scott case (to which, incidentally, Buchanan had made reference in his inaugural address, stating his belief that the case would settle the question of slavery in the territories once and for all).

Under different circumstances, the case might not have caused such a

furor, but because of the heated congressional and national debate over the issue of slavery, the decision that Scott was not a free man despite his residencies in nonslave states further divided the parties and polarized the nation. Coming on the heels of the outrage expressed over the Kansas-Nebraska Act, nearly all of the remaining moderates in the North expressed their anger

ABOVE: *Having been a strident abolitionist for years, John Brown entered freely into the bloody guerrilla warfare in Kansas, killing several unarmed southerners in the process. After raising funds in the North, he began to plan to incite a full-scale slave uprising. On October 11, 1859, Brown led his small band of supporters into Harper's Ferry, Virginia, the site of a major arsenal. U.S. troops under Colonel Robert E. Lee subdued Brown and his men. After a highly publicized trial, Brown was hanged on December 2, 1859.*

LEFT: *John Brown spread violence in "Bleeding Kansas" and gathered a band of followers—including his sons—who attempted to attract runaway slaves to his cause, arm them, and lead them in a revolt against slavery. A hero to much of the population of the North, Brown's name became a rallying cry for northern abolitionists as secession and, eventually, Civil War became realities.*

by adopting increasingly abolitionist sentiments. Events had shown that the will of the majority of the population—and the will of their elected representatives in congress—were insufficient to halt the spread of slavery into the new territories, which were certain to become new states. They had seen the Missouri Compromise trivialized in the struggle to gain control of the transcontinental railroad and the prosperity that it would bring. And they had watched in anger as radical and combative southerners rushed to settle the new Kansas Territory and set into place a de facto proslavery constitution before sufficient numbers of "Free Soilers" could arrive to dispute the control of the new region's government.

It was, however, the actions of a single man—John Brown—that galvanized the as-yet-uninvolved populations of both sections and pushed them closer to embracing the radical elements of both the North and South who were struggling for control of the entire political process. John Brown and a few radical followers struck a highly visible blow in retaliation for the beating of Senator Charles Sumner by a South Carolina congressman, "Bully" Brooks. Brooks' attack on a member of the U.S. Senate, coupled with such "border ruffian" provocations as the attack on the town of Lawrence, Kansas, had angered Brown to the point that he felt action had to be taken.

The morning sun on May 24, 1856, rose on a terrible scene on the Kansas plains, where Brown and his men had massacred a half dozen people. Six proslavery settlers—all unarmed and two of them teenage boys—had been hacked to death and several of the bodies had been mutilated as a grim reminder that people with similar beliefs might suffer the same fate. It is a good indicaton of the unusual state of the nation at the time that Brown's murderous reprisal for the beating of Senator Sumner was not seen for the clear-cut murder it was.

Unfortunately for the fate of the nation, Brown was not immediately arrested and soon after, confused reports about the event began to appear in newspapers. A congressional investigation into the affair was essentially canceled as abolitionist members of the committee interfered with the testimony of key witnesses. By the end of the investigation, Brown's brutal slaughter was seen in the North just as he had seen it—as a major blow for the freedom of slaves.

As gruesome as was Brown's first assault, it was his second strike against slavery that sent a collective shudder of

fear through the entire South. Brown and twenty-one of his followers, backed by both funds and material from abolitionist supporters in the North, marched into Harper's Ferry on October 16, 1859, in an attempt to capture the United States Armory located there. His plan was to capture weapons that would then be used to arm the slaves expected to rally to him throughout the deep Virginia valley. Hostages were taken, but in the process of capturing the armory, some citizens (including the mayor) and some of the attackers (including two of Brown's sons) were either killed or wounded. This was the state of affairs when Federal troops, marines under the command of Colonel Robert E. Lee, arrived on the scene to take control of the situation.

After a short period of negotiation carried out by another Federal officer who would serve in the Confederate army, Lieutenant J.E.B. Stuart, Lee ordered the marines to assault the firehouse where Brown and his followers had taken refuge. Soon Brown and his men were in custody and awaiting justice at the hands of Virginia's court system.

As with his killings in Kansas, Brown's latest outrages held only a local significance, and if the case had been left to local courts Brown's attack would have been tried as the criminal act it was. Unfortunately, the entire raid and its aftermath gained national prominence as political players on both sides clamored from the sidelines.

Rather than the attack itself, what captured the attention of the southern population was Brown's intention to rally, arm, and lead slaves out of a mountain fastness to attack slave owners. The slave-holding areas had experienced rebellions in the past—certainly all the South recalled vividly Nat Turner's rebellion, which had left nearly sixty whites dead during more than a week of terror in Virginia in August 1831. The thought of a large-scale slave uprising was understandably horrifying to slave owners in the South, where approximately 3.5 million slaves were held in bondage. Many southerners knew that this condition of forced labor was wrong and that the slaves had every reason to rise in revolt. Slave owners anticipated that deadly vengeance would be exacted should

their slaves manage to organize and arm themselves.

Southerners' fears were also augmented by recent historical events, specifically the slave revolt that had occurred in Haiti at the turn of the century. Slaves on the French-controlled island were able to take advantage of the chaos created by the French Revolution, staging a bloody insurrection. The whites began to flee northward to the United States; those who remained in Haiti were all massacred by 1803. Thanks to the refugees arriving in the United States, terrifying stories of the revolt were circulated among southerners, who must have seen the parallels with their own situation.

The white population in the South had a great deal to fear from a major slave revolt, which John Brown knew only too well. And to white southerners, the Republicans were seen as conspirators with Brown and the other abolitionists in the North. By the end of the trial of John Brown, much of the population of the South had moved toward accepting the strategy staked out by the region's radical politicians—secession.

The trial of John Brown occurred as the nation prepared for the 1860 national elections, and emotions were running high in both sections of the nation. After winning only 40 percent of the popular vote, but carrying every free state other than New Jersey, Abraham Lincoln—the nominee of the Republican party—was elected president. Since the new party had been associated with the abolitionist movement, most southerners felt that the tall midwesterner was an antislavery sympathizer. To a large degree, they were right.

OPPOSITE: *The United States' new president, Abraham Lincoln, was fifty-two years old when he made the journey from Springfield, Illinois, to Washington, D.C., for his inauguration. Convinced there would be an ambush set for Lincoln in Baltimore, his bodyguards slipped him into the city after dark. He would soon call for seventy-five thousand volunteers to suppress the southern rebellion. Rather than participate in an effort to coerce their sister states under force of arms, the remainder of the southern states joined the new Confederacy. Lincoln would preside over the nation during the most difficult period in its history.*

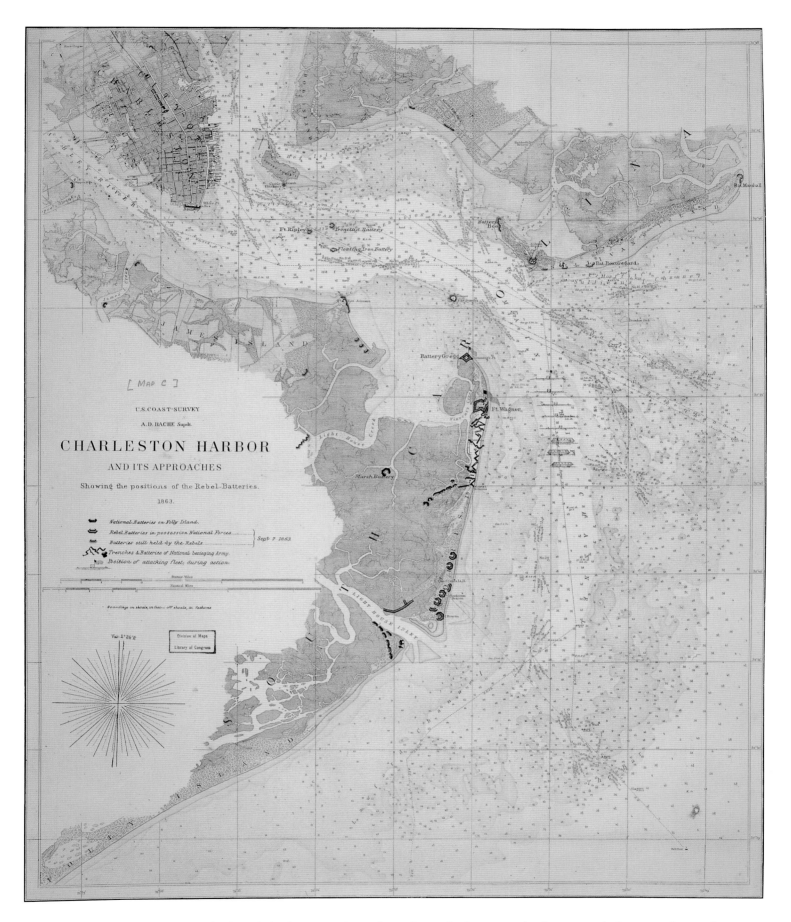

ABOVE: *The Civil War began in the harbor of Charleston, South Carolina, when Federal troops under the command of Major Robert Anderson evacuated their position at Fort Moultrie on Sullivan's Island for more defensible positions at nearby Fort Sumter. Within two weeks, the supplies intended for the besieged Federals, shipped aboard the* Star of the West, *were turned back by South Carolina's artillery batteries. Nonetheless, the trapped garrison was able to hold out in Fort Sumter as the state troops reinforced their positions. War became a grim reality at 4:30 in the morning on April 12, 1861, when secessionist Edmund Ruffin fired the first cannon on the fort. Anderson returned fire from Sumter's lower, protected batteries, but the weight of arms against him was too great for his troops to resist for long. By 1863, as this map shows, the Confederates were solidly in control of the region.*

Lincoln opposed slavery and was quite clear on his feelings about that peculiar institution, but he was no abolitionist. He was squarely on the record as opposing any extension of slavery into the new territories and he called the institution "an unqualified evil," but he was also born in the South. He was from Kentucky (as was Jefferson Davis) and he and his party had carefully crafted a political platform that avoided a single-minded opposition to slavery. The Republicans continued to favor a liberalized immigration policy, high tariffs, the Homestead Act, and funding for the transcontinental railroad. There appeared to be a concerted Republican effort to show the South's population that they were a national party with broad appeal, not the group of antislavery fanatics that they had been painted. The Republicans had rejected as potential nominees such nationally recognized politicians as William H. Seward and Salmon P. Chase because both had made strongly antisouthern statements that were a part of the public record. In an effort to be conciliatory toward their angry cousins in the South, the Republicans had selected a candidate who was really a moderate on the subject of slavery. Unfortunately, passions had been running at such a fevered pitch for so long that many of their efforts went unnoticed in the South.

The radicals of South Carolina were the first to react to Lincoln's election. On December 20, 1860, the state's secession convention voted to leave the Union. In January 1861, six additional states joined her. All of this was occurring as Buchanan sat in the White House as a "lame duck" president, with a cabinet that was essentially useless to him. One member of his cabinet, Secretary of War John B. Floyd, was actively engaged in the transfer of arms and war materials from Federal armories in the North to new locations in the South. Floyd, a former governor of Virginia, was on the verge of indictment thanks to possible congressional hearings regarding his involvement in the embezzlement of Indian Trust Funds and the outright selling of an army post to real-estate developers. By working for the cause of secession, this southern partisan was actively sabotaging any effort on the part of President Buchanan to mediate the dispute, leaving the president in a helpless position.

One of Kentucky's senators, John J. Crittenden, developed a plan that would require a constitutional amendment and would result in a division of the new territories into free and slave sections across the continent instead of splitting up the country by following the old Missouri Compromise line. Lincoln's opposition to the spread of slavery in the territories put an end to this effort. Former president John Tyler, a Virginian, managed a peace conference that was held in Washington, D.C., in February 1861, but it failed to bring any new initiatives forward, concentrating instead on a rehashing of Crittenden's earlier proposals. Lincoln and the congress made one attempt at reconciliation by passing an amendment that would guarantee forever the existence of slavery in the states where it was currently allowed, but this didn't offer the South anything that it didn't already have. And anyway, the excitement that had been generated by the thought of creating a new nation—many southerners were by this point prepared to fight "a second American Revolution" to make it a reality—precluded any interest among southern secessionists in further attempts at compromise.

ABOVE: *Once South Carolina seceded from the Union, its leaders knew they would be able to assert their full independence only by gaining control of the Federal forts inside Charleston Harbor. Major Anderson, the local Federal commander, managed to prevent any actions on the part of his soldiers that could have precipitated an attack by the secessionists, but once he understood the magnitude of the threat facing his small, isolated garrison, he ordered a general evacuation from the weaker positions at Fort Moultrie for a stronger position nearby—Fort Sumter.*

Although fewer than half of the slave states had actually left the Union, seven states that had seceded met in Montgomery, Alabama, to establish the new nation just before Lincoln was inaugurated. The new Confederate States of America retained nearly all of the laws of their former nation—and left the Constitution nearly untouched. Passions ran high and militia companies began drilling in the streets of small towns across the country as both sides prepared to fight.

The South had an initial advantage in that it could accomplish its military goals by simply avoiding conflict with the North. It had already achieved all of its leadership's stated goals by seceding from the Union. The North, however, had taken the position that secession was illegal and prepared to take steps to preserve the Union by force. The momentum generated by the events of the day was mounting rapidly by the time of Lincoln's inaugural address, in which he stated: "In your hands, my dissatisfied fellow-countrymen, and not in mine is the momentous issue of civil war. The government will not assail you. You can have no conflict without yourselves being the aggressors. You have no oath registered in heaven to destroy the government, while I shall have the most solemn one to 'preserve, protect, and defend it.'"

One part plea for reconciliation, one part threat, President Lincoln's words were nonetheless insufficient to prevent the devastating events of the next four years.

RIGHT: *Located within the harbor at Charleston, South Carolina, Fort Sumter became a target for Confederate guns as the southern army attempted to force the sur-render of the Federal garrison. In early 1864, toward the end of the war, the mason-ry structure became a target of Union guns as Federal forces began to pound the fortress into rubble. In the later bombardment, the old fort suffered far more damage than it had in April 1861, when South Carolina's gunners had forced the surrender of Major Robert Anderson and sparked the Civil War.*

The Civil War in 1861

The defensive posture adopted by the Confederacy was well-matched to the social, political, and military realities the new government faced. Besides their safety, the southerners' very way of life was threatened, making the region's defense a cause everyone could passionately support; this made for a committed, inspired army that enjoyed the nearly unequivocal support of the population it was sworn to protect. Politically, the new government would have to win recognition in the eyes of the world before it could establish itself as a nation; the fact that the southern army had their backs to the wall ensured sympathy from outside observers, if not actual recognition. Finally, the South was geographically well-suited to a defensive campaign. In the eastern portion, the Blue Ridge and Allegheny mountain ranges provided a natural barrier that ran roughly north to south. And although the Union navy would shortly establish control of the ocean approaches, many of the east-west running rivers that supplied the Chesapeake Bay belonged to the South and provided decent protection against invasion. In addition, the soldiers of the Confederate army were more intimately familiar than their Union counterparts with the terrain over which the war would be fought.

Of course, the southerners had other advantages at the beginning of the war, too. For one thing, the military was blessed with many of the most talented of the country's commanders, whereas in the North the antiquated beauracracy of the army was populated with many commanders who owed their positions to political favoritism rather than ability. The ineptitude and back-stabbing of the northern commanders proved to be a major disadvantage: in the opening years of the war, the overwhelmingly better-equipped and more populous armies of the North were nonetheless repeatedly bested by far-smaller but more competently led Confederate armies.

Unfortunately, the South was not able to extract itself from Union affairs quite so smoothly as might have been hoped. By not actually playing the role of the aggressor, the South could have left the northern government in a position where it could accomplish its stated goal—preservation of the Union—only by attacking the Confederacy, a move that would have caused an outcry from many camps, both domestic and foreign. As it turned out, the South was forced into an act of aggression that weakened its political advantage. While the last strains of the overture to war were being played throughout the distintegrating country, the old symbol of national unity, "Old Glory," was being removed from all national property in the South as the slave-holding states assumed control of their own affairs. In two places in the South, however, the Federal presence continued to make itself felt: at Fort Pickens, near Pensacola, Florida, and at Fort Moultrie, located in Charleston Harbor, South Carolina. These symbols of Federal occupation were an embarrassment to the Confederacy.

Fort Moultrie was far too large to be defended by the small garrison stationed there to defend it. Accordingly, its Kentuckian commander, Major Robert Anderson—clearly seeing the threat to his troops posed by the first stirring of the winds of war—decided to withdraw to a smaller, more easily defended fortification nearby: Fort Sumter.

Fort Sumter

The commander of the Federal facilities at Fort Moultrie in Charleston Harbor had been an interesting selection. Major Robert Anderson's father had had the honor of the same command during the Revolutionary War and had been forced to surrender his colonial garrison to the British. The younger Anderson was a southerner by birth and had married a woman from Georgia. He had arrived at Charleston in late November 1860— only a short month prior to South Carolina's secession. He had been assigned to the post by John B. Floyd, the man who as Secretary of War of the United States of America under Buchanan had been transferring arms from Federal arsenals to armories in the South. Floyd had assumed that the southern-born Anderson would swiftly join the secessionists when he was selected for his assignment, but the commander at Fort Moultrie was a professional army officer who followed his conscience according to the dictates of personal honor. He resolved to defend his position if he were attacked. The first test of his resolve as well as his leadership was not long in coming.

On January 9, just before daybreak, the chartered paddle-wheeler *Star of the West*

entered Charleston harbor with supplies and two hundred soldiers to reinforce the Union garrison at Fort Sumter. As it came within two miles (3.2km) of the Federal fort, Confederate gunners at the Morris Island Battery opened fire, but the steamer passed by with only slight damage. As the vessel neared Fort Sumter, Confederate gunners at nearby Fort Moultrie (which had fallen after Anderson and his garrison had abandoned it) opened fire as well. The ship's captain was forced to turn the boat about to escape destruction or capture as an armed schooner approached.

South Carolina's armed forces had fired on the national flag for the first time, and Anderson would have been fully justified in returning fire upon Fort Moultrie, which lay well within the range of the guns at Fort Sumter. Lacking clear orders and hoping to avoid civil war, however, Anderson didn't direct his gunners to fire and the incident was allowed to pass without erupting into open war between the two sides. President Buchanan would have been justified in ordering the army and navy into action against South Carolina, but the president—as well as the nation's armed forces—were totally unprepared to go to war.

Jefferson Davis, the president of the Confederacy, acted swiftly by sending commissioners to Washington, D.C., to discuss the

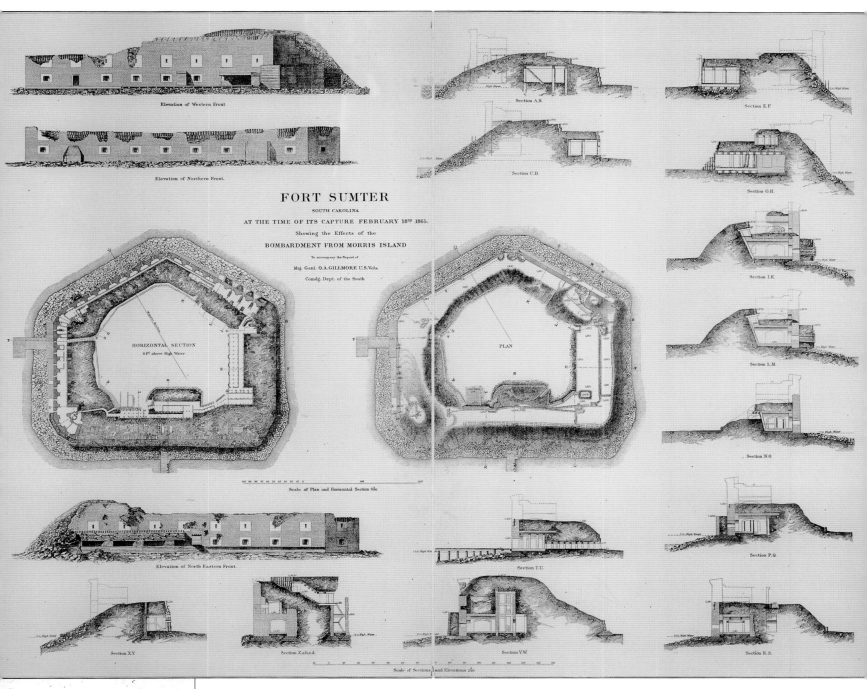

FORT SUMTER

SOUTH CAROLINA

AT THE TIME OF ITS CAPTURE FEBRUARY 18TH 1865.

Showing the Effects of the

BOMBARDMENT FROM MORRIS ISLAND

To accompany the Report of

Maj. Genl. Q.A.GILLMORE U.S.Vols.

Comdg. Dept. of the South

problem presented to the new country by the presence of Federal forts within their national boundary. Informed that the forts would not be resupplied without sufficient formal notification, the commissioners departed as Lincoln—in office for only a few days—struggled with the enormous problem facing him. The forts were militarily insignificant, but what happened to them was of the utmost political importance. Should Lincoln decide to evacuate the forts, there was the possibility that his supporters in the North would lessen their enthusiasm for the Union and become accustomed to having a new nation on their southern border, particularly since the alternative was to fight an expensive war with a neighboring enemy. If Lincoln were to order the military to reinforce either of the forts, however, Davis would be able to cite it as Federal provocation

ABOVE: *Fort Sumter was positioned strategically at the entrance to Charleston's harbor, the apex of the fort's pentagon shape pointing directly toward Fort Moultrie. Moultrie was evacuated by the Union force stationed there for the comparative safety of Sumter, where some of the defenders ignored orders to occupy the safety of the lower levels, instead climbing to the upper positions to fire preloaded heavy guns at the Confederates. Despite these efforts, the northern soldiers were eventually captured and the fort reduced. With revealing before-and-after profiles of its defensive works, this map from 1865 shows the even more severe beating that the relatively well-protected Sumter took toward the end of the war as the Union army recaptured it.*

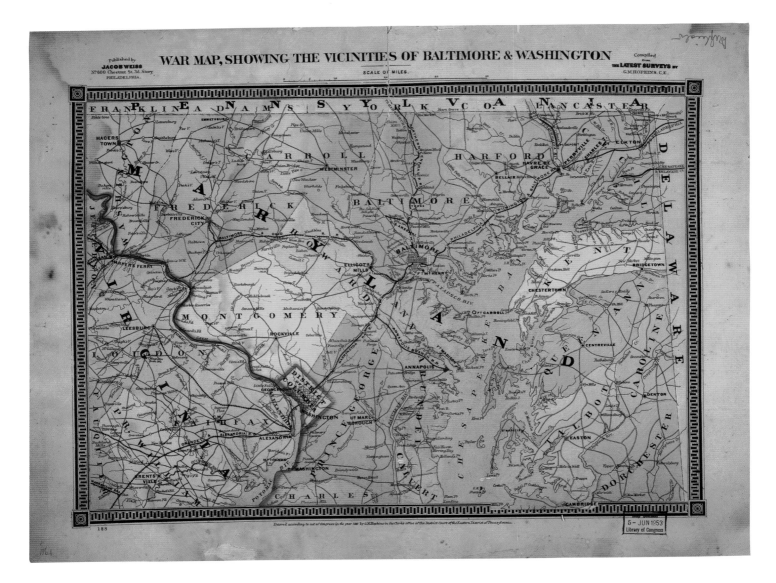

ABOVE: *Reinforcements arriving to defend Washington, D.C., had to pass through the streets of Baltimore, Maryland, a city with strong pro-Confederate sentiments. As one volunteer Union regiment, the 6th Massachusetts Infantry Regiment, marched to a connecting rail station, a mob attacked one company of soldiers. When one soldier was killed by a gunshot from the crowd, the volunteer company opened fire, leaving twelve bodies in the streets as the New Englanders marched away. Initially, President Lincoln avoided any form of conflict with the citizens of Baltimore, fearing that any action on his part could propel slaveholding Maryland, which bordered Washington, D.C., into the new Confederacy. Once sufficient numbers of troops were on hand to adequately defend the nation's capital, Lincoln moved to deal with the unruly citizens in his neighboring city to the north. Union soldiers entered Baltimore on May 12, 1861, and arrested many pro-Confederacy citizens, imprisoning them without the benefit of trial. This map clearly demonstrates the vulnerable location of Washington, D.C., which was surrounded by slave states and had only a single supply line, which passed through nearby Baltimore, to the industrial centers of the North.*

and thereby rally the remaining slave states to the support of the Confederacy. Lincoln faced a monumental problem that would cost him either way he went, but a decision had to be made soon because the food supply at the besieged Fort Sumter was growing short.

Lincoln chose a third route, one that might not offend the new leaders of the Confederacy but at the same time would demonstrate a commitment to maintaining the Federal garrison. On March 29, 1861, he gave the order to resupply only the provisions of the garrison at Fort Sumter, and on April 8, he notified South Carolina's governor of his decision. The next move was up to Jefferson Davis and the members of South Carolina's militia encircling Sumter.

Davis was faced with a problem not unlike that recently faced by Lincoln. Each had to maintain the sovereignty of his respective nation; any wavering would result in loss of support within a large block of undecided states, primarily those of the all-important upper South where the decision to secede had not yet been made, and the border states of Missouri, Maryland, and Delaware. Lincoln and Davis were both playing to this large audience. The balance of political and military power would depend on the alignment of these key states.

In retrospect, just as Lincoln had had little choice other than to provide provisions to Fort Sumter's garrison or lose the post to the Confederacy in an embarrassing surrender, Davis had little choice in his actions either. Once Lincoln had chosen to resupply or reinforce Sumter, the Confederacy had to attack it. The new Confederacy would be seen as a pretender—not only by the undecided states but by foreign nations, important for trade, as well—if it proved unable to remove the remaining Federal troops from within her borders. If the troops were captured or destroyed, however, the uncommitted slave states could be expected to rally to the new nation, which would have proven its strength. Part of the attraction to the undecided states was that a strong Confederacy capable of managing its internal security considerably allayed fears of any future northern-inspired slave rebellions. Thus, Davis decided to allow an attack at either Fort Pickens in Florida or against Fort Sumter in South Carolina. Once notified that supplies were being dispatched to Anderson, Davis sent orders to his on-the-scene

BELOW: *Commanding General Winfield Scott, America's leading Mexican War hero, was seventy-five when Fort Sumter was fired upon. The overall commander of the Federal army planned a gigantic siege of the Confederacy that would rely on the Federal navy to blockade the South's coastal areas while a large army was recruited and trained for an invasion of the South. Once a superior force was assembled, he proposed a methodical campaign to dismember the Confederacy by using the Mississippi River to move Union troops into southern territory, thereby splitting the South in two. This derisive cartoon map published by J.B. Elliot of Cincinnati, Ohio, in 1861, was representative of the scorn expressed in the northern media for Scott's plan, which seemed to anticipate a prolonged conflict and war of attrition. In the end, the embargo proved decisive in crippling the South's ability to wage a lengthy war in a conflict that must have seemed by just the second year that it might never end. History has proven Scott to be one of the few Union strategists who had a competent grasp of the big picture early on in the war.*

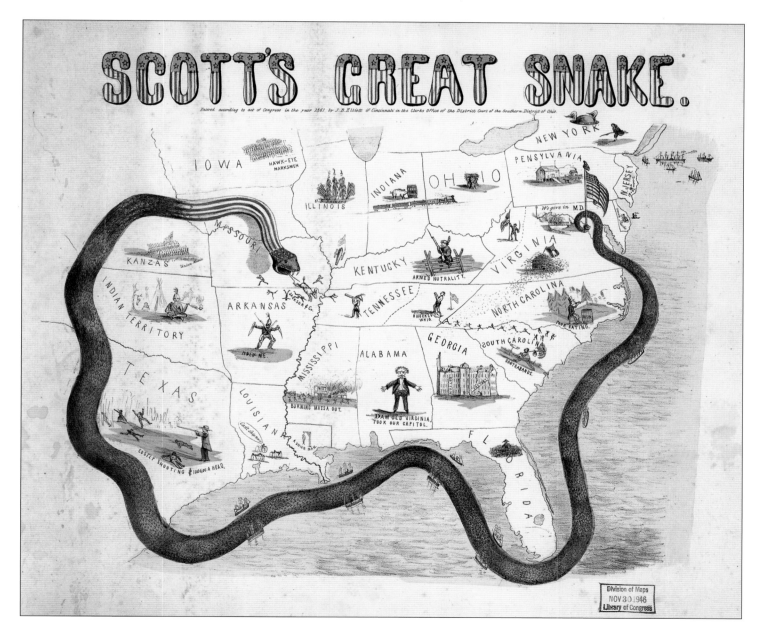

commander, Brigadier General P.G.T. Beauregard: no provisions were to arrive at Fort Sumter.

In the afternoon of April 11, 1861, a small boat was rowed from Charleston, into the harbor, and then out to Fort Sumter with three passengers bearing a note from Beauregard to Major Anderson demanding the surrender of the small fortress. As would happen in countless engagements throughout the Civil War, there had been a previous association of these two officers in the U.S. Army. Anderson had taught artillery tactics to Beauregard when the latter attended West Point. A part of the note mentioned: "The flag which you have upheld for so long and with so much fortitude...may be saluted by you on taking it down."

Anderson made one final attempt to prevent the war he feared would soon break out once Beauregard ordered his batteries to commence firing. Short of food and unable to obtain additional rations, Anderson admitted frankly to the officers delivering Beauregard's ultimatum that he would be "starved out" in only a few days. With this statement, he provided an opportunity for the Confederacy to capture Fort Sumter without firing the shots that would have swiftly led to full-scale combat.

Davis had already decided that he must assert the authority of the new nation during this time, however, and informed Beauregard that unless Anderson could provide a precise time of surrender, Fort Sumter should be "reduced." Anderson told them that he would be forced to surrender by noon on April 15, unless he was provided supplies or additional instructions from his superiors. Although he had in good faith met the letter of the demand made upon him by Davis' messengers, Anderson was shortly given a note by the Confederates informing him that he would be fired upon within one hour. Shaking hands with the emissaries, Anderson prepared to face a bombardment. Jefferson Davis ordered the attack he felt the Confederacy needed to make if it were to attract additional support and survive as a nation. He had chosen to strike in a location where the Confederacy was strongest and where Federal authorities were at their most vulnerable.

The attack itself was nearly anticlimactic. The Confederate batteries opened a heavy barrage against the brick sides of the fort as Anderson and his troops remained sheltered in the covered casements and withheld their fire. Initially concerned that the Federal garrison would not fire back—and thereby deny

Beauregard a military victory—the Confederates fired round after round toward the fort.

Lacking effective rear sights on the cannon and short of powder, Anderson's men were able to respond with only a few guns. Little damage was done to the Confederate gun positions, but Fort Sumter was in dangerous straits. Fires had broken out on two occasions and threatened the powder magazine on April 13. A shell snapped the flag staff at the fort, but it was quickly nailed back together under fire.

Colonel Louis Wigfall, a former Texas senator now on Beauregard's staff, arrived in front of the fort waving a white handkerchief on the tip of his sword, demanding Sumter's surrender. At the moment, the fires were dangerously close to the magazine and the powder necessary for firing the cannon was nearly gone. The gates had been blown down by shells and Fort Sumter was in danger of being captured by ground attack. Anderson agreed to evacuate under the same terms offered by Beauregard, who had given permission to the captured men to salute the U.S. flag as it was lowered, and the battle came to an end.

Permitted to fire a final salute using improvised powder bags, the garrison fired cannon until midway through the salute a heavy gun exploded, instantly killing one man, mortally wounding another, and injuring four others. Daniel Hough was the first man to die in a war that would see the deaths of more than 600,000 other men and boys.

A Confederate boat took the captured garrison from Sumter to Federal vessels that had been sent south with a relief force. The skirmish was over, but the conflagration was soon to follow. Davis' men had struck the first blow and Lincoln was now free to "assail" them in order to preserve the Union.

The Civil War Begins in Earnest

The opposing forces were not equal adversaries when gauged by any comparison of strength. The Union states had a population of nearly twenty-two million while the South had only about nine million (3.5 million of whom were slaves). In practical terms, this disparity meant that the North would be able to maintain its army by enrolling—with volunteers and

BELOW: *Surrounded by slave states (Maryland and Virginia) and a slaveholding city itself, Washington, D.C., was vulnerable to attack when the Civil War opened. Symbolically, the nation's capital had a great amount of significance—its loss would have been a great blow to the North and to newly elected President Lincoln, a blow from which there may have been no recovery, especially if France and England were consequently to recognize the Confederacy. Anxiously awaiting the arrival of troops to defend Washington, Lincoln declared in frustration: "I don't believe there is any North." Soon, however, volunteer regiments began to fill the city, drilling in every open area they could find as they attempted to refine their fledgling military skills.*

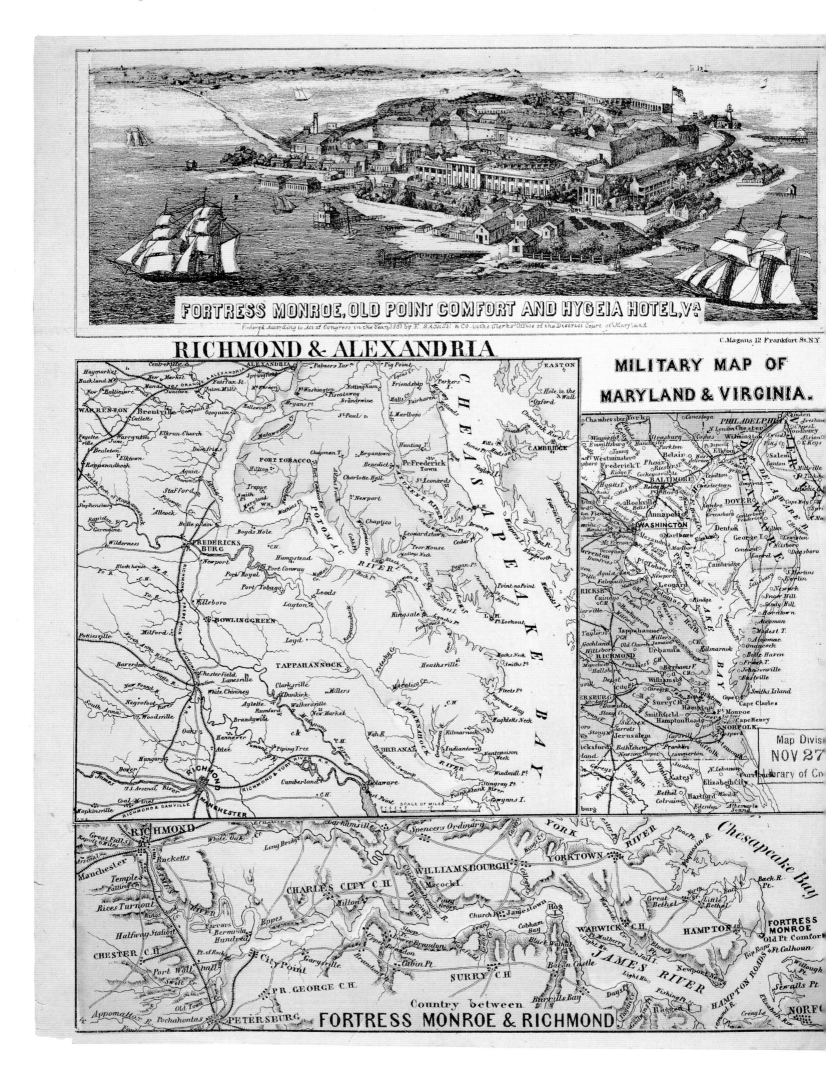

FORTRESS MONROE, OLD POINT COMFORT AND HYGEIA HOTEL, VA.

Entered According to Act of Congress in the Year 1861 by E. SACHSE & CO. in the Clerks' Office of the District Court of Maryland

C. Magnus 12 Frankfort St. N.Y.

RICHMOND & ALEXANDRIA

MILITARY MAP OF MARYLAND & VIRGINIA.

Country between FORTRESS MONROE & RICHMOND

conscripts—approximately 40 percent of its male population between 1861 and 1865. By comparison, the South was forced to rely on 90 percent of its male population to sustain a smaller force in the field. Nearly 2.1 million men would eventually serve in the northern armies while between 800,000 and 900,000 would serve in the southern, with peak strength being one million and 600,000, respectively.

The North was also much better supported by industry, and had better railroads, greater commercial seapower, and much more mineral wealth. Northern farms also produced a vast amount of food to support armies in the field. Horses and mules were in abundance, as well—especially when compared to the South—completing a transportation network that could only be envied by the southerners.

The South was not, however, without some significant advantages. It possessed good interior lines of communication, which allowed for rapid movement of troops, and a long coastline that made it difficult to fully blockade—initially, at least. Southerners also had a rich military tradition thanks to numerous campaigns against Native Americans, the British, and Mexicans. This allowed the Southerners an early advantage in the formation of excellent cavalry units that would (especially in the early days of fighting) help the South fight for its independence as the North sent its forces southward in its attempt to reestablish the Union. The South also had the advantage of being a defender on its home soil, a strategic boon as well as an inspiring cause. Whatever the relative advantages of each side, the conflict upon which they were embarking would prove to be costly, painful, and have long-lasting effects on the young country.

The nation was experiencing its first taste of tragedy as spring was changing into summer. Individual soldiers were facing terrible decisions that involved choosing between their conflicting loyalties. At the time, national influence was seldom felt by the ordinary citizen, whose personal contact with any form of government at all, much less the national government, was limited to the county seat to which his taxes were paid. The larger, national government was far away from the daily lives of the country's citizens. Not surprisingly, large groups of men in the South volunteered to defend their "homes, hearths, and altars" from the anticipated invaders from the North. Equal passion was felt by the new soldiers from the North who chose to follow the example of their new president in preserving the Union.

One of the men with conflicting loyalties was the soldier who had been selected by the Federal army's commander, Winfield Scott, to lead the national army in the field. Robert E.

Lee, a Virginian, chose to resign his colonel's commission in the national army rather than fight against his native state. He soon thereafter accepted a general's commission in Virginia's state forces. This was a time in which many others were faced with similar, painful choices as officers in the small national army returned to their states or remained in their regiments until called upon to accept higher responsibilities in the armies of their respective sections.

This was a confusing and trying time for the military profession. Men who had trained together at West Point and had become close friends in the Mexican War were beginning to serve in opposing armies. Many a soldier in the field had the experience where he was well acquainted with the man commanding or among the troops opposing him; knowing both the strengths and weaknesses of each other, opposing commanders often modified their tactics in ways not seen in previous wars.

The politicians and general population of the country managed to ignore the warnings of professional military officers regarding the probable length and severity of the war. Lincoln had come to believe that the war would be both short and painless despite Winfield Scott's warning that the war would require 300,000 men and three years to effectively prosecute. Ignoring the warning, Lincoln requested volunteers from the various state militias to serve for only ninety days. The southern leadership was equally misguided as to the severity and length of the adventure on which they were about to embark. They all spoke of "one southerner being worth ten Yankees" and believed they would be in their newly independent nation by autumn as they prepared to fight what they believed was a "second American Revolution."

The war was fought not only on the military front but on the political front as well. When Virginia joined the Confederacy, the new national capital was swiftly moved from Montgomery to Richmond—not far from the Union capital—and the war began to resemble a "war between two cities." Federal troops under Nathaniel Lyon moved against their secessionist-minded neighbors in St. Louis; these extralegal methods helped secure Missouri for the Union. Equally unconstitutional means were utilized in maintaining Union control in Maryland, a slave state, whose secession would leave Washington, D.C., entirely surrounded by enemy forces. Members of the legislature and prominent citizens of Baltimore were arrested and imprisoned, illegally, and were confined until the Unionist governor had firm control of this crucial state.

Soon after the secession of Virginia, Lincoln's troops began to move. On May 23, Union forces crossed the Potomac River to

OPPOSITE: *Troops under the command of Massachusetts' General Benjamin Butler were sent to reinforce the Federal garrison at Fortress Monroe, located at the tip of the Virginia Peninsula, near the naval base at Norfolk. Butler's troops moved out of Fortress Monroe (lower right corner) on June 10, 1861, but they were repulsed by the Confederates under Colonel John B. Magruder at Big Bethel, Virginia. This early battle showed that neither combatant was adequately trained nor prepared for combat at this early stage of the Civil War, but both sides continued to prepare for major engagements in the naive hope that the war could be won with a single climactic engagement.*

ABOVE: *A great battle was fought between the soldiers of Union General Irwin McDowell and Confederate General P.G.T. Beauregard on July 21, 1861. Neither commander was able to bring the full weight of his army to the battlefield, but McDowell's Federals were forced to retreat to their previous positions near Washington, D.C. While the entire Confederate defensive line had held, the southern army failed to develop a substantial pursuit, which could have resulted in the capture of the Federal capital. This detailed map shows troop positions, roads, houses, and includes the names of residents, rivers, and terrain features. Many of the locations on this map by topographical engineer James L. Bowen would see bloodshed in the coming conflict.*

occupy Arlington Heights and Alexandria; in conjunction with these movements, Lincoln extended a naval blockade that isolated both Virginia and North Carolina and cut off the rest of the Confederacy's coastal areas. Shortly afterward, Union soldiers from Ohio and Indiana began to move toward the east.

Virginia's western counties had historic grievances against the state government in Virginia's tidewater and piedmont regions. While taxes had been uniform throughout the state, most of the state's public works had been done in eastern Virginia, home to the wealthy population of the state. Understandably, there was a great deal of resentment over this in Virginia's western counties. As Virginia voted to leave the Union, considerable numbers of western Virginians began to openly discuss the possibility of leaving Virginia to form a new state. Ohio's Governor Denison decided to support these new Unionists, and ordered his soldiers under the command of General George B. McClellan to cross the Ohio River to aid them.

McClellan's regiments crossed into Virginia and marched along the strategic route of the Baltimore and Ohio Railroad to prevent its destruction by Virginia's secessionist forces. The key town of Grafton was occupied from May 26 to 30 as the Union regiments continued toward a concentration of Virginia troops at Philippi. Arriving near the town early on the morning of June 3, 1861, Federal troops under the command of Benjamin F. Kelley opened fire on the unprepared—and untrained—Virginia troops under the command of George Porterfield. The swift retreat of the Confederate troops in the town

was derided by the Union soldiers as the "Philippi Races." The Union's superiority of numbers had given them a false sense of power, as they would soon learn. Nonetheless, the initial battle involving large numbers of soldiers had been fought and the first maneuver campaign of the Civil War had opened.

On June 10, Union soldiers—including one colorful regiment of brightly clad zouaves—marched toward Confederate positions in the vicinity of Newport News, Virginia. Soon after watching them go into the field, flamboyant Federal commander Benjamin Butler was watching them return to the relative safety of the sanctuary of Fortress Monroe in the wake of a less-than-decisive battle at Big Bethel. Casualties had been inflicted by both sides in this small but significant battle, a harbinger of the more widespread destruction that would soon begin to occur.

The Bull Run Campaign

The romantic outlooks of both sides were soon to be replaced by a far grimmer reality during a sobering sequence of events that took place near Washington, D.C., itself. Relatively large forces had begun to assemble in the area as northern newspapers and politicians began to demand that a move "on to Richmond" be ordered soon. A new brigadier general who had recently been a major in the regular army, Irwin McDowell, had been attempting to assemble his volunteer, militia, and regular forces into an effective fighting unit for nearly three months with little success. He had been charged with the defense of the capital with the fifty thousand men at his disposal as the Confederates began to assemble a large force to the southwest near the small town of Manassas, Virginia.

General P.G.T. Beauregard, the Confederate commander who had taken over Fort Sumter, was in charge of the twenty thousand Confederates who were gathering there. Immediately to the north of Manassas was another large force of Confederates—eleven thousand men—under the command of General Joseph Johnston in the Shenandoah Valley town of Winchester. McDowell had placed an eighteen-thousand-man army at Martinsburg, twenty miles (32km) to the north of Winchester, to hold Johnston in place as the remaining Union forces prepared to move against Beauregard.

Despite the warnings from experienced army commander Winfield Scott, Lincoln had decided to use the raw troops available to McDowell in an attempt to drive toward Richmond and bring the war to a swift and early conclusion. Feeling

LEFT: *General P.G.T. Beauregard was the Confederate commander at Charleston, South Carolina, when Fort Sumter was fired upon. He was later the commander at the battle of Bull Run, and later still served as Albert Sidney Johnston's second-in-command at Shiloh, where he directed his army's withdrawal to Corinth, Mississippi, after Johnston was mortally wounded. Back in Charleston in the fall of 1862, he helped defend the city from naval attacks. He did well in May 1864, bottling up General Benjamin Butler's army at Bermuda Hundred, in Virginia. He also held off Grant at Petersburg until Lee arrived to defend the city.*

Union General Irwin McDowell's march against the Confederate defenses at Manassas (see map, opposite) was hastened by demands for immediate action by congressmen, newspaper editorials, and northern public opinion. Lincoln, anxious to use the ninety-day militia volunteers before their term of service expired, reasoned the South was equally unprepared for war and pressed for an offensive campaign. Believing that a single defeat in battle would force the South to surrender, Lincoln continued to demand an advance by the new army assembled in Washington, D.C. In July 1861 the largest army ever assembled on the continent began to march toward an uncertain future along the banks of a small stream called Bull Run.

MAP
OF THE
BATTLEFIELD OF BULL RUN VIRGINIA
Brig. Gen. IRVIN McDOWELL Commanding the U.S Forces,
Gen. G.T.BEAUREGARD Commanding the Confederate Forces.
JULY 21st 1861.

Compiled from a map accompanying the report of Brig. Genl McDowell
and a map made under the direction of Genl Beauregard.

Published by authority of the HON.THE SECRETARY OF WAR
in the Office of the CHIEF OF ENGINEERS U.S.Army.

1877.

Scale, 3 inches = 1 mile

Note. Dotted lines near Centreville indicate sites of bivouacs
on the night of July 20th.
Full lines denote the position of the Forces on the next day
at the commencement of the engagement at Sudley's Springs;
Blue marking the United States Forces, and Red the Confederate.

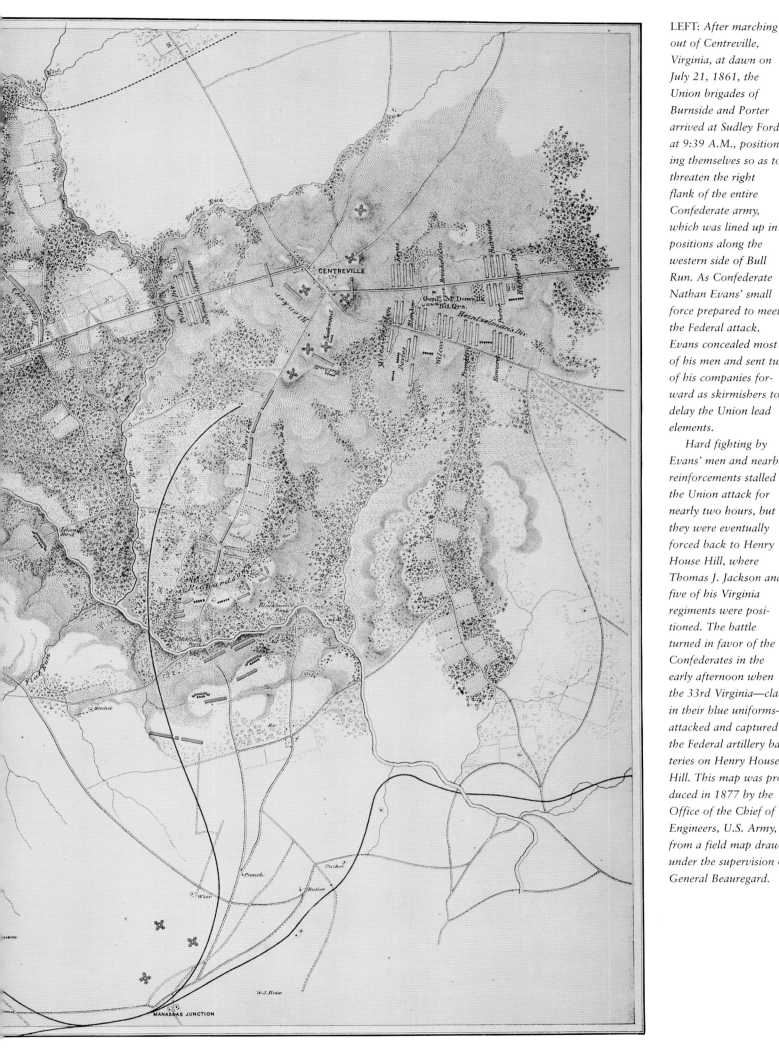

LEFT: *After marching out of Centreville, Virginia, at dawn on July 21, 1861, the Union brigades of Burnside and Porter arrived at Sudley Ford at 9:39 A.M., positioning themselves so as to threaten the right flank of the entire Confederate army, which was lined up in positions along the western side of Bull Run. As Confederate Nathan Evans' small force prepared to meet the Federal attack, Evans concealed most of his men and sent two of his companies forward as skirmishers to delay the Union lead elements.*

Hard fighting by Evans' men and nearby reinforcements stalled the Union attack for nearly two hours, but they were eventually forced back to Henry House Hill, where Thomas J. Jackson and five of his Virginia regiments were positioned. The battle turned in favor of the Confederates in the early afternoon when the 33rd Virginia—clad in their blue uniforms—attacked and captured the Federal artillery batteries on Henry House Hill. This map was produced in 1877 by the Office of the Chief of Engineers, U.S. Army, from a field map drawn under the supervision of General Beauregard.

that the Confederates were equally raw and that McDowell had superior numbers available to him and wanting to use the ninety-day volunteers before they were released, Lincoln ignored the old army commander. McDowell's soldiers marched out of Washington toward their opponents near Manassas. On July 16, the largest army ever assembled in North America began to march slowly over four parallel routes toward Manassas. McDowell had advantages of numbers, but his raw troops would be expected to attack over terrain where the "equally raw" Confederates would be able to take advantage of landscape to defend themselves against the attackers.

New developments in technology became a factor in the maneuvering of the large armies in the region. While McDowell marched out of Washington, spies told of his departure, swiftly telegraphing messages that led to a concentration of forces at Manassas. Unheard-of movements of large numbers of soldiers were managed as Johnston sent his cavalry commander, J.E.B. Stuart, in a wide sweep designed to confuse the Federal commander at Martinsburg, Virginia, as to the Confederate general's intentions. As swiftly as the cavalry was ordered out, Johnston arranged with local railroad officials to transport his four infantry brigades, including the lead brigade of Thomas J. Jackson, to reinforce Beauregard. With the use of the railroad and telegraph Johnston had been able to move Jackson's brigade more than fifty-seven miles (91.2km) in twenty-five hours—the troops reached Manassas on July 20.

McDowell meanwhile had taken too much time in getting to Manassas and once there, delayed his attack. Certain that his untried troops would be unable to strike the Confederate

right flank, he delayed an additional two days while his engineers searched for a route that would permit the Union force to hit the Confederate left flank. Finally prepared to strike on July 21, three of McDowell's brigades and a 30-pounder rifle opened the fight at the Stone Bridge over Bull Run. Simultaneously, McDowell led five of his brigades over an eight-mile (12.8km) march to an undefended ford near Sudley Springs, where he hoped to strike the Confederate left flank and destroy the nearby railroad.

The first phase of McDowell's attack struck eleven Confederate companies that were supported by only two guns. For the first hour, McDowell timidly ordered his regiments to attack one at a time as the Confederate commanders, fully aware of their danger, moved ten additional regiments to form a second defensive line on Henry House Hill. Full brigades of Federal troops were soon committed to combat and the Confederate line to the north of the Warrenton Turnpike began to lose its cohesion. Johnston, senior to Beauregard in rank, wisely turned over the management of the battle to his subordinate and rode to the rear to direct arriving Rebel reinforcements to locations where they were most needed.

Jackson and his brigade had arrived on the field and formed up just behind the Henry House. It was here that the sorely pressed Brigadier General Bernard Bee told his men, "Look at Jackson's Brigade; it stands like a stone wall." Three brigades were able to reorganize in the woods to the rear of Jackson's lines, and McDowell's attack was slowed as a general two-hour lull developed. It was during the next phase of the battle, renewed at 2:00 P.M., that a change in momentum occurred.

McDowell ordered two batteries of artillery into the line at the Henry House, but he provided little infantry support. In the confusion of the battle, a blue-uniformed regiment of Confederates, the 33rd Virginia Infantry Regiment, appeared to the right front of the Union artillery batteries. The artillery commander ordered his men to fire canister, large loads of small shot that was capable of cutting broad swathes through assaulting infantry, but he was overruled by McDowell's chief artillery officer, who believed these blue uniforms were worn by friendly soldiers who were arriving to provide the anticipated—and very much needed—infantry support.

Pulling up to within seventy yards (63.8m) of the Union artillery, the Virginia regiment leveled its muskets and fired a volley into the Union artillerymen. The decimated artillerymen could not hold their guns in the face of this concentrated fire. For the remainder of the day, these guns stood unused between the two contending armies.

By 4:00 P.M., Beauregard had been reinforced by two fresh brigades, and he ordered a general advance of his entire line. The tired Federal force, lacking sufficient artillery support, began to withdraw along the routes they had used to march into battle. The raw Federal troops became increasingly confused as they retreated and the withdrawal soon became a rout. By 6:30 in the evening, the roads were filled with panic-stricken Union soldiers fleeing eastward to seek the safety of the defenses of Washington, D.C.

Jefferson Davis had arrived in the field late in the day, and after a meeting with both of his commanders, Johnston and Beauregard, he ordered a general pursuit by the fresh men who had been on the Confederate right side of the line. As with many Civil War battles, the general pursuit was never fully developed. As a result, the retreating Union army was able to save itself and the Confederacy lost a grand opportunity to use captured supplies to sustain themselves in an attack against the Federal capital. The Confederacy had won a lopsided victory in the first major battle of the war.

At this point, the northern leaders were forced to consider the nature of the conflict they had entered into for the first time. The reality of the situation was that they had engaged in a war with a serious challenger, and the entire resources of the North were going to have to be marshalled if they were to win. Military leaders had to be taken seriously if they were given the authority to plan campaigns—that is, without interference from politicians—in the quest to bring the insurgents under control. Finally, and most significantly, the North was alarmed to find that the European powers, particularly Britain and France, had begun to view the new Confederacy as a potentially viable nation—one that could become a profitable source of trade—that deserved recognition. Clearly, the challenges faced by the North in the aftermath of the battle of Bull Run were great.

The Confederate leadership was not overconfident as it reviewed the battle's outcome.

BELOW: *The large stone house at the foot of the slope from Henry House Hill was located along the Warrenton Turnpike. Three Confederate brigades struggled against two Union divisions on nearby Matthew's Hill, but by noon they fell back past this house and across the turnpike until they were positioned on the crest of Henry House Hill. This small area was the location of some of the most decisive fighting in this battle, where Thomas Jonathan Jackson earned his legendary epithet: "Stonewall."*

There had been several moments during which the battle of First Manassas could have gone the other way—and they knew it. For all of their bravado, the Confederate army had engaged and barely escaped destruction at the hands of a formidable opponent. Quickly, the new government called for an additional 400,000 volunteers.

Lincoln soon called for a force of 500,000 men to serve for three years as the optimistically assembled ninety-day volunteers were released from duty. The northern leadership was finally recognizing that the Civil War would be long and costly.

It was at this time that the Union navy began to make its most important contribution to the war effort. Despite the blockade, there was a great movement of goods and military materials flowing toward Confederate ports; money was being made rapidly in the trade of contraband goods. In response to this, measures were undertaken to enforce the blockade; by the end of the year, two hundred Union ships were on patrol, intercepting Confederate blockade runners seeking to profit from the sale of goods that had become increasingly scarce in the South.

As both sides rushed additional men into training camps, there was a general lull in combat operations as each side examined the daunting challenges ahead. The front—to be defended by the South and assailed by the North—was enormous, stretching from the shores of Maryland in the east to Fort Craig, New Mexico, in the far west. Federal troops were swiftly moved westward in an attempt to control the central portion of the nation along the Mississippi River. Specifically, large numbers of soldiers were sent to Missouri, where the population quickly divided into two hostile camps. The trans-Mississippi Rebels won a victory at Wilson's Creek in August.

A border state, Kentucky had concluded that neutrality was the best option. Both sides appeared at first to respect the decision of Kentucky's governor. But the area was both populous and, like Missouri, located strategically within the center of the nation. The side that eventually won Kentucky—and Missouri— would control the critical terrain (especially the Mississippi and Ohio rivers) that would permit attacks deep into the heartland of the opponent.

The greatest peril for the Union, however, was at the national capital. Following the Confederate victory at Bull Run, the Potomac River was threatened by a concentration of southern forces. In addition, the Confederates were actively recruiting men in Maryland. The

BELOW: *Missouri was critically important to the Confederacy's western strategy in the early days of the war. With a population of 1.3 million people, the territory lay adjacent to some of the most important river junctions in the country—the Missouri and Mississippi—at a time when rivers were the main transportation routes. Missouri's former governor, Sterling Price, and Texan General Ben McCullough combined forces to defeat a Federal army at Wilson's Creek, Missouri, on August 10, 1861 (shown in this sketch by Captain N. Boardman of the Missouri Light Artillery). Price soon won another victory at Lexington, Missouri, a month later. Despite these modest successes, the Confederate loss at Pea Ridge ensured Union control of Missouri. The state would be ravaged by guerrilla warfare, but remained in the Union for the entire war.*

loss of Maryland would leave Washington, D.C., surrounded by hostile forces. This grave danger was sensed by President Lincoln.

Lincoln called on the new national hero, General George McClellan—fresh from victories in a series of campaigns in western Virginia—to take command of all of the troops in the Washington, D.C., region. Having an unrivaled reputation at the time and popular with both the public and his men, McClellan began to train his soldiers, whipping them into a formidable military machine, the Army of the Potomac. Shortly afterward, the aging commander-in-chief of the army, Virginia's Winfield Scott, retired from service and McClellan was assigned the retired general's responsibilities. As McClellan was stabilizing the situation in the Washington, D.C., area, Confederate pressure began to mount in the west.

Kentucky's neutrality began to be seriously threatened on September 4, 1861, as Confederate troops crossed from Tennessee to occupy the strategic river port and railroad town of Columbus, Kentucky. The following day, two additional river towns were seized by an unknown brigadier general, Ulysses Grant, commanding Illinois troops. By the end of the month, Kentucky's state government had joined the Union as both sides began to fill the western part of the state with troops. Battle lines were drawn throughout the state and both sides began to consider offensive spring operations. The fighting at Fort Sumter and Bull Run had shown both sides that a hard war was coming, and in light of this grim realization both combatants began to gather their resources for the grueling campaigns that would begin in only a few short months.

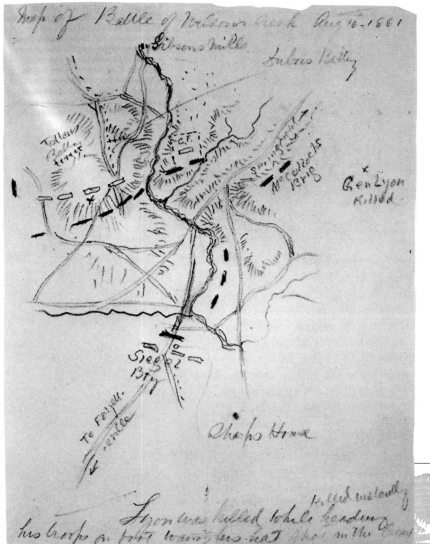

RIGHT: *General Nathaniel Lyon, riding at the head of the 1st Iowa Infantry Regiment, led a desperate charge at Wilson's Creek, Missouri, on August 10, 1861. Lyon was wounded three times, but insisted on continuing to lead the fight. He was killed after sustaining a fourth wound; tragically, his Federal force lost the battle.*

CHAPTER TWO

The Civil War in 1862

During 1862, the young volunteer soldiers serving on both sides discovered war to be less of a romantic adventure than they had imagined when donning their new uniforms in 1861. The political leaders of both sections were also beginning to understand the high cost (in money and lives) associated with the decisions they had made.

A statement made after the war and attributed to Union General William T. Sherman accurately sums up the results of the next three years of war. Sherman averred, "Lee was valiantly fighting flames that threatened the whole dwelling from the front porch as it burned down behind him." This description of events is revealing. Scholars have traditionally studied the war in the eastern theater, where Lee sought to defend his "Native State," Virginia, from northern invasion, but it was in the west that the Union armies were able to sow the seeds of the Confederacy's destruction.

In the east, McClellan had organized and drilled his Army of the Potomac to near perfection and put into place a group of competent commanders. Unfortunately, these preparations amounted to very little. Both North and South were preparing for a conclusive engagement on a Napoleonic scale that neither side was prepared to lose. Lincoln was especially keen to end the war quickly, and directives were developed with the intent of pushing McClellan into action. For his part, McClellan repeatedly deferred launching his army, exaggerating to the president the problems he faced (and failing to recognize that the Confederacy faced many similar problems). Lincoln wrote dispatches to McClellan in efforts to get the Federal army into motion, once stating: "Are you not over cautious when you assume that you can not do what the enemy is con-

stantly doing? Should you not claim to be at least his equal in prowess and act upon the claim?" The president even went as far as to issue his General War Order No. 1 in January 1862 in an additional effort to get McClellan moving. Despite the president's entreaties, little happened in the eastern theater.

In the west, however, Union troops had been assembled into two separate commands, one under Don Carlos Buell, in Louisville, and the other under Henry Halleck, in St. Louis. The opposing lines stretched from the Appalachian Mountains westward to Kansas, but most of these opposing forces were concentrated in a region east of the Mississippi River. Buell had forty-five thousand men under his command and Halleck was in charge of approximately ninety thousand soldiers.

Opposed to this relatively large force was a forty-three-thousand-man Confederate army under the command of General Albert S. Johnston, an experienced and capable officer. Confronting a larger force that was intent on attacking southward, Johnston's men occupied a system of forts and camps stretching across northern Tennessee along a line just south of Kentucky's southern boundary. Two large forts had been constructed in the area to defend against the anticipated Union attacks, Fort Henry on the Cumberland River and Fort Donelson on the nearby Tennessee River, but the region was far from being uniform in its sympathies.

Large numbers of pro-Union men lived in the mountainous areas of east Tennessee and Lincoln hoped to rally them. These hardy mountaineers, like the Unionists found in the mountains of western Virginia, were a source of potential recruits in an area

PAGE 36: *This map
details the considerable
defenses of Washington,
D.C., in place by 1862.
The young nation's capi-
tal was less than sixty
years old as the Civil
War began to erupt
around its boundaries.
Still under construction
at that time, the city
soon began to serve as
the national headquar-
ters of the Union's war
effort. Because the city
had enormous political
significance, the north-
ern states began to rush
troops southward to
defend it. The city soon
became an enormous
military camp that was
home to thousands of
soldiers and the site of
mighty supply depots
filled with items neces-
sary to sustain the men.
Fittingly, the city was
surrounded by a protect-
ing ring of strong
fortresses and entrench-
ments, complete with
huge artillery pieces
weighing as much as
twenty-five tons (25.4t),
well positioned to shell
attacking Confederates.*

RIGHT: *General Henry
W. Halleck, known
irreverently within the
prewar national army as
"Old Brains," graduated
from West Point in
1840 and had written or
translated several books
on the art of war.
Initially in command of
the western theater, the
skilled administrator
became general-in-chief
of all the Union's armies
until 1864, when he
became chief-of-staff,
an administrative assign-
ment that freed Grant
from heavy paperwork
as he planned the
destruction of Lee's
Army of Northern
Virginia.*

whose loss would severely damage the
Confederacy. Lincoln had urged action to support
these people in their hopes to rally to the North,
as had been done with the population of western
Virginia. Buell successfully penetrated the
Confederate defensive lines at Mill Springs,
Kentucky, in January, but no moves were made to
develop this victory into a general offensive. And
so matters stood until a campaign proposed by
Ulysses S. Grant was adopted by General Halleck.

Fort Henry and Fort Donelson

The campaign under question would have a defi-
nite effect on the outcome of the entire Civil
War. One of Halleck's subordinates at the time,
Grant had been proposing a river-borne operation up the Tennessee to assault and capture Fort
Henry, one of the primary positions in Johnston's
defensive line. Curiously, junior commanders
Grant and naval officer Andrew H. Foote were
taking the initiative by encouraging their more
senior commanders into action. At any rate,
Halleck agreed to the plan.

Ordered into motion by
Halleck on January 30,
1862, Grant and Foote were
in the vicinity of Fort Henry
by February 6. Meanwhile,
most of the men in the
doomed fort were marched
to reinforce nearby Fort
Donelson while the commander, Lloyd Tilghman,
remained with his gunners to
defend against Foote's
attack. Positioned low on the
water, Fort Henry's gunners
soon felt the wrath of Foote's
guns as they fired directly
into their works, reducing
guns and gunners to pieces.
By the end of the day, Fort
Henry was in the hands of
the Union army and the
Tennessee River was open to
Federal gunboats along a
watercourse that led into
northern Alabama.

Grant soon wrote a sim-
ple telegraph message to
Halleck that took the senior
commander by surprise: "I
shall take and destroy Fort
Donelson on the 8th and
return to Fort Henry." His
men were delayed a few

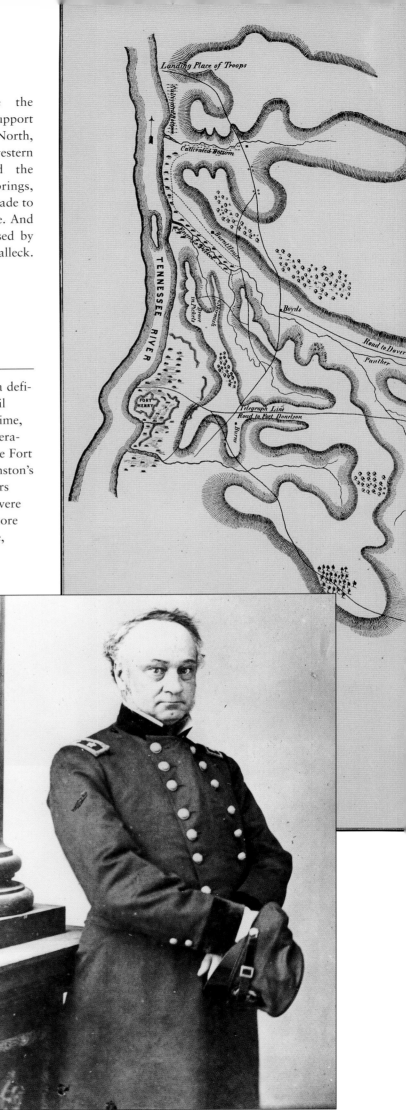

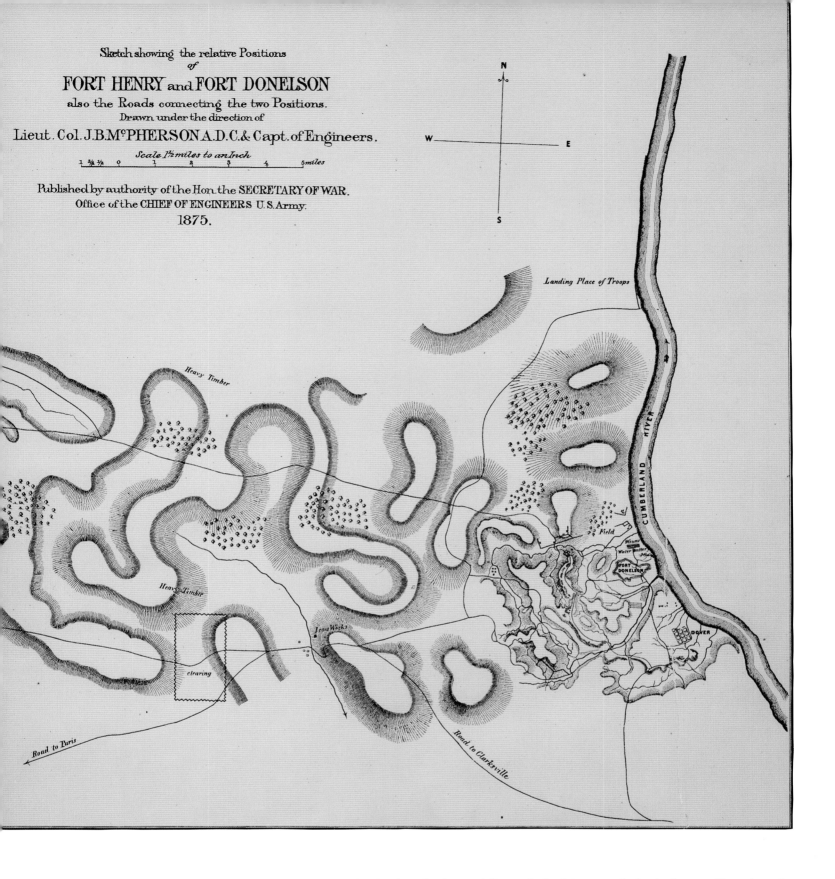

Sketch showing the relative Positions
of
FORT HENRY and FORT DONELSON
also the Roads connecting the two Positions.
Drawn under the direction of
Lieut. Col. J.B. McPHERSON A.D.C. & Capt. of Engineers.

Scale 1½ miles to an Inch

Published by authority of the Hon. the SECRETARY OF WAR.
Office of the CHIEF OF ENGINEERS U.S. Army.
1875.

Landing Place of Troops

Heavy Timber

Heavy Timber

Iron Works

clearing

Road to Paris

Road to Clarksville

CUMBERLAND RIVER

Field

FORT DONELSON

Water Battery

DOVER

ABOVE: *One of the pivotal battles of the Civil War was fought along the shores of the Cumberland River, on the border between Kentucky and Tennessee. A mighty squadron of ironclad gunboats was assembled and coordinated with the Union army, under an aggressive young commander, Ulysses S. Grant, in operations against the Confederate's defensive lines. Fort Henry (left, center) surrendered after a short bombardment, and Grant was soon investing nearby Fort Donelson (lower right). A poor command structure within the doomed fort and the inability of the Confederates to provide reinforcements and provisions resulted in a defeat of the Rebel soldiers and brought General Grant to the attention of senior planners in Washington, D.C. This Union map shows the Confederate defenses, including gun pits and water batteries, and the Union disposition around Fort Donelson. The Federal attackers under General Ulysses S. Grant had marched a long distance in springlike weather, discarding their heavy blankets and overcoats along the way. As the warm weather turned back to an icy blast of winter, the freezing men were forced to endure the terrible conditions while in the open. They hardly dared to kindle a small flame for fear of attracting fire from Confederate sharpshooters in the nearby fort. The trapped Confederates sallied from their doomed fortifications and pushed a large part of the Union army back nearly two miles (3.2km), but incompetent commanders missed the opportunity to lead their men out to safety. Grant took the fort after demanding "unconditional surrender" from his old friend, Confederate General Simon Bolivar Buckner. This postwar map was prepared by the Office of the Chief of Engineers, U.S. Army.*

days, but were soon in motion toward their target. Some troops were moved aboard Foote's boats, but the bulk of Grant's twenty-seven-thousand-man army marched overland in mild weather that induced many of them to discard their heavy coats and blankets. They dearly regretted having discarded their warm clothes when the winter weather returned with a vengeance as they invested Fort Donelson and the Confederate earthworks surrounding the small town of Dover, Tennessee.

The garrison at Fort Donelson was composed of approximately fifteen thousand men, but there was a serious problem with the command hierarchy. There were three brigadier generals present, and the ranking officer who assumed command at this hour of danger was the least qualified to do so.

John B. Floyd had served both as Virginia's governor and Buchanan's Secretary of War before being commissioned in the Confederate army. While in Buchanan's cabinet, Floyd had been actively transferring arms and supplies into depots and armories in the South and had been accused of the embezzlement of Indian Trust Funds right before the crisis at Fort Sumter presented him with an opportunity to resign his position and return to the safety of Virginia. Once in the Confederate army, Floyd was given command of some troops and won a skirmish at Cross Lanes, in western Virginia; upon being aggressively attacked by a small army under William S. Rosecrans in late 1861, however, Floyd ordered a retreat from his positions at Carnifex Ferry and Cotton Hill. He and his brigade, mostly Virginians, were then sent to reinforce the garrison at Fort Donelson, and he arrived there in time to assume command just as Grant and Foote were under way.

The other general officers in the doomed fort were Gideon Pillow and Simon Bolivar Buckner, a West Point graduate and a prewar friend of Grant. Unfortunately, the best of these generals was the third in command, and the Confederacy was soon to suffer a disaster from which they would never fully recover.

Grant and Foote were hoping to reduce the fort with naval gunfire as they had Fort Henry, but they were met by accurate return fire that disabled some of Foote's gunboats. As it turned out, Fort Donelson was positioned on higher ground, which gave the defenders the advantage: their plunging fire took its toll while the Federal cannonade frequently passed overhead without doing any damage at all. Disappointed at losing the opening round, Grant invested the fort and prepared for a long siege. But the defenders soon reacted to the presence of Grant's army.

On February 15, a large force attacked out of their trenches and pushed one of Grant's divisions nearly two miles (3.2km) to the rear of

their earlier positions before sufficient numbers of Federals were able to react to the attack. Unfortunately, the men were recalled to their former positions by Pillow, and Grant took the opportunity to order a general counterattack all along his lines. By the end of the day, part of the Union army had penetrated the fort's outer defensive works. The three commanders of Fort Donelson knew that they were doomed.

Floyd, fearing arrest and imprisonment (and the "iron cage" in which he was sure the Union army would display him), passed command to Pillow, who just as swiftly passed the command of the fort over to the professional soldier, Buckner—essentially so that the young commander could preside over the surrender of the garrison.

Floyd escaped with two of his Virginia regiments on a steamboat that had just arrived to deliver corn to the fort and Pillow was rowed to safety in a skiff as Buckner asked Grant, a man to whom he had once loaned money, for terms. Grant was a man of few words and he answered in a terse message: "No terms except unconditional and immediate surrender can be accepted. I propose to move immediately upon your

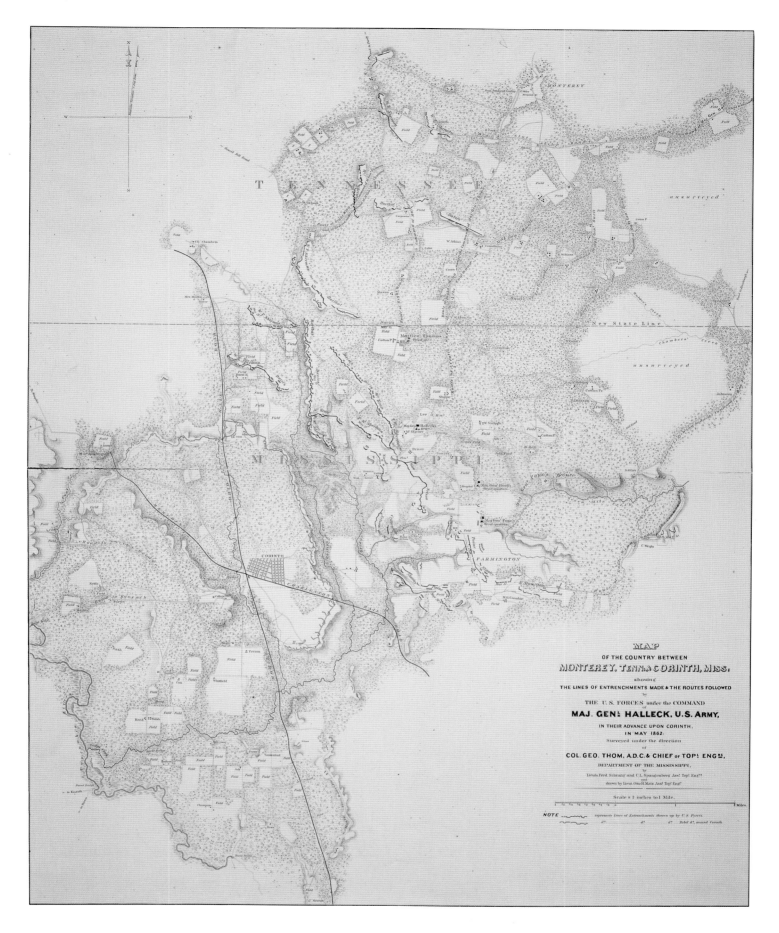

MAP
OF THE COUNTRY BETWEEN
MONTEREY, TENN. & CORINTH, MISS.
showing
THE LINES OF ENTRENCHMENTS MADE & THE ROUTES FOLLOWED
by
THE U.S. FORCES under the COMMAND
of
MAJ. GEN! HALLECK, U.S. ARMY,
IN THEIR ADVANCE UPON CORINTH,
IN MAY 1862.
Surveyed under the direction
of
COL. GEO. THOM, A.D.C. & CHIEF OF TOP! ENG!S,
DEPARTMENT OF THE MISSISSIPPI,
by
Lieuts. Fred. Schraag and C.L. Spangenberg Ass! Top! Eng!s
drawn by Lieut. Otto H.Matz Ass! Top! Eng!

ABOVE: *Once the bloody battle of Shiloh was over, Confederate Brigadier General P.G.T. Beauregard withdrew his battered army to Corinth, Mississippi, giving up control of western Tennessee in the process. Halleck had been placed in command of the Union army in the region, and moved toward the goal of Corinth with his customary degree of caution. The Federal troops arrived at Corinth on May 28, 1862, and began to shell the Confederate defenses the next morning. Beauregard ultimately withdrew, leaving the Union army in control of western Tennessee and in an excellent position to commence operations designed to capture the entire length of the Mississippi River. This map of the territory around Corinth, the most important Confederate railroad junction in the west, was drawn by Lieutenant Otto Matz, a topographical engineer with the Federal army.*

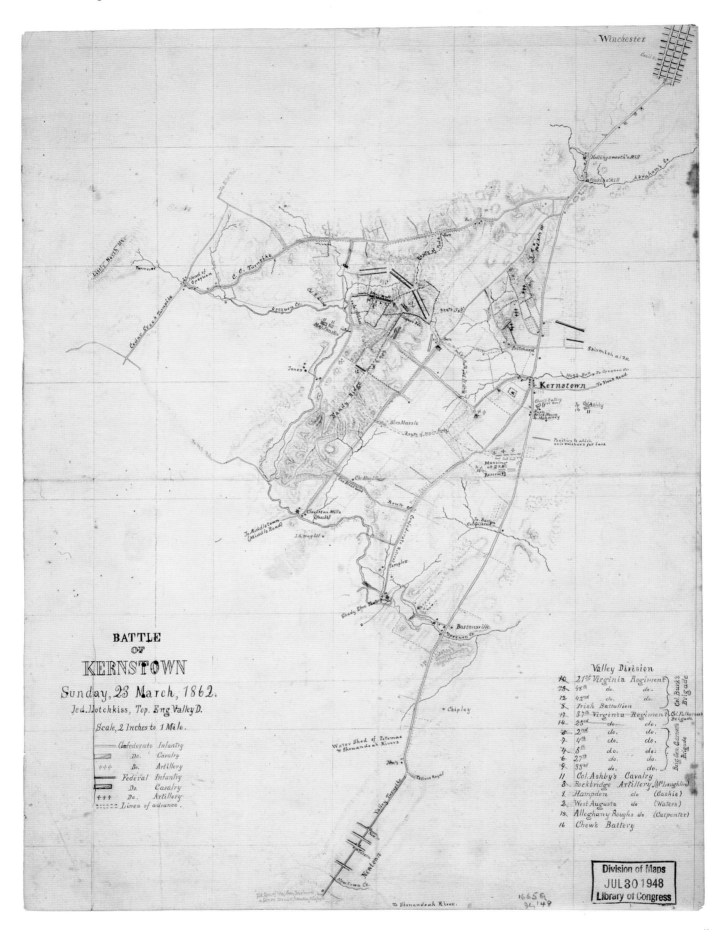

ABOVE: *As General George B. McClellan moved his troops toward Richmond during his Peninsula Campaign, General Thomas J. "Stonewall" Jackson was ordered to begin a bold diversion in the Shenandoah Valley. From March 23 to June 9, 1862, Jackson fought six battles against Union forces: Kernstown, McDowell, Front Royal, Winchester, Cross Keys, and Port Republic. Only the battle at Kernstown was lost by the aggressive Confederate commander. Prior to that initial engagement, Jackson's tired men had marched twenty-five miles (40km) on March 22 and an additional sixteen miles (25.6km) on March 23 (a Sunday, a day Jackson took quite seriously). Encountering stout resistance and outnumbered, Jackson had been forced to withdraw from Kernstown. This excellent field map was drawn by the remarkable Confederate topographical engineer Jedediah Hotchkiss, many of whose maps appear in this book. Amazingly, the majority of his detailed sketches were done on horseback.*

1ˢ BACON'S MILITARY MAP OF AMERICA.1ˢ

**BACON'S
MILITARY MAP OF THE
UNITED STATES
Shewing the
FORTS & FORTIFICATIONS.**

Published by BACON & Cᵒ 48 Paternoster Row

LONDON 1862

EXPLANATION.

works." Only the men with Floyd and the cavalrymen under the command of Colonel Nathan Bedford Forrest—some bearing an infantryman with them in the saddle—were able to escape.

Extremely poor leadership at a critical part of the Confederate defensive line, the violation of a cardinal military principle—unity of command—and the recall of the attacking Confederates who had successfully sortied against Grant's right wing had doomed much more than the just the men of Fort Donelson.

Albert S. Johnston wrote: "The blow was most disastrous and almost without remedy." The Confederacy had lost somewhere between twelve and fifteen thousand men and munitions to match, and their defensive line had been penetrated by a large force. As a result of the victory, Federal gunboats and steamboats filled with rested troops were now able to move at will deep into the heart of the Confederacy. Kentucky was secured for the Union by this victory, and the armies of the North moved into Tennessee—a large state filled with diverse agricultural and industrial capacities. The Confederacy spent the remainder of the war attempting to recover from the disastrous blow it had been dealt at Fort Donelson. Though nobody could have known

this at the time, it would prove even more disastrous for the Confederacy that Ulysses S. Grant had emerged as a capable combat commander.

President Lincoln, impressed with the victories in the west, wisely unified the armies in that theater of operations under Halleck (known as "Old Brains" in the prewar army for his translation of famous military historian Jomini's work on tactics and his general knowledge of the literature of war). With the Confederates' defensive line now broken, swift movement followed: soon, John Pope's Army of the Mississippi and Foote's naval force were successful in attacking a number of Confederate positions, including New Madrid, Missouri, and Island No. 10, on the Mississippi River.

Halleck made the decision to coordinate Grant's army, fresh from the victories along the Tennessee River, and Buell's army, then at Nashville, in an attack against Johnston, whose army was stationed at the crucial rail junction in Corinth, in northeastern Mississippi. This set the stage for the next great encounter between the opposing forces. The plan was for Grant and Buell to meet at Pittsburg Landing on the Tennessee River before moving southward against Johnston.

ABOVE: *This fine map from 1862 is one of a series of six published during the Civil War by an English firm, Bacon and Company, that used colors to differentiate the slave and free states. It also shows which states were border slave states and which ones had seceded, demonstrating a more-than-passing interest in the details of the war. This was the first major war since the end of the war in the Crimea and many Europeans followed its progress closely, in particular as diplomats from both the Confederacy and Union were busily trying to either engage the European powers or discourage them from getting involved.*

Shiloh

Johnston learned of the Union troop movements and ordered his forty thousand men north out of Corinth on April 3 with hopes to surprise the Union forces at Shiloh and thereby regain the initiative. Muddy roads, poor staff coordination, and undisciplined troops resulted in delays, so the command wasn't able to put the twenty-two-mile (35.2km) route to Shiloh behind them until

April 5. Johnston then delayed an attack on the Federals until the following morning, an error that would cost him dearly, though luckily for him Grant was also making errors.

Foolishly, the Union army had established camp with the Tennessee River at its back and creeks on each of its flanks. The entire army, including Grant, seemed to be overconfident in its abilities after the lopsided victories at forts Henry and Donelson. No defensive works were constructed as the entire army moved into its

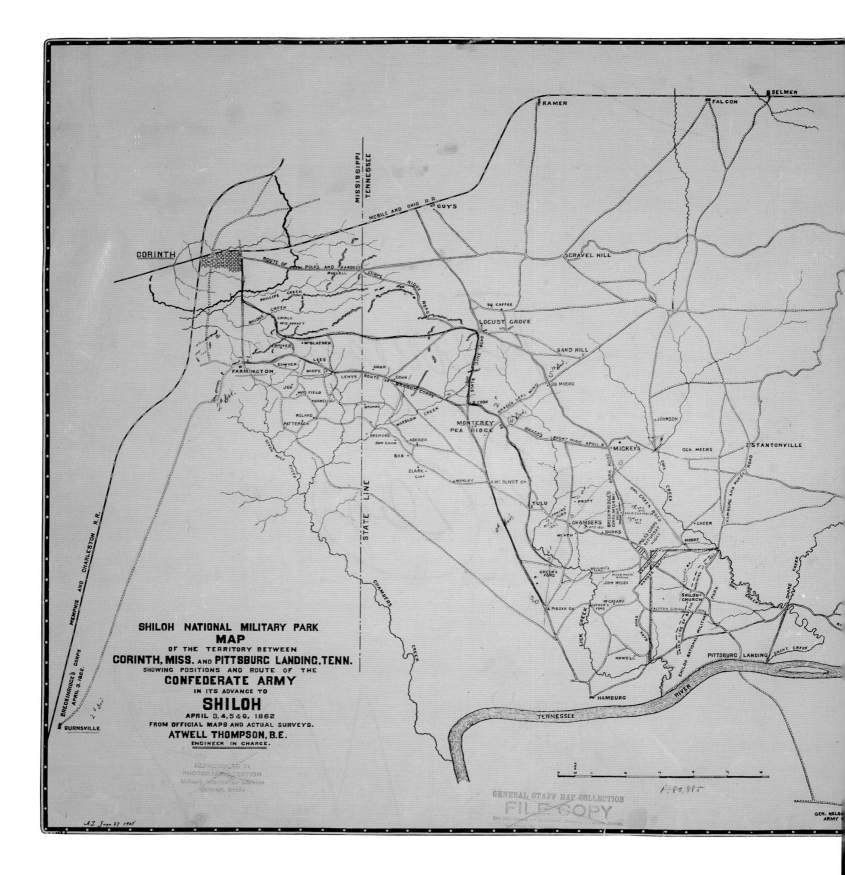

SHILOH NATIONAL MILITARY PARK
MAP
OF THE TERRITORY BETWEEN
CORINTH, MISS. AND **PITTSBURG LANDING, TENN.**
SHOWING POSITIONS AND ROUTE OF THE
CONFEDERATE ARMY
IN ITS ADVANCE TO
SHILOH
APRIL 3, 4, 5 & 6, 1862
FROM OFFICIAL MAPS AND ACTUAL SURVEYS.
ATWELL THOMPSON, B.E.
ENGINEER IN CHARGE.

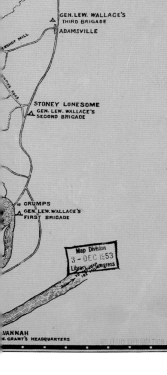

ABOVE: *General Albert Sidney Johnston was fifty-nine years old in 1862 and he had served in the nation's Regular Army with distinction. He served as a colonel of the elite 2nd U.S. Cavalry and his decision to join the Confederacy made him one of the South's most experienced field commanders. On the morning of April 6, 1862, he led the 9th Arkansas in a surprise attack against Grant's Army of Tennessee, stationed at Pittsburgh Landing. Riding along the brigades that composed his army at Shiloh later in the day, Johnston stopped to address his men to inspire them to greater efforts. Above his head he waved a tin cup he had taken from the captured Federal encampments. Later still, he led his troops toward the Union lines opposing him in a peach orchard and was wounded in the right leg. Ignoring his injury, Johnston remained on his horse until he collapsed from blood loss and died.*

LEFT: *Grant's positions at Shiloh were not good, and since the Union army was on the attack, no orders were given to build defensive positions. The Union army had its back against the river and creeks at each flank. They conducted little or no active patrolling, leaving them fatally unaware of the presence of 40,000 Confederate troops within two miles (3.2km) of where the Federal soldiers lay sleeping. When General Albert S. Johnston's men burst from the woods early in the morning of April 6, many Union soldiers rushed from their tents to fight. Johnston received a mortal wound and was replaced by General P.G.T. Beauregard, who suspended attacks for the rest of the day. As the day was ending, one of Grant's divisions that had lost its way and advance elements of General Don Carlos Buell's army began to arrive on the field. Grant counterattacked on April 7 and soon regained all the ground lost the previous day. The Confederates began to withdraw toward Corinth, Mississippi. The bloodiest battle of the war (to this point) had been fought at a cost of 13,000 Union casualties. The Confederates lost 11,000. This 1957 tour map of Shiloh National Park includes the scene of fighting from Pittsburg Landing to Shiloh (north is to the right).*

RIGHT: *A scene from the Shiloh battlefield. During the engagement in and around the ten-acre (4ha) peach orchard (located beyond the fence in this postwar photograph), showers of pink petals fell incongruously as shell fragments struck the flowering trees. In order to break the Union line, Johnston ordered an attack, personally leading part of the assault, which forced the Union defenders back to the relative safety of the Sunken Road. The brave general bled to death on the field; ironically, he had ordered his personal physician to care for a group of wounded Federals and no one on his staff knew how to use the tourniquet he carried in his pocket. By the time he collapsed from the saddle, it was probably too late for a tourniquet anyway.*

night camp and no one seemed to be aware that a forty-thousand-man force of Confederates was camped within two miles (3.2km) of them. Grant himself had stopped at the town of Savannah and spent the night nine miles (14.4km) upriver from his army.

Early on the morning of April 6, Johnston's men charged out of the woods that had sheltered them as they assembled for their attack. Achieving total surprise, the Confederates were engaged by Union troops, who rushed out of their tents onto the company streets to assemble and fight as best they could. Most of the Union regiments fought hard and yielded ground slowly—and some even rallied in defensive positions from which they punished the attackers severely. Some minor setbacks aside, however, the Confederates were prevailing, and by the afternoon they had managed to push the Union army back all along the line. Unfortunately for the Confederates, the ferocity of the fighting had also managed to disrupt their attack formations, and many of the newly formed regiments became disorganized. As Johnston gathered his men to him and charged the Union lines in a peach orchard, he was mortally wounded.

General Beauregard assumed command, and immediately decided to halt the fighting for the day in order to reorganize his columns. Because of this, the Confederate army lost the advantage of momentum it had gained through surprise, and at around the same time Grant received rein-

forcements. Lew Wallace had managed to stop the Confederate breakout at Fort Donelson, saving the entire operation, but became lost on the way to the fighting at Shiloh. He arrived at the end of the day on April 6 and his fresh division helped stabilize Grant's faltering lines. Advance elements of Buell's army from Nashville also began to arrive on the field and swell the Union ranks during the period of suspended Confederate operations.

The rest of the battle was somewhat anticlimactic. Grant counterattacked the following day and the Confederates withdrew to Corinth. As with many of the early Civil War battles, there was no attempt to pursue the retreating army and finish the job, probably because the Union army had been so severely handled.

The battle of Shiloh had been particularly bloody. Out of sixty-five thousand Union soldiers present on the field, thirteen thousand died; meanwhile, the South lost eleven thousand men it could ill spare. Although the Union had lost more men, it had secured the victory and narrowly averted disaster. The key to the victory had been Lincoln's decision to unify the western commands under a single officer (Halleck). If this had not been done, Johnston and Beauregard probably would have been able to defeat Grant before moving on and engaging the smaller force under Buell at a later date and at a different location. By ordering the army to adhere to the principle of unity of command,

Lincoln had saved his armies in the west from suffering a major disaster.

Halleck cautiously led the men of Grant's and Buell's forces against Corinth. He had seen what the Confederates were capable of at Shiloh and he was in no hurry to let them repeat the performance. The Federals entered Corinth on May 30, the town having been evacuated. Events were clearly favoring the Union army in the west at this point in the war.

BELOW: *The Battle of Shiloh was one of the hardest-fought encounters in the western theater of operations because the stakes were high for both sides. A victory for the Confederacy would represent a first step toward regaining the crucial resources of western and central Tennessee and Kentucky. A victory for the Union would consolidate the North's control over a large portion of the central Mississippi Valley (a process completed in July 1863 with the capture of Vicksburg). This scene shows the Union troops defending the peach orchard near Pittsburg Landing, where Grant had been awaiting the arrival of Buell before moving on to Corinth.*

LEFT: *Ulysses S. Grant won an important pair of victories at forts Henry and Donelson, but came under some criticism for being poorly prepared, possibly overconfident, at Shiloh. Lincoln defended Grant, saying, "I can't spare this man, he fights."*

BELOW: *Jackson was able to bring a superior force of ten thousand Confederates to oppose six thousand Federal soldiers at McDowell, Virginia, on May 8, 1862. Slowed by rough terrain in placing his artillery into positions from which retreating Federal troops would be decimated, Jackson kept his infantry on a hill from which he could oppose any Union attack. The Federal commander, General Robert H. Milroy, ordered an attack designed to hold Jackson's army in place until the bulk of the Union force could retreat. While the repeated attacks failed to dislodge Jackson, the Federal tactic allowed the bulk of the Union force to escape after nightfall. This unfinished map was prepared by Jedediah Hotchkiss.*

OPPOSITE: *On June 8, 1862, Jackson found himself between two Federal generals, John C. Fremont and James Shields, at the head of forces poised to converge against the Confederate commander near Port Republic, Virginia. Jackson ordered Jedediah Hotchkiss to prepare a map of the area. Once he was familiar with the region's terrain, Jackson arranged his troops. He placed most of his army along the hills overlooking the small town of Port Republic to hold off Shields as he sent a full division to confront Fremont at Cross Keys (left, center). After halting Fremont, Jackson shifted most of his remaining force across North River to attack Shields, forcing him to withdraw. Fremont slowly resumed his advance against Jackson, but was unable to cross the river. Jackson had ordered the burning of the single bridge. If the Union force had thought to burn the bridge earlier, Jackson would have been trapped between two large Federal forces and the outcome of the Civil War might have been altered considerably. This sketch by Hotchkiss has a series of squiggles in the lower left-hand corner where the cartographer tested his pens and ink.*

Kentucky-Tennessee Campaign

As Halleck moved into Corinth, Pope and Foote took control of the Mississippi River as far south as Memphis. Meanwhile, a combined attack by Admiral David Glasgow Farragut and Benjamin Butler managed to break through the coastal defenses near the mouth of the Mississippi River and secure New Orleans for the Union. By the middle of 1862, Federal control over the Mississippi was firmly established—with the exception of the 150-mile (240km) stretch of the great river that lay between Port Hudson and Vicksburg.

Due to sustained and far-reaching operations in the west, the Federal forces were becoming increasingly vulnerable as their lines of communication stretched thin and Confederate cavalry raids struck deep into their rear areas. Over the

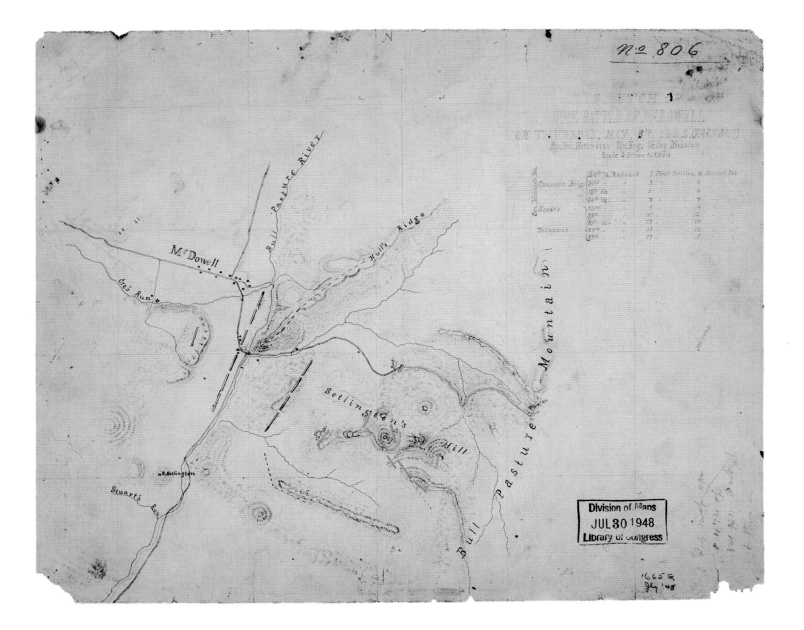

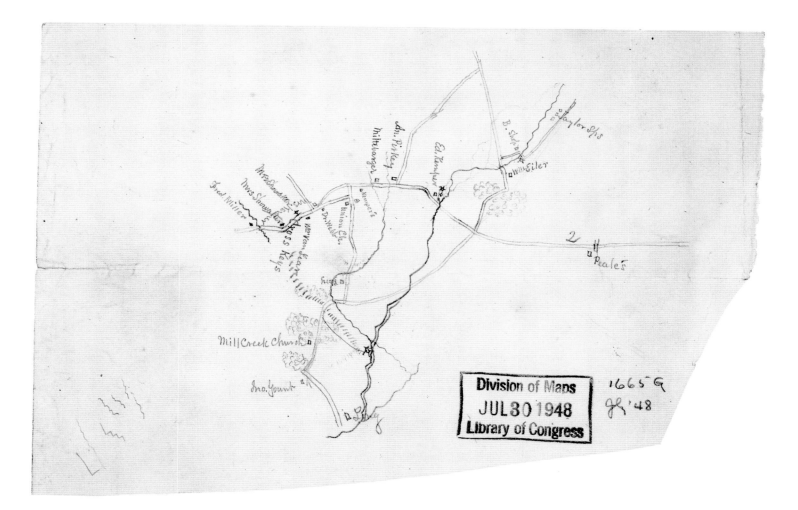

course of the summer, the Confederate commanders began to prepare for a major offensive with the objective of regaining the advantage in the western theater of war. The plan was relatively simple and involved armies on both sides of the Appalachian Mountains. Braxton Bragg and Kirby Smith were assigned the task of attacking into eastern Tennessee before turning north into Kentucky. Meanwhile they would be supported by a force under Earl Van Dorn, who was assigned the job of attacking Grant in western Tennessee before moving to unite with Bragg and Smith in Kentucky.

The movements of the Confederate forces in the west were to be closely coordinated with advances in the east by the Army of Northern Virginia, under Robert E. Lee, as it moved to strike deep into Maryland. The strategy of the entire plan involved regaining the overall initiative against the Union army in both theaters; success would depend on swift movement, coordination between the forces, and the rallying of new troops from Kentucky and Maryland as the respective armies entered those border states.

Initially, things went well with the Confederates. Buell withdrew from his positions in Alabama and Tennessee, but his army engaged Bragg at Perryville, Kentucky, on October 7, 1862. The fighting began when troops under Philip Sheridan took possession of a creek where

both sides hoped to get drinking water (it had been one of the hottest, driest summers on record). The battle of Perryville was filled with confusion—Buell was at his headquarters during most of the conflict and was unaware that the fighting was severe until it was nearly over—and ended in a stalemate. Heavy casualties sustained by Bragg's army compelled the Confederates to withdraw. Additionally, the failure of Van Dorn to complete his portion of the plan—he was killed later in the war by a jealous husband—halted any further planned advances in the region.

On Christmas Day that year, William S. Rosecrans replaced Buell, and was cautious in moving against Bragg, who was occupying central Tennessee. After gathering sufficient supplies at the base at Nashville, which freed him from dependency on a vulnerable railroad supply line, Rosecrans marched out of Nashville on December 26 toward Bragg's positions on Stones River, where the Confederate commander planned to meet the Federals in battle. Both commanders entered into the fight with identical battle plans: attack the opponent on the right flank. Rosecrans intended to strike hard at Bragg's right flank and pin his army against the river. Bragg planned a similar move against Rosecrans.

The battle of Stones River opened on December 3, with Bragg ordering a swift attack that he hoped would give him the advantage. Attacking Confederates under the command of Major General William J. Hardee struck hard on the Union army's right flank, which was forced back. Having struck swiftly and with authority, Bragg had gained the upper hand in the conflict with Rosecrans, who as a result was forced to modify his original battle plan. Federal units that had struck against Bragg's right flank were recalled while Sheridan's division—as it had done at Perryville—successfully repelled attacks along the center of the Union line. As the right wing of Rosecrans' army was pushed back, Confederate cavalry further harrassed the army, striking hard in the Federal rear areas.

As Rosecrans' right elements were forced back, they were compressed and began to put up a stiff resistance. As a result, further Confederate assaults began to bog down and the attackers began to tire. Rosecrans met with his senior commanders during the night to discuss their options. Receiving support from his corps commanders, major generals Thomas L. Crittenden and George H. Thomas, Rosecrans decided to remain on the field instead of ordering a general retreat.

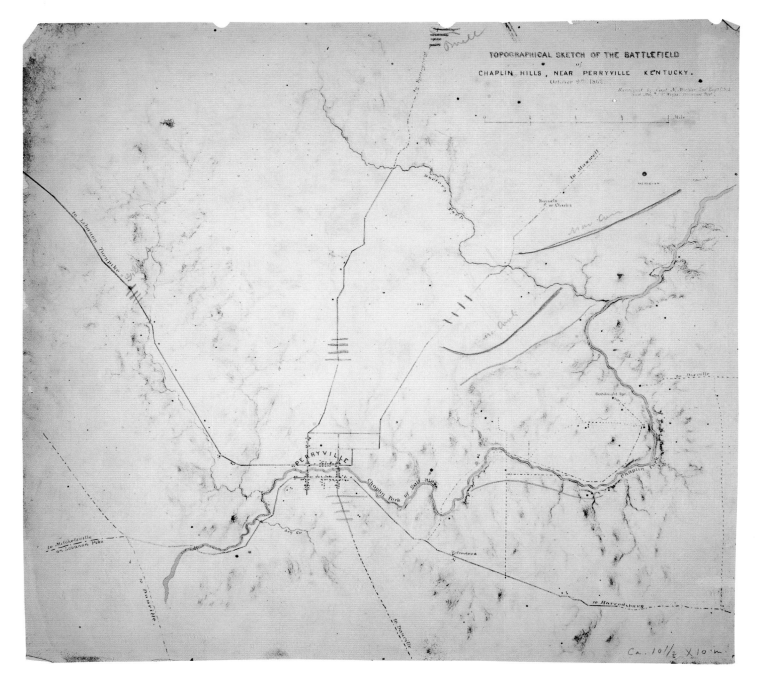

ABOVE: *Confederate strategy in the west during 1862 involved an invasion of Kentucky. General Braxton Bragg was able to force General Buell out of northern Alabama and central Tennessee without fighting, but his progress was slowed once he arrived in Kentucky. Severe fighting began at Perryville, Kentucky, on October 8, 1862, over the possession of drinking water. General Philip H. Sheridan's division fought well and held their ground. Union troops later pushed the Confederates out of Perryville and the battle ended as a stalemate. Heavy casualties and the presence of numerically superior Union forces compelled Bragg to withdraw. Kentucky was lost to the Confederacy. This topographical sketch of the battlefield of Chaplin Hills, or Perryville, by Captain Nathaniel Michler and Major John Weyss shows the vicinity as it appeared on October 9.*

ABOVE: *The Union artillery of the Army of the Potomac served George B. McClellan well during the Peninsula Campaign, easily outclassing the guns and gunners available to the Confederates. When Lee assumed command of the Army of Northern Virginia after the fighting at Seven Pines (called Fair Oaks by the Union), he initiated an aggressive campaign, known as the Seven Days' Battles, that forced the Union army back from the outskirts of Richmond. It was the massed Union artillery on Malvern Hill that allowed McClellan's army to escape to the relative safety of Harrison's Landing, ending the campaign with an intact Union army. This photograph shows Captain Horatio Gibson's battery of Union horse artillery near the battlefield of Fair Oaks, Virginia.*

RIGHT: *Thomas "Stonewall" Jackson managed to achieve greatness in a relatively short period of time. Referred to as "Tom Fool" by many students at Virginia's Military Institute, where he had taught, he became "Stonewall" by the end of the battle of Bull Run. By the time of his death at the Battle of Chancellorsville in 1863, Jackson had achieved a well-deserved position of honor in the military history of the nation. It was believed that Jackson felt "praying and fighting...to be his ideal of the whole duty of a man."*

ABOVE: *This photograph of the Union army's camp at Cumberland Landing shows troop formations drawn up for inspection in May 1862. McClellan's large Army of the Potomac was fully supplied with all the necessities of camp life, including the mud-spattered portable forge (foreground) used by farriers responsible for the shoeing of the enormous numbers of horses and mules needed to transport this huge force toward Richmond.*

OPPOSITE: *After occupying Winchester on November 5, 1861, Jackson began to analyze the tactical situation facing him. Major General Nathaniel Banks and eighteen thousand Federal troops were located in nearby Maryland, just across the broad Potomac River from Virginia. Brigadier General William S. Rosecrans and twenty-two thousand troops were inside nearby western Virginia. And Brigadier General Benjamin F. Kelley and five thousand troops occupied nearby Romney, barely forty miles (64km) away from Winchester over an excellent turnpike. Jackson's immediate goal was Romney. By taking the town and forcing Kelley's withdrawal, Jackson could preempt any plans for the concentration of Kelley's and Banks' forces against him in Winchester. The winter march to Romney was terrible—bitterly cold, with snow and sleet falling—but the Confederate army managed to occupy the recently abandoned Romney on January 13, 1862. Jackson returned to Winchester, and shortly thereafter several of his officers signed a petition to Jefferson Davis to be withdrawn from the freezing mountain town. Once Jackson learned his orders had been reversed, he sent a letter of resignation to the Confederate War Department. Only the intervention of a close friend prevented the South from losing one its most skilled and aggressive commanders.*

Little fighting occurred on New Year's Day, 1863, but Bragg ordered forward Kentuckian Major General John C. Breckinridge, a former vice president of the United States, to attack the Union army's left wing. They were successful at first, but Federal counterattacks and withering fire from massed artillery drove Breckinridge's men back to their original positions. Bragg was somewhat surprised to find the Union army still standing firm, and took January 1 and most of January 2 to consider his position before ordering an attack against the Federal left flank. The Confederates initially drove their opponents back, but then were decimated by heavy artillery fire and forced to retreat. The contending armies remained in their positions until the evening of January 3, when Bragg withdrew from the field. Although the fighting had ended in a stalemate, the Federals fared better in the end, having secured much of the state.

Overall, the large offensives planned by the Confederate army in the west had failed to achieve significant results during 1862, and they had suffered severe losses in personnel, their most precious and irreplaceable resource. On the Federal side, Rosecrans had survived the test at Stones River, but his Army of the Cumberland was so badly damaged that it would be unable to engage in offensive operations for nearly six months. The war in the west ended in a tactical draw at the end of 1862.

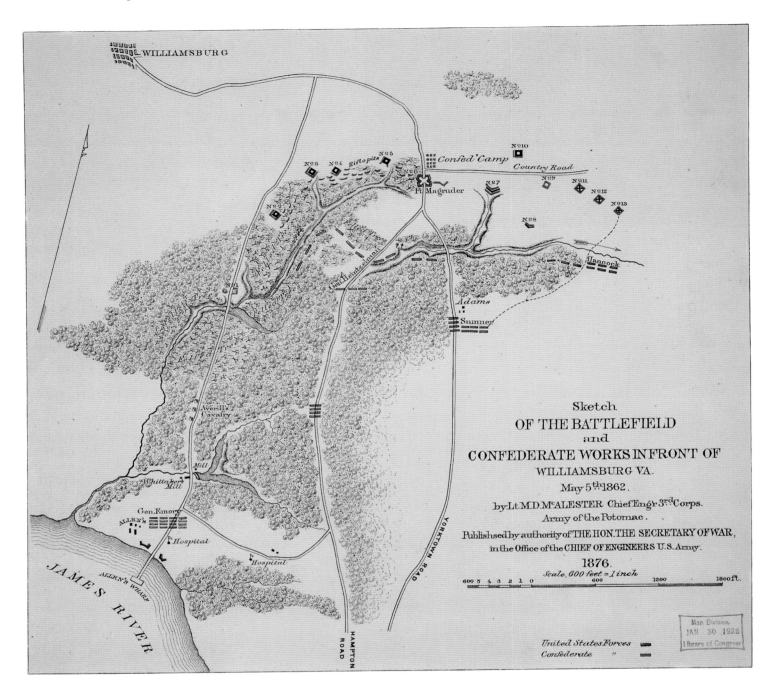

Sketch
OF THE BATTLEFIELD
and
CONFEDERATE WORKS IN FRONT OF
WILLIAMSBURG VA.
May 5th 1862.
by Lt. M.D. McALESTER Chief Engr 3rd Corps.
Army of the Potomac.
Published by authority of THE HON. THE SECRETARY OF WAR,
in the Office of the CHIEF OF ENGINEERS U.S. Army.
1876.
Scale, 600 feet = 1 inch

United States Forces
Confederate "

ABOVE: *As the Confederates were fighting to cover the withdrawal of their army past the former colonial capital of Williamsburg, generals Daniel Harvey Hill and Jubal Early were granted permission to attack in an attempt to silence Winfield S. Hancock's artillery (upper right). Moving his infantry behind the crest of a hill, Hancock waited until the Confederate regiments were within thirty paces before ordering his men to fire. After firing successive volleys, Hancock ordered a charge that swept the Confederates to the rear. Afterward McClellan wrote, "Hancock was superb," providing an apt nickname, Hancock the Superb. This battlefield sketch was made by Lieutenant Miles McAlester, Chief Engineer of the 3rd Corps, Army of the Potomac, and published later by the Office of the Chief of Engineers, U.S. Army.*

There was one bright spot for the Confederates, however, who still had control of Chattanooga and eastern Tennessee—the region that the Union would have to capture if they were to penetrate into and capture Georgia.

The Peninsula Campaign

There was a different approach to warfare in the eastern theater of operations, where the conflict had narrowed to become a "war between two cities." War plans formulated in Washington concentrated on the capture of Richmond instead of the destruction of the Confederacy's fighting capability—that is, the elimination of the Army of Northern Virginia. The two armies

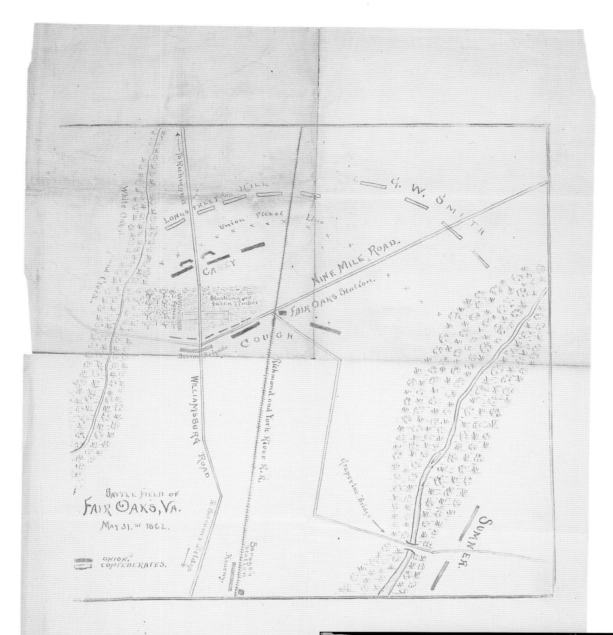

LEFT: *The Battle of Fair Oaks—or Seven Pines—began on May 31, 1862, when an impatient General Daniel H. Hill ordered his men to attack the entrenchments and camp of Union General Silas Casey's division along the Williamsburg Road. The Confederates were unable to exploit their initial success, and Union reinforcements were able to cross the flooded Chickahominy River to stop additional attacks by Confederate General Joseph Johnston. At dusk, Johnston rode forward to evaluate the situation and was wounded by a spent minié ball and a shell fragment. The battle was not renewed the following day, when Lee was placed in command. This is one of several excellent maps drawn by Charles W. Reed, of the 9th Massachusetts Battery.*

RIGHT: *Aerial observation over Fair Oaks by the Union's Professor Thaddeus Lowe during the battle was the first use of aerial observation by American forces in combat. Observers made sketches later converted into maps, but if speed in reporting was needed, the observers could communicate with their headquarters by telegraph. The innovative Lowe also modified a barge into history's first aircraft carrier during McClellan's Peninsula Campaign.*

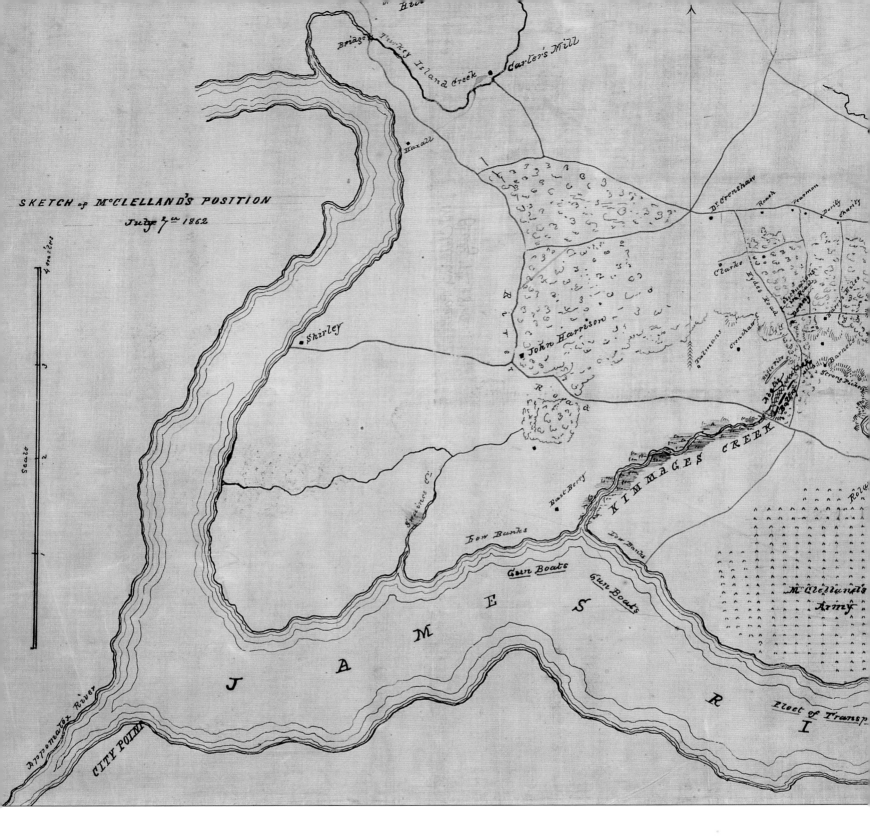

faced one another in northern Virginia, where Joseph Johnston, now commander of the entire Confederate army in Virginia, faced the enormous war machine that had been trained and equipped at great expense under George B. McClellan, the Army of the Potomac.

Lincoln and McClellan, both of whom were opionated and had strong personalities, differed in their ideas about operations against the Confederate capital. Lincoln wanted the Army of the Potomac to use a land route in order to keep the entire army between Johnston's force and Washington. McClellan preferred a water route, which would allow him to get between Johnston's army, located in the vicinity of Manassas, and the intended target, Richmond.

McClellan believed the fortifications that had been constructed around Washington would adequately protect the capital from attack. Both men put their differences aside when Johnston moved his army away from Manassas to better protect Richmond.

Once Johnston had shifted his army to Fredericksburg, which was on McClellan's prospective route to Richmond, McClellan refined his plans for a waterborne assault. He planned to take advantage of the Federal superiority in naval capabilities and move his troops to a safe location under Union control, Fort Monroe. Fast-moving troops could cover the seventy-five miles (120km) up the peninsula to Richmond before Johnston would be able to

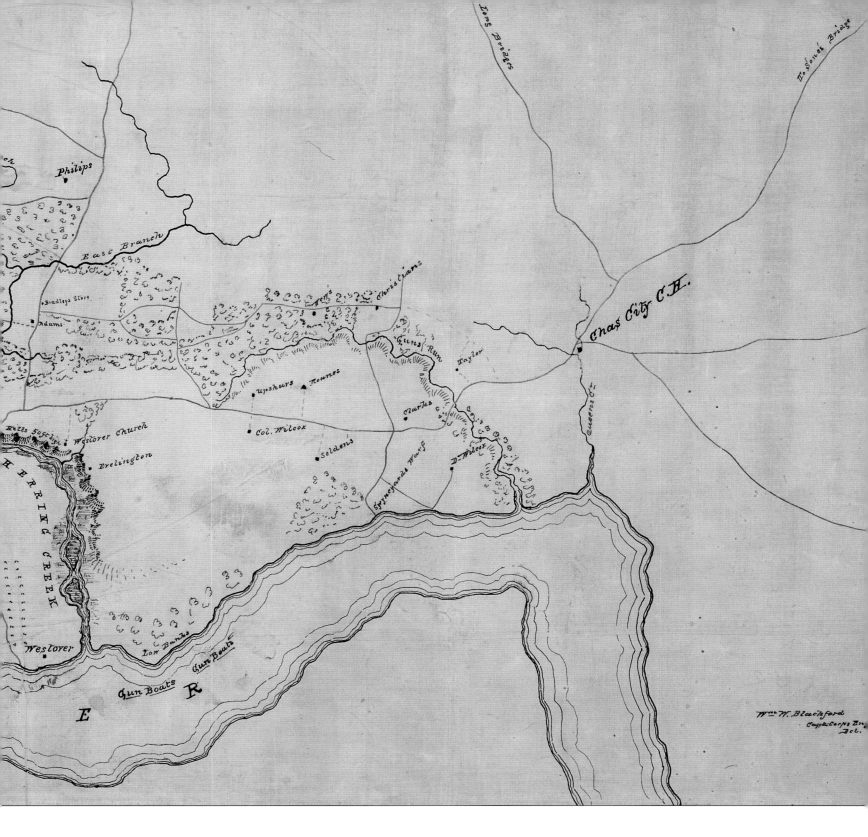

ABOVE: *Following the disaster at Bull Run, McClellan spent months training and developing his splendid Army of the Potomac. With the better portion of this formidable body at his back, McClellan approached Richmond during the Peninsula Campaign in 1862; unfortunately, his characteristic slowness in the face of combat cost him dearly when aggression might have secured the capture of the strategic town. Even more significantly, the Union commander failed to grasp the weakness of the Confederate army that faced him under the untried Robert E. Lee. In contrast, Lee quickly assessed the situation and took immediate steps to fortify his defensive lines around the Confederate capital, Richmond. Demonstrating the aggression for which he would become famous, Lee then launched a tactical offensive against McClellan in the Seven Days' Battles, which forced the Union army back from Richmond and into a general withdrawal from the Virginia Peninsula.*

By the end of the Seven Days' Battles, McClellan's army sought refuge at Harrison's Landing, having faced the military genius of Robert E. Lee for the first time. After the fighting at Malvern Hill, the Army of the Potomac marched eight miles (12.8km) to the relative safety of the landing, where nearby Union gunboats along the James River could provide protective fire. Lee had lost one quarter of his army in the defense of Richmond, while McClellan managed to save his once-proud army by withdrawing. Lee wrote: "Under ordinary circumstances, the Federal army should have been destroyed." This map illustrates the positions of McClellan's army on July 7, 1862. Part of the Hotchkiss collection of maps and papers at the Library of Congress, this map was prepared by Captain William W. Blackford of the Corps of Engineers.

ABOVE: *The peninsula over which McClellan proposed to march toward Richmond narrowed significantly near Yorktown (a Revolutionary War site) and was protected by fifteen thousand Confederate troops. Yorktown's defenses were on Abraham Lincoln's mind on April 5, 1862, as he anxiously awaited for news of McClellan's progress on the peninsula and the march toward Richmond. The president's general anxiety was increased by the news that Grant was heavily engaged at Shiloh. Meanwhile, convinced he was too short of men to successfully defeat the number of Confederates he had imagined there to be, McClellan decided to besiege Yorktown instead of attacking it directly. His concerns were increased by an excellent deception created by Confederate John B. Magruder, an amateur actor who marched a few hundred troops around and around in a circle, a section of which was visible to McClellan's lines. Thinking this column represented huge numbers of reinforcements, the cautious McClellan delayed until huge siege guns were in place. The guns were in position by May 3, but by then the Confederate commander had ordered a general withdrawal. They had managed to delay McClellan for a full month, allowing additional Confederates to be assembled near Richmond to resist McClellan's advance. This illustration shows the seige of Yorktown.*

TOP: *Huge, ten-ton (10.1t) cannon capable of firing shells weighing two hundred pounds (90.6kg) were hauled into positions by teams of 100 horses. McClellan delayed any thoughts of attack until 114 of these enormous guns were in place to reduce Yorktown's defenses. Combined with heavy mortars capable of hurling 220-pound (99.7kg) shells into the Confederate trenches, this overwhelming force convinced the Confederates to withdraw. Meanwhile, the Union force had wasted precious time.*

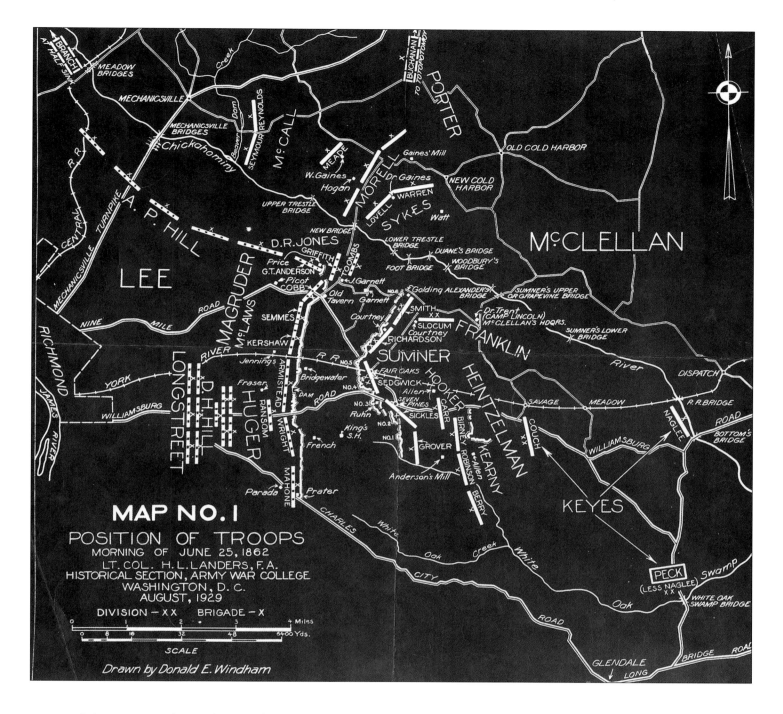

MAP NO. 1

POSITION OF TROOPS
MORNING OF JUNE 25, 1862
LT. COL. H. L. LANDERS, F. A.
HISTORICAL SECTION, ARMY WAR COLLEGE
WASHINGTON, D. C.
AUGUST, 1929

DIVISION – XX   BRIGADE – X

SCALE

Drawn by Donald E. Windham

react to their presence and move his men from Fredericksburg and thereby halt the invasion.

The plan was good and the troops were well-trained and in sufficient numbers to accomplish their assignments. Unfortunately for the Army of the Potomac, Thomas J. "Stonewall" Jackson began wreaking havoc in the Shenandoah Valley just as McClellan was planning to set out.

As Johnston made swift preparations to move his army from Fredericksburg to confront McClellan on the peninsula, Robert E. Lee, then military advisor to Jefferson Davis, sent orders to Jackson to initiate a campaign in the Shenandoah Valley, knowing full well that any threat against the capital would result in additional troops being withheld from McClellan.

Jackson, one of the best field strategists in American history, was a decisive and brilliant commander whose use of deception, swift

movement, surprise, and hard strikes soon left the equivalent of three Federal divisions defeated. For their part, the Union forces were under separate commanders, moved more slowly than Jackson's force, and were hampered by the fact that orders arriving from Washington frequently lacked any realistic grasp of the local situation.

Jackson fought six battles between March 23 and June 9, 1862: Kernstown, McDowell, Front Royal, Winchester, Cross Keys, and Port Republic. He won clear victories in each of these confrontations, with the exception of Kernstown, and his actions prevented a full corps of Union soldiers from being sent to reinforce McClellan in his efforts to take Richmond: upon being informed that there were too few men to protect Washington, D.C., Lincoln ordered that one of the two corps waiting to board the transport ships be held back. With this, McClellan lost thirty thousand men from his attacking force.

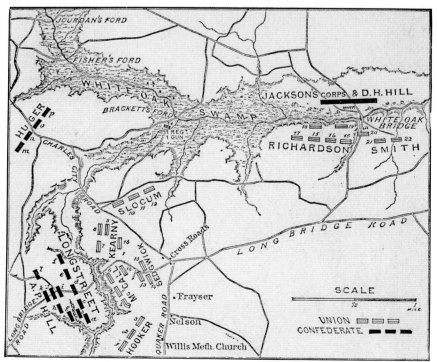

ABOVE and RIGHT: *The battle of Frayser's Farm (or Glendale) was fought on June 30, 1862. McClellan was in the process of shifting his base from the York River to the relative safety of the James (where Federal gunboats offered some protection) as Lee attempted to interdict the maneuvering Union columns. Near the center of Lee's line, five Alabama regiments charged forward against the Federal line. As the 11th Alabama charged at the Federal defenders, a Union artillery battery fired canister into them. The color bearer of the 11th Alabama, Charles McNeil, jumped to the top of a Union cannon before being shot down. The Federal defenders counterattacked to regain the captured battery, but the guns were lost a second time. The 11th Alabama paid a terrible price: seven of their ten company commanders were lost and one company emerged from the battle with only three men remaining. Curiously, one of the columns assigned to attack the Union army at a critical road junction, led by Jackson, bogged down because its commander seemed to lose some of his normal energy on the battlefield. The painting is by Don Troiani. The map was published in* Century *magazine in July 1885.*

PREVIOUS PAGE: *McClellan hoped to use his superior artillery force to break through Lee's defensive positions in front of Richmond, but was hit hard by the Confederate army before the Union attack could be coordinated. Aware that his Union counterpart tended to be overcautious, Lee left just twenty-five thousand men in defensive positions to guard Richmond and sent 65,000 soldiers north of the Chickahominy River to attack Fitz-John Porter's isolated V Corps. Porter was fortunate: he survived the ensuing battle on the outskirts of Mechanicsville and was able to retreat to a position near Gaines' Mill (where Lee again attacked), and eventually rejoined McClellan on the southern shore of the Chickahominy. With his bold actions, Lee had gained the initiative and continued to attack the Federals throughout the remainder of the week. This map, produced in 1929 under the auspices of the U.S. Army War College, shows the positions of the forces the day before the attack outside Mechanicsville.*

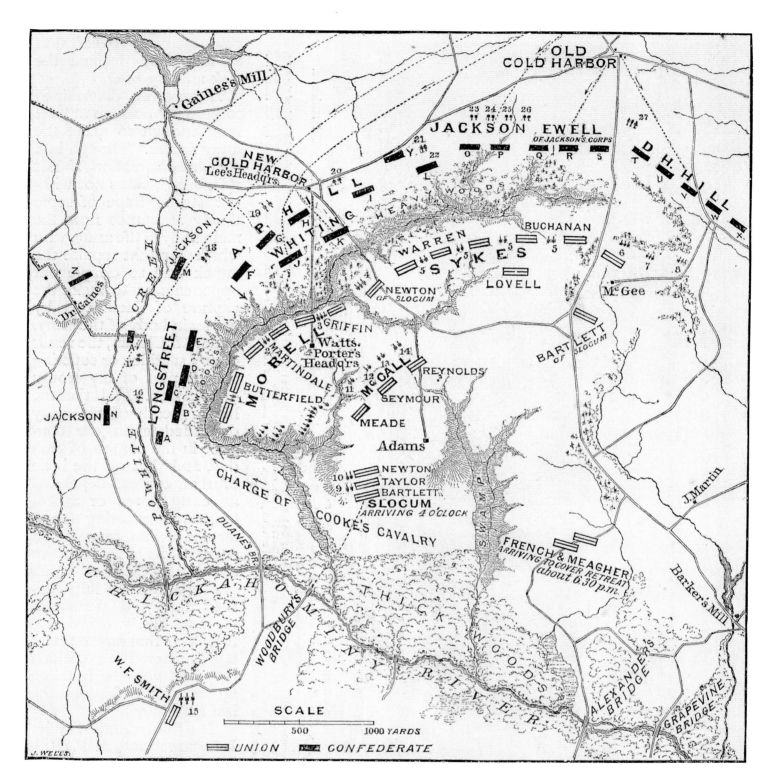

ABOVE: *Following the devastating defeat at Bull Run in July 1861, General George B. McClellan was given the job of rebuilding the Union army. For eight months, McClellan did nothing but drill the army, honing it into a well-equipped, well-drilled fighting machine, which was thereafter known as the Army of the Potomac. Taking advantage of the transport capabilities of the northern navy, McClellan mobilized his new force, taking them south to the peninsula between the York and James rivers, where he planned to mount a northwesterly offensive with the ultimate goal of taking Richmond. Landing at Fort Monroe, the Federal troops headed northwest toward the first Confederate stronghold, Yorktown. After several daring delaying moves by the Confederates, the Union army had finally come within six miles (9.6km) of Richmond. During fighting at Fair Oaks, also known to the South as Seven Pines, Confederate General Johnston was wounded, which elevated Lee to his first major command. Believing that only by mounting aggressive offensive operations would Richmond be preserved, Lee recalled Jackson's army from the Shenandoah Valley and mounted a daring attack on the superior Union army on June 25, 1862, touching off a series of battles that would be known as the Seven Days' Battles. After the bloody stand-off at Seven Pines, Lee quickly invigorated his weary army and battered the Union army, forcing McClellan to order the retreat of Fitz-John Porter's V Corps to Gaines' Mill. Lee continued to press his advantage, striking the Federal right along a swamp near Gaines' Mill on June 27, 1862. Initial frontal assaults by the Confederate divisions were repulsed, and new attacks were ordered. In the afternoon, John B. Hood and his Texas Brigade were able to break through the Union center and hold their position against a counterattack. The Union army was forced to retreat during the night across the Chickahominy River, ultimately setting the stage for a gigantic confrontation at Malvern Hill. Reproduced from a battlefield map made by Jacob Wells on June 27, 1862, and published in the June 1885 edition of* Century *magazine, this map shows the disposition of troops at the battle of Gaines' Mill.*

RIGHT: *Malvern Hill was the location of the final showdown between Lee and McClellan in the Seven Days' Battles. The battle began on July 1, 1862, when the Confederates attacked Union skirmishers at the foot of the hill; their apparent success led Lee to believe he would be able to trap McClellan against the James River. Massed Union artillery pieces—250 of them—positioned on the top of the hill soon were able to silence Confederate guns with effective counter-battery fire. In addition, nearby Federal gunboats fired their large naval guns across the summit of Malvern Hill in support of McClellan's soldiers, and by the end of the day, Lee had lost more than five thousand men. McClellan's artillery had made the difference; one battery alone had fired 1,392 rounds at the attacking Confederate lines. The undamaged Union army withdrew to the safety of Harrison's Landing while the Confederate army counted their dead. This map is based on the battlefield sketch of Jacob Wells and was first published in* Century *magazine in the August 1885 issue.*

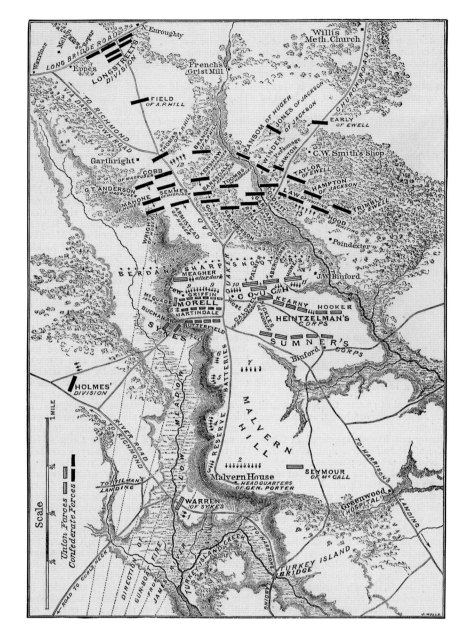

LEFT: *Union wounded were treated in field hospitals, such as this one at Savage's Station, where men of the 16th New York Infantry received care. Such injuries were horrendous in Civil War battles, where there was a common ratio of 4- or 5-to-1 wounded to killed. Wounded soldiers faced primitive medical treatments, and amputation was a common procedure for any gunshot wound that resulted in a fractured bone of the arm or leg. Chest, head, and abdominal wounds were normally fatal.*

Incorrectly informed by his secret service advisors that he was faced by large numbers of Confederates, McClellan cautiously moved the forces he had assembled at Fort Monroe in a northwesterly direction along the peninsula formed by the York and James rivers. At Yorktown, he was delayed for a full month by Major General John B. Magruder and his fifteen thousand men. Magruder skillfully utilized deception techniques to convince McClellan that his numbers were far greater than they actually were. Not long after fighting free of Magruder's men, McClellan was delayed again, this time at Williamsburg, where he encountered even stiffer Confederate resistance from Major General James Longstreet's rear guard.

McClellan's army marched close to Richmond on May 25, and two of his corps crossed the Chickahominy River while the remaining three corps remained on the north side. When the river was flooded by severe rains on May 30, Johnston saw an opportunity to defeat the divided Union army, one half at a time. He ordered his army to strike the isolated corps south of the river on May 31. But his commanders were not up to the complex tasks assigned them, and the Federals held their ground. On June 1, the Union forces counterattacked, but gained little. Johnston was wounded in this fighting, known as the battle of Fair Oaks to the Union and Seven Pines to the Confederacy.

With Johnston wounded, President Davis ordered Robert E. Lee to take command of the army in front of Richmond. Lee was a confident and supremely able commander, and true to his nature he moved swiftly to deploy the Confederate army in an effort to destroy the Army of the Potomac in a climactic battle. As part of the plan, Lee ordered Jackson to return to the Richmond vicinity from the Shenandoah Valley.

Lee hit the Union army hard. Leaving only a small portion of the Confederate army to defend Richmond, on June 26 Lee moved the bulk of his army, sixty-five thousand men, against McClellan's V Corps, under the command of Fitz-John Porter, which was isolated on the north side of the Chickahominy River. Then the unexpected happened—Jackson was late in arriving at the battlefield, and Porter's corps managed to survive the battle of Mechanicsville after a severe fight.

McClellan ordered the V Corps to withdraw to stronger positions at Gaines' Mill, where Lee struck them on June 27. While the Federal line was able to hold for a while against the fifty-seven thousand Confederates attacking them, their lines eventually broke. Fortunately for the Union force, darkness fell before Lee could order additional attacks to exploit his advantage. McClellan took the opportunity provided by the lull in the fighting to withdraw Porter's men, ordering them to rejoin the main army on the south side of the Chickahominy.

McClellan chose to retreat to the James River, which was fully open to the gunboats of the Union navy, and the Army of the Potomac began to move over two roads. Lee attacked the Federal rear guard units as the main force continued to withdraw. The two forces fought at Savage's Station on June 29 and again at Frayser's Farm on June 30.

On July 1, McClellan concentrated his large army near his new base of operations, Harrison's Landing, where nearby Federal gunboats could bring supporting fire against any attacking

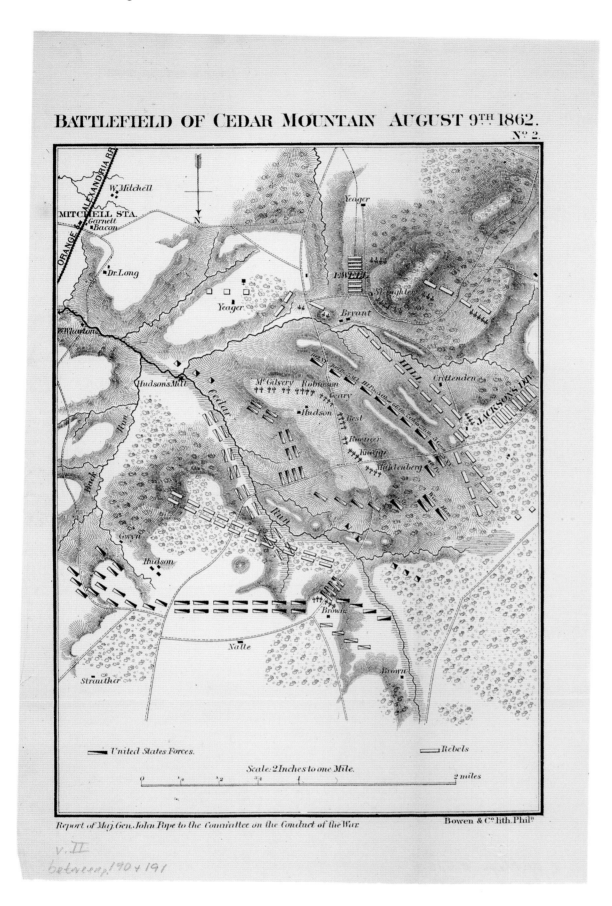

BATTLEFIELD OF CEDAR MOUNTAIN AUGUST 9TH 1862.

Nº 2.

Report of Maj. Gen. John Pope to the Committee on the Conduct of the War.

Bowen & Cº. lith. Philª

ABOVE: *During the afternoon of August 9, 1862, Jackson ordered several brigades to secure Cedar Mountain, Virginia, as his remaining troops were deployed to the west. The Union troops, commanded by General Nathaniel Banks, attacked from the north, across Cedar Run, to strike Jackson's left flank. Severe fighting developed and Jackson's entire left wing began to break apart. Jackson rode forward to rally the retreating men as he ordered General Ambrose P. Hill's division into the fight. By the end of the day, the Union line began to break and the bloody battle ended. Produced by the commercial lithographer Bowen & Co. of Philadelphia, this map of the Cedar Mountain battlefield accompanied an official report by General John Pope to the Committee on the Conduct of the War in 1866.*

Confederates. McClellan occupied the high ground on Malvern Hill, where his artillery was placed nearly hub to hub and his infantry was ordered into strong supporting positions.

Initially convinced that McClellan's position was too strong to be assaulted, Lee later reversed himself when he saw movements within the Federal lines that convinced him that they were once again retreating. He ordered his troops forward, but subordinate commanders moved into assault slowly, attacking the Union line piecemeal. The Federal artillery cut broad swathes through the attackers' formations and the gunboats on the river delivered additional fire. The attack ground to a halt. Lee had been unable to mass his regiments to attack McClellan all at once and thereby overwhelm the Union position.

The following day, McClellan withdrew his army to Harrison's Landing, where it assumed defensive positions under cover of the heavy guns of the Union navy vessels. The series of engagements that would become known as the Seven Days' battles had come to a bloody end. Lee withdrew his battered army, which had done all of the attacking and lost more than twenty thousand men, back to Richmond to rest and reorganize for the next phase of the campaign.

Lee was in a difficult position even though he had forced McClellan's Army of the Potomac away from the Confederate capital. Major General John Pope, with forty-five thousand men, had been ordered south to the vicinity of Fredericksburg, Virginia, leaving Lee's Army of Northern Virginia caught between the armies of McClellan and Pope. He sent Jackson toward Pope with a small force of twenty-four thousand men, and the two armies fought a battle at Cedar Mountain on August 9.

LEFT: *Encountering the retreating men from his own Stonewall Brigade on August 9, 1862, at Cedar Mountain (pictured here), Jackson rode into his demoralized men, attempting to rally them by drawing his sword. Unaccustomed to using the weapon, he found that it had rusted into its scabbard. Drawing the entire sword, scabbard and all, Jackson grabbed the regiment's battle flag and led his men back into the fight. This painting is by Don Troiani.*

Second Manassas

In a bold maneuver—given that McClellan was still on Richmond's very doorstep—Lee decided to take the war northward and move against the smaller force protecting Washington, D.C., under the command of Major General John Pope. Pope became aware of Lee's intentions and withdrew across the Rappahannock River, where Lee had hoped to trap him. Jackson was sent on a swift march over sixty miles (96km) of Virginia countryside and he was able to get into Pope's rear areas. Jackson destroyed the Union army's supplies on August 26 in Manassas, Virginia, and was able to draw away before being located by Pope.

Pope was so occupied with locating Jackson that he overlooked the nearby presence of Lee and the rest of the Army of Northern Virginia. On August 29, Pope's men attacked Jackson's troops, who were sheltered behind the unfinished and abandoned railroad whose embankments provided ready-made trenches. Porter's corps from the Army of the Potomac arrived on the battlefield with the intention of attacking Jackson's right flank, but Longstreet also arrived on the scene, having just transited Thoroughfare Gap, and blocked Porter's advance.

On August 30, Pope assumed that Jackson was retreating and ordered his men to pursue.

This gave Lee the opportunity that he had been awaiting, and he ordered Longstreet to strike immediately at Pope's exposed flank. As with the other Union army that had fought here at Manassas, or Bull Run, in 1861, Pope led his men back from Manassas to the safety of the defenses of Washington, D.C., though not until they had fought an additional battle with a Confederate force at Chantilly.

Lee had managed to win a great battle against a large army while another Federal army loitered nearby. It was his audacity and ability to make the most of speed, surprise, and deception that allowed him to win this major battle.

Lincoln recalled McClellan from the Richmond area to Washington, D.C., to resume command of the home forces while John Pope was ordered to a new command in faraway Minnesota. McClellan planned to take the time to reorganize and resupply the Army of the Potomac after its long campaign and hard fighting near Richmond, but Lee had different ideas.

At this time, Braxton Bragg was invading Kentucky as part of a grand strategy with the aim of bringing that slave state under control of the Confederacy. Lee and Jefferson Davis reviewed the strategic situation, which revealed that McClellan had left the routes into the north relatively uncovered. There was a garrison at Harper's Ferry, but little else stood in the way of a Confederate move into either Maryland or

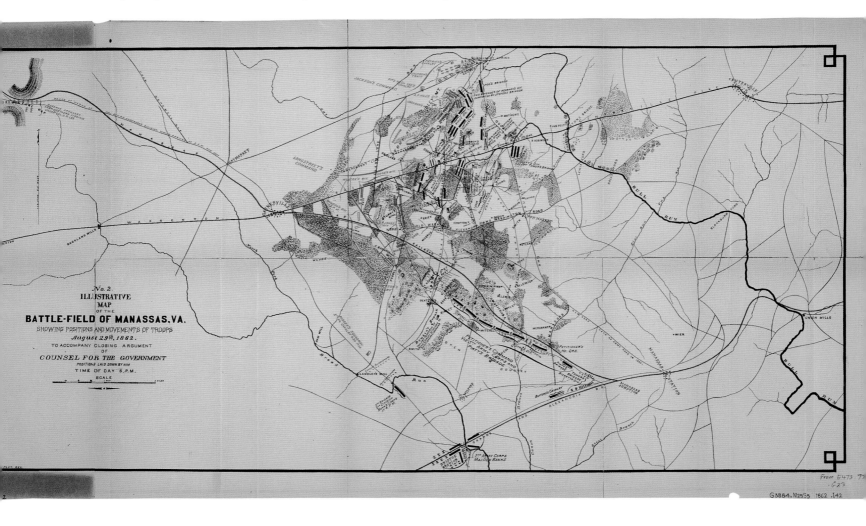

No. 2.
ILLUSTRATIVE
MAP
OF THE
BATTLE-FIELD OF MANASSAS. VA.
SHOWING POSITIONS AND MOVEMENTS OF TROOPS
August 29th, 1862.
TO ACCOMPANY CLOSING ARGUMENT
OF
COUNSEL FOR THE GOVERNMENT
POSITIONS LAID DOWN BY HIM
TIME OF DAY 6 P.M.
SCALE

LEFT: *After the battle of Second Manassas was over, Pope was in full retreat toward the defenses of Washington, D.C. This photograph shows Stone Church in Centreville, located on the Warrenton Turnpike, where Pope stopped along the retreat, perhaps to reflect on the dismal turn of events. The Union army had lost another major battle along with nearly 15,000 men, who were lost between the Rappahannock crossings and the Potomac River. In only three short months, the military situation had reversed itself. When Lee had taken command of the southern army, McClellan was pressing forward at the defenses of Richmond, but now Lee was approaching Washington, D.C., driving Pope before him.*

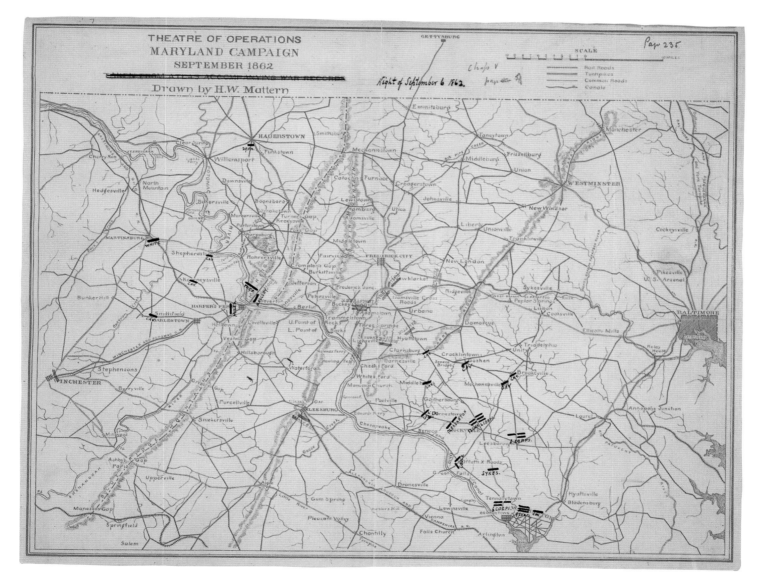

ABOVE: *Robert E. Lee had defeated the Army of the Potomac, clearing the region of opposition, and planned to take the war into the North for the first time. By invading Maryland, Lee hoped to be able to draw the Army of the Potomac into a climactic battle and destroy it as he cut rail communications between the eastern and western sections of the country. A Confederate move into Maryland would also expose the major cities of Washington, D.C., Baltimore, and Philadelphia to the horrors of war and (hopefully) demoralize their populations. Moreover, it was hoped that victory on northern soil would spur international recognition of the Confederacy. Opposing Lee was the battered Army of the Potomac under its old commander, George B. McClellan, recalled into active service. The two armies would meet once again along Antietam Creek. This map was drawn by H.W. Mattern and shows the position of troops from September 6 to 14, 1862 (the troop markings were added later by General Ezra Carman).*

ABOVE: *After his success at Second Manassas, Lee didn't pause to rest and refit his divisions. He ordered his army forward to cross the Potomac River, and once across, to camp near Frederick, Maryland. His Potomac River crossing is observed by Union pickets in this sketch by Alfred Waud.*

RIGHT: *General George B. McClellan, "Little Mac" to the men of the Army of the Potomac, had been recalled to command after the Union defeat at Second Manassas under Pope. Learning of Lee's campaign plan when a copy of Confederate orders were found wrapped around some lost cigars, McClellan still delayed any decisive movements and Lee was able to concentrate his scattered forces and fight the Union army into a bloody stalemate at Antietam.*

Pennsylvania. Shortly, a decision was made to invade Maryland—like Kentucky, a slave state with many Confederate sympathizers—while drawing the damaged Army of the Potomac into a location where it could be defeated or destroyed in an enormous battle that would leave Washington unprotected. Other major cities in the east—Baltimore, Philadelphia, and Harrisburg—would also be threatened by this move, and the line of march would allow the Confederate army to destroy the major connecting link with the Union's western states, the Baltimore and Ohio Railroad. With these objectives in mind, Lee invaded Maryland in the first offensive operation by the Confederate army in the east.

Lee's fifty-five-thousand-man army marched from Manassas to Leesburg, Virginia, the site of the Federal disaster at Ball's Bluff, and crossed the Potomac River to march to camps near Frederick, Maryland. From there, Lee quickly sent Jackson to capture the Federal garrison at Harper's Ferry while the rest of the army marched toward Hagerstown, Maryland.

McClellan's Army of the Potomac was forced to march from their camps near Washington and follow Lee, keeping themselves between the Confederates and the national capital. The Federals arrived at Frederick, Maryland, on September 12. It was at this point in the campaign that McClellan had an incredible stroke of luck: a copy of Lee's campaign plan fell into his hands.

Two Union soldiers found an extra copy of orders meant to go to Major General D.H. Hill wrapped around cigars and rushed the precious document to General McClellan. After delaying for an additional sixteen hours before mobilizing, McClellan began to move, but by then Lee had learned of the lost orders and moved all

available men into positions at the gaps in South Mountain through which the Army of the Potomac would have to travel. It was not until the night of September 14 that McClellan was able to force his way across South Mountain.

Antietam

Lee retreated to the town of Sharpsburg, near Antietam Creek, where he prepared to meet McClellan. The Federal commander delayed until September 17 before ordering a series of three uncoordinated attacks throughout the day. Major clashes ensued, the names of which entered into the pages of American military history in infamy: West Woods, East Woods, The Cornfield, Bloody Lane, and Burnside's Bridge. Major General A.P. Hill and his "Light Division" arrived on the field after a swift march from Harper's Ferry just in time to halt what might have been a decisive assault on Sharpsburg by Major General Ambrose Burnside and his IX Corps.

The day ended with thirteen thousand of the seventy thousand Union soldiers committed as casualties and nearly the same number out of the forty thousand Confederates in the battle. The bloodiest day in American military history was over, and in the end McClellan allowed Lee to depart from the field. The battle had been a bloody draw, but when the Army of Northern Virginia was forced to withdraw, Lincoln was

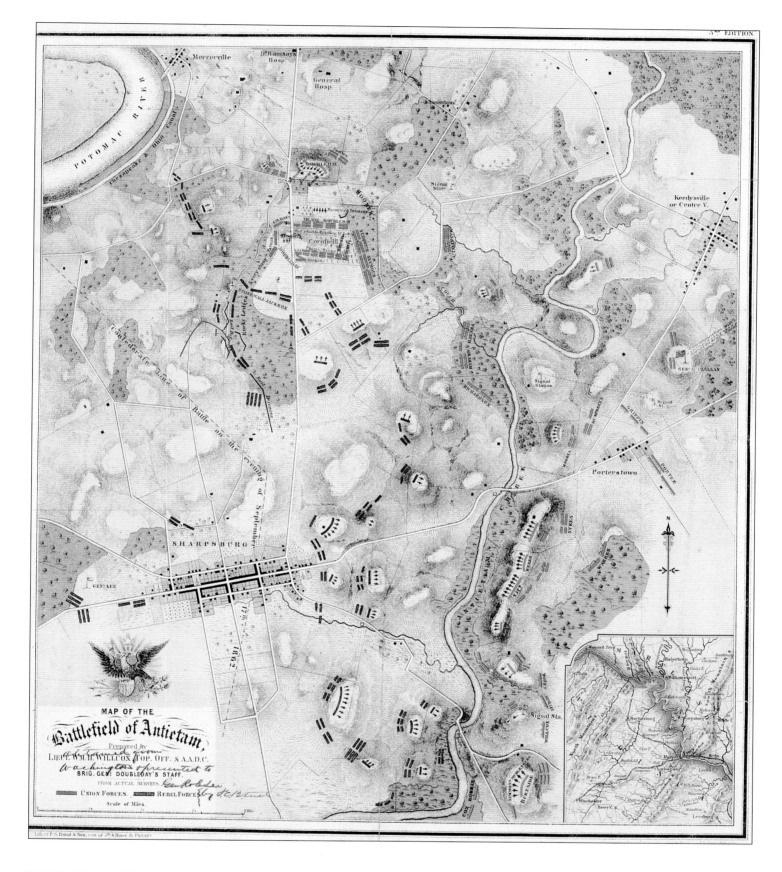

ABOVE: *After the defeat of General John Pope at Second Manassas, command of the Army of the Potomac was returned to George B. McClellan. The conceited commander soon wrote to his wife, saying, "under the circumstances no one else could save the country, and I have not shrunk from the terrible task." After recovering a lost copy of Lee's orders to the Confederate commanders (Special Orders No. 191), McClellan moved his large army into battle against a widely dispersed Confederate force. McClellan's naturally cautious approach, however, cost him the opportunity of a lifetime: Lee was able to hastily assemble his forces after fighting a battle at nearby South Mountain, and on September 17, 1862, the two armies fought a battle in which McClellan committed his forces piecemeal. By the end of the day, the two armies had fought the bloodiest single-day battle of the entire Civil War—Antietam. This lithograph was made by the commercial firm P.S. Duval & Son, Philadelphia, from a map by Lieutenant William H. Willcox. This particular copy is inscribed to General Lee from J.E.B. Stuart.*

RIGHT: *Confederate soldiers sheltered themselves in a shallow depression called the Sunken Road, but so many men lost their lives there that this stretch of battlefield has been called Bloody Lane since the battle of Antietam.*

BELOW: *McClellan delayed his assault at Antietam until the early morning of September 17, when a series of uncoordinated attacks were ordered. Confederate lines were hard-pressed, but they held as fighting raged across rolling terrain that entered history as the West Wood, the Cornfield, the East Wood, Bloody Lane, and Burnside's Bridge. Massed volley fire from muskets and cannon struck extended lines of assaulting soldiers, who were "dropped like a scythe running through our line." The proud regiments, like the Irish soldiers of the famous Irish Brigade pictured here, moved forward in lines that looked as if nothing could halt their progress. By the end of the day, the Union army had lost 13,000 men out of 70,000 engaged. The Confederates, with 40,000 men present on the field, lost nearly as many troops in the bloodiest single-day battle of the Civil War.*

able to claim that a strategic victory had been won by the Union at Antietam.

Lincoln took this opportunity to issue the Emancipation Proclamation, a political pronouncement that freed few—if any—slaves at the time it was issued, but nonetheless had a great emotional and moral impact on the population and on the war. The Emancipation Proclamation was a carefully crafted piece of political manipulation: although the slaves of the four slave states remaining in the Union were unaffected by it and none of the slaves living in areas held by the Union army were free to leave their masters, Lincoln had managed to appeal to antislavery opinion everywhere, but especially in Europe. From the time the proclamation was delivered, open recognition of the Confederacy by the European powers became unlikely.

Earlier in the year, Congress had passed the Second Confiscation Act, a part of which authorized the recruitment of blacks, but the Emancipation Proclamation provided additional

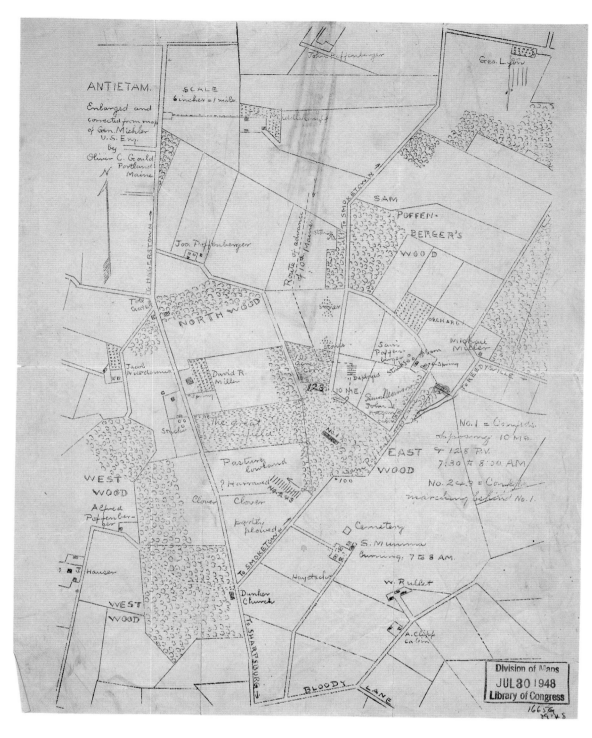

LEFT: *Early on the morning of September 17, 1862, Lee had positioned his army along a line between the town of Sharpsburg and Antietam Creek. The Union battle plan resulted in a series of uncoordinated attacks, McClellan typically hesitating to commit his two reserve corps against Lee's exhausted defenders. If McClellan had ordered his reserves forward, Confederate resistance might have collapsed, but instead the battle ended in a grisly stalemate. This map illustrates the first phase of the battle. This map of the battlefield was drawn by Oliver Gould from the earlier sketch by General Nathaniel Michler of the U.S. Engineers Corps.*

RIGHT: *Major General George B. McClellan (fifth from left) emerged from the initial maneuver campaign of the Civil War in western Virginia to assume command of the largest military force ever assembled in the western hemisphere up to that point. After organizing the army into a formidable military body, McClellan proved inept at leading it into battle. He was relieved of his command, but was called on to lead the Army of the Potomac once again when Pope proved even less able to guide the Union army to victory. Alas, the same timidity that had prevented success during the Peninsula Campaign caused McClellan to make costly mistakes during the Maryland Campaign and the battle of Antietam.*

LEFT: *Federal attackers planned to assault the Georgia defenders at the lower bridge over Antietam Creek by driving directly across the bridge while additional troops forded the creek downstream. Union General George Crook's brigade was assigned the task of attacking over the bridge, but Crook uncharacteristically had failed to scout to his front, and his attack actually missed the bridge, arriving at the creek four hundred yards (365.6m) upstream. General Ambrose Burnside ordered another attempt, but the assaulting columns fell apart under heavy fire before they arrived at the bridge.*

ABOVE: *McClellan ordered yet another attempt to take the lower bridge over Antietam. Burnside was ordered to take the bridge "if it costs 10,000 men." After receiving a promise that their long delayed whisky ration would be delivered, the 51st Pennsylvania and 51st New York Infantry Regiments prepared to cross the bridge. Federal cannon were pushed close to the crossing and double canister shots were fired at the Confederate defenders. Initially pinned down by heavy fire, the 51st Pennsylvania's color bearers and color guard rushed the bridge as Confederate fire slackened. Shortly afterward, the men of both regiments were across the bridge and the surviving Georgians (now out of ammunition) withdrew to preselected positions after they learned a large Federal force had crossed downstream and would soon attack their flanks.*

incentives to recruitment. By spring 1863, the War Department had established a Bureau of Colored Troops and segregated units controlled by white officers began to enter Federal service in significant numbers. In contrast, black men who chose to serve in the Confederate army served in fully integrated units.

After Antietam, both armies returned to base areas in Virginia, where they recuperated from the terrible effects of their recent battle. McClellan was relieved of his command by President Lincoln for political arrogance and obvious disrespect for the president as much as for his inability to fight effectively with the powerful military machine at his command, the Army of the Potomac. Ambrose Burnside reluctantly accepted, on November 7, the position vacated by McClellan and worked to develop a campaign plan for early winter.

Fredericksburg

With Lee near Culpeper, Burnside planned to march rapidly to Fredericksburg, then advance along the railroad to Richmond before Lee could move his army to block a movement against the Confederate capital. This swift movement of the 120,000-man Union army would also place the entire Army of the Potomac squarely between Lee and Richmond and would certainly bring on a general engagement on ground selected by Burnside. The excellent plan, however, still was dependent upon the inefficient commanders at lower levels within the army.

Burnside attempted to remedy this situation through the creation of additional headquarters at a level above the corps. He assigned two corps and cavalry to each of three Grand Divisions— Right, Left, and Center—each of which was placed under an experienced commander. Once they began their march, the troops were able to reach Fredericksburg by November 17, well in advance of Lee's arrival and all according to plan. But problems delayed the construction of pontoon bridges over the Rappahannock River that were needed by the assaulting columns of infantry. The Confederate army was given sufficient time to make a hasty march to Fredericksburg, where they moved on to high ground to the rear of the town as they waited for Burnside to make his next move.

Position meant everything to Civil War commanders, and Lee's army now enjoyed some of the best defensive positions they would occupy during the entire war. From their camp on the high ground, they could observe Burnside's preparations for river crossings that were

BELOW: *On November 7, 1862, President Lincoln replaced McClellan with General Ambrose Burnside. The new commander of the Army of the Potomac decided to march rapidly to Fredericksburg before Lee could move to block the advance. Once he was located between Lee and Richmond, Burnside planned to move against the Confederate capital. As planned, Burnside arrived at the Rappahannock River crossings well ahead of Lee, but a series of delays in building pontoon bridges allowed Lee to occupy the high ground before Burnside's men could cross the river.*

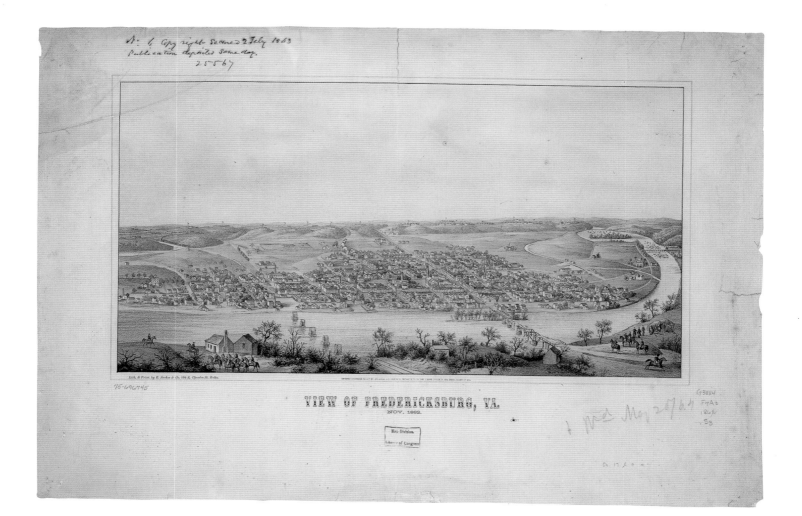

VIEW OF FREDERICKSBURG, VA.
NOV. 1862.

RIGHT: *When General Ambrose Burnside took over the Army of the Potomac from the dismissed McClellan, he surprised Lincoln by moving swiftly to take the offensive. Seeing an open avenue to Richmond through Fredericksburg, Burnside quickly moved his army southward, but then bogged down at the Rappahannock River, which was flooding and therefore too high to ford. Delaying three weeks while he waited for pontoon bridges to arrive and then to be built (the Union's efforts were delayed by a combination of bad weather, an inefficient bureaucracy, and good marksmanship by the Mississippi sharpshooters of General William Barksdale's brigade), Burnside lost the initiative. To counter the sharpshooters firing on the engineers, the Union artillery fired on the small town as the pontoons were built. By the time the bridges were built, it was too late: Lee had organized a near-impenetrable defense.*

BELOW: *Massed Union artillery stationed outside Fredericksburg proved meaningless in the doomed Federal assault in late 1862.*

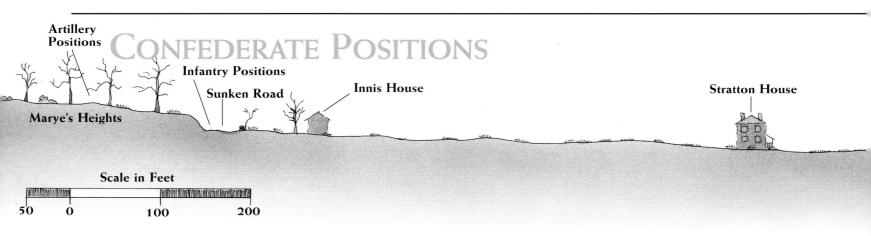

Artillery Positions

CONFEDERATE **P**OSITIONS

Infantry Positions

Sunken Road

Innis House

Stratton House

Marye's Heights

Scale in Feet

50   0   100   200

necessary if the Confederate army were to be engaged. The situation that Lee had recently faced at Malvern Hill was completely reversed: Burnside's Grand Divisions prepared to march uphill to attack strongly positioned veteran troops of the Army of Northern Virginia.

Burnside's engineers began laying their pontoon bridges on December 11, but a steady harassing fire from concealed Confederate sharpshooters delayed their progress. Burnside ordered troops to cross in open boats to secure parts of the intended bridgeheads; with the assistance of this forward guard, the bridges were completed on December 12. After the artillery shelled Fredericksburg on December 13, Union assault columns crossed the river and formed up to attack the strong positions occupied by Lee's army. The Left Grand Division had some early success against Jackson's defenders, but local counterattacks soon forced them back. On the opposite side of the field, the Union soldiers had to cross a full mile (1.6km) of open terrain before arriving at Marye's Heights, where they encountered a withering fire from Confederate riflemen placed by General Longstreet in four ranks beyond a high stone wall. Bravely, the Union soldiers attacked again and again against the strongly positioned Confederates, but they were unable to break through; soon, piles of dead and dying Federal soldiers lined the slopes of the hills adjacent to Fredericksburg.

Burnside planned to repeat the attack the following morning, but was convinced by his corps commanders to abandon the attempt. He had already lost twelve thousand men without any gain to justify the losses. Protected by the high stone walls and other terrain defenses they had occupied, the Confederates had lost fewer than half as many men, just more than five thousand, in a lopsided victory over Burnside. Both armies soon went into winter quarters to prepare for the next series of campaigns that would begin in spring 1863.

Fredericksburg
December 11–13, 1862

The battle of Fredericksburg might have proven decisive in ending the war much earlier, but for weather-related and beauracratic delays that cost the Union forces precious time in implementing Burnside's plan to strike at Lee before the end of the fighting season. The plan was sound, but the delays involved in crossing the Rappahannock, which gave Lee time to orchestrate a formidable defense, rendered the plan foolhardy by the time the pontoon crossing was actually complete. Surveying the terrain from foot of the slope (right) that culminated in Marye's Heights (left), Burnside probably should have realized the danger in attempting to take the Confederate position from below. As happens in so many conflicts, however, the momentum of the Union offense carried it inexorably forward.

By December 11, the Federal forces had completed the pontoon bridges across the river and the troops began to cross over, marching by the dead bodies of the soldiers who had made their passage possible. On December 13, the assault began, with Burnside ordering troops forward past the outskirts of Fredericksburg to the position behind the town occupied by the Confederates. As the Union soldiers traversed the ground below Marye's Heights, they scrambled to take shelter from the hail of bullets behind the few outlying houses that dotted the terrain. But to actually get at the Rebels behind the wall they had to leave the scant protection of the brick houses behind. Wave after wave of Union soldiers were mown down as they pursued the hopeless frontal assault.

The possibility of missing the Union soldiers was so slim that Confederates who feared taking a bullet themselves simply lifted their guns above their heads as they hid behind the stone wall and unloaded in the general direction of the enemy. Despite the devastating loss of life, Burnside stubbornly continued to order attacks into the late afternoon, when darkness finally provided a break from the slaughter. The next day, the Union dug in among their dead and awaited orders. Reluctantly, and only at the urging of his officers, Burnside finally ordered a retreat. By December 16, the Union army was gone.

UNION POSITIONS

Ditch

❦ Fredericksburg ❦

RIGHT: *Following the stalemate at Antietam, Union General George B. McClellan was replaced by Major General Ambrose E. Burnside. In order to forestall a second invasion of the North by Lee, Burnside returned to the offensive by marching south toward Richmond. Burnside's course intersected that of Lee and his Confederate army at the river town of Fredericksburg. Fortifying his forces on high ground, Lee met Burnside's attacks with a merciless hail of fire that cost the Federal army dearly as the 1862 campaign season ground to a bloody halt. This map was drawn by Confederate topographical engineer Samuel Howell Brown on December 13, 1862, and shows the pontoon crossings over the Rappahannock River and the clearly superior positions of the Confederate troops and batteries.*

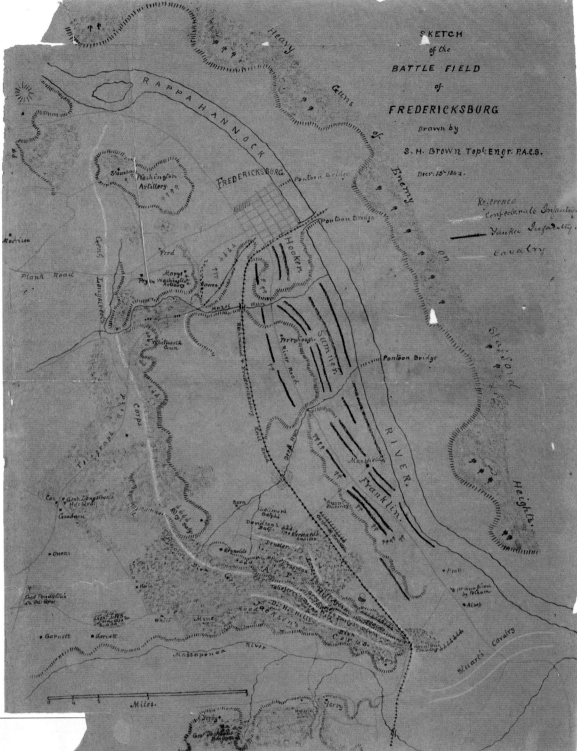

LEFT: *Fredericksburg, Virginia, was positioned on the Richmond, Fredericksburg & Potomac Railroad. Burnside planned a swift march down the railroad's trackage, but delays in bridging the Rappahannock permitted Lee time to occupy high ground. Despite Lee's tactical advantage, Burnside felt the sheer weight of the Army of the Potomac would be sufficient to dislodge the Confederate army. This was one of the more fatal miscalculations of the entire war. The destruction visited on the town was widespread, and even churches were damaged by the fighting.*

1862 in the West

The vast trans-Mississippi west was a region that held the attention of planners in both Washington and Richmond. Large amounts of mineral and agricultural wealth and outlets to the Pacific Ocean were the major attractions to the Confederacy—advantages that the Union hoped to deny their southern neighbors. Brigadier Henry Sibley moved up the Rio Grande valley with a Confederate column and managed to enter Santa Fe, New Mexico, before Union soldiers and volunteers from Colorado attacked the advancing Confederates at Glorieta Pass, New Mexico, on March 26 and 28.

Soon additional Union columns were converging on Sibley, forcing him to withdraw through the Rio Grande valley into Texas. This dashed the hopes of Confederate leaders to gain an outlet to the Pacific.

Fighting developed early in 1862 in Missouri and Arkansas as both sides attempted to gain control of this strategic region. The Federal army gained control over Missouri early in the year when they were able to force the Confederates to retreat into northwestern Arkansas. Not long afterward, however, the Confederates were able to regroup and attack the Union army at Pea Ridge on March 7 and 8. General Van Dorn simultaneously attacked both flanks of Major General Samuel Curtis' Federal army. Curtis was able to turn his men and overpower Van Dorn, and the Confederate army was soon forced to withdraw once again. Curtis had won a special prize for the Union: Missouri, with 1.3 million people and a strategic location in the center of the nation, would remain under Federal control from that point forward.

The year had seen severe fighting, and both sides realized that the worst was still to come. The Union had managed to win two impressive victories, at Fort Henry and Fort Donelson, in the early part of 1862 and Missouri had been held firmly under Federal control. On the Confederate side, Braxton Bragg had failed to capture Kentucky and Lee had been unable to gain control of Maryland. The strategic scales—particularly in the west—had tipped significantly in the favor of the Union while the fighting in the eastern theater had been extremely bloody but inconclusive.

BELOW: *The battle of Pea Ridge was fought on March 7 and 8, 1862. Confederates under generals Earl Van Dorn and Sterling Price managed to execute a double envelopment of Union General Samuel Curtis' left and right rear simultaneously. In doing so, however, the Confederates attacked in two isolated wings that limited the impact of their assaults. The Confederates were forced to withdraw, leaving Missouri firmly under Union control for the remainder of the Civil War. This postwar map shows the final positions of the participants in this important battle.*

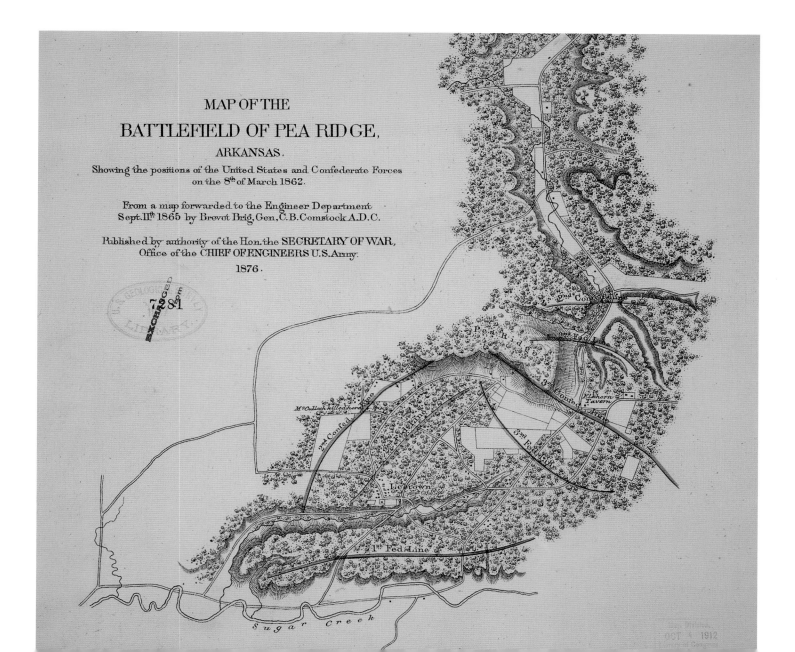

CHAPTER THREE

The Civil War in 1863

The Confederacy still had a chance for victory as 1863 opened. In spite of the critical Union successes in the west, the Confederates still had partial control of the Mississippi River (namely the strongholds at Port Hudson and Vicksburg), and in the east, the Army of Northern Virginia under Lee had won several dramatic victories (culminating with the rout at Fredericksburg). This meant that the war was essentially a draw at this point, though the North's superiority in both manpower and industrial strength would soon begin to have a dramatic impact during this pivotal year. Whereas the Union forces were able to reequip themselves during the winter lull, the southerners struggled, short on supplies of every sort, including clothing, food, and ammunition.

The Union strategy for 1863 would involve a three-pronged assault to be carried out in the west, the south, and in the east. In the western theater, Lincoln saw the best opportunities for a decisive engagement. He and his Secretary of War, Edwin Stanton, began to develop a campaign plan of attacks on the Confederate strongholds along the banks of the Mississippi. Dangerously, they appointed field commanders without first consulting their military commanders, Halleck and Grant. As a result, several politicians were appointed generals; true to their natures, these men had used their political status to gain the appointments just as they had used their influence to gain favors while holding public office.

Lincoln and Stanton—who were at best amateur strategists—selected General Nathaniel Banks, a political appointee general from Massachusetts, to command the force ordered to move northward from Louisiana and take the Confederate bastion at Port

Hudson from Major General Franklin Gardner. At the same time, one of the more political of Lincoln's generals, John A. McClernand, was given command of the troops to be ordered to march south toward Vicksburg, the capture of which Grant had been attempting to accomplish since the previous year. This plan sorely tried the cardinal principle of unity of command because it meant that McClernand would be operating independently within Grant's area of responsibility. A worse situation could hardly have been conceived. In the end, reason (in the form of Henry Halleck's strenuous objections) prevailed, and Lincoln was convinced to place Grant in command with McClernand as his subordinate. Also under Grant were William T. Sherman and James B. McPherson.

Midway through the year, the northern strategists turned their eyes south, to Tennessee. Seeing that the Tennessee River, which ran north to south, could provide the Confederates a route by which to attack Kentucky and that the eastern portion of the state was a transportation hub in general, Lincoln ordered William Rosecrans (stationed at Murfreesboro) to move against the nearby Confederate army under Braxton Bragg. These two generals would spar for control of the area beginning in July.

In the eastern theater, meanwhile, the tactical standoff between the Army of Northern Virginia and the Army of the Potomac continued outside of Fredericksburg. Not surprisingly, Burnside was replaced because of the disaster at Marye's Heights. Command of the Army of the Potomac was placed in the hands of Joseph "Fighting Joe" Hooker, a hard-drinking, aggressive commander who had been one of Burnside's severest critics.

PAGE 78: *Sketch maps prepared by cartographers in the field were later used to develop finished maps for use by commanders and as a part of after-action reports. The rough sketches normally included the distances between significant landmarks, compass bearings from point to point, and key terrain features. From these rough sketches, cartographers were later able to compile accurate maps in a remarkably short period. This map is one of a series of sketches made by Jedediah Hotchkiss in May 1863 of the battle of Chancellorsville, Virginia.*

OPPOSITE: *Once the city fortress of Vicksburg fell, on July 4, the last Confederate fort on the Mississippi, Port Hudson (left, center), surrendered. Although Banks' assault on the fortress had been a dismal failure, Gardner saw no hope in resisting once Vicksburg had been captured. Lincoln described the Union objective in the west best when he said that the Mississippi should "roll unvexed to the sea," but it was General John Fremont (a former presidential candidate who was eventually relieved of his command) who had best summed up the significance of the Mississippi: "[T]he immediate possession of the valley of the Mississippi River would control the result of the war. Who held the Mississippi would hold the country by the heart." This detailed map was drawn for Nathaniel Banks in 1864 and later published by the Office of the Chief of Engineers, U.S. Army.*

BELOW: *The siege of Vicksburg had been terrible for both the Confederate soldiers and the 2,500 civilians who had chosen to remain. As the long siege continued, the soldiers of both sides began to dig deep "bomb proofs" in which to remain when fired upon by artillery (civilians, too, availed themselves of the protective burrows). The shelters in this photograph were at the north end of the Union line of earthworks facing Vicksburg's defenders. The large house belonged to New Englander James Shirley, a Union supporter who was moved to safety with his entire family by General Grant.*

Vicksburg

Vicksburg, Mississippi, was clearly the key to controlling the mighty Mississippi. Once the bastion was taken, the remaining Confederate fortress, Port Hudson, Louisiana, would capitulate as its isolated position at that point would be untenable. Unfortunately for Grant, Vicksburg lay in a location that was entirely favorable for the defense.

Bluffs as high as 250 feet (76m) rose above the water and extended for nearly 100 miles (160km) on either flank of the city. The ground south of the city was swampy and nearly impassable for large military units; the region to the north was the delta of the Yazoo River, a swampy area that extended sixty miles (96km) to the east and almost 200 miles (320km) on its north-south axis. The Confederate army had fortified the high bluffs from the Yazoo in the north, about ten miles (16km) above Vicksburg, to the mouth of the Big Black River forty miles (64km) south of the city.

The city and vicinity had become a great fortress—it was dangerous to attempt to pass by it on the Mississippi in armored boats. In addition, the city could not be assaulted across the

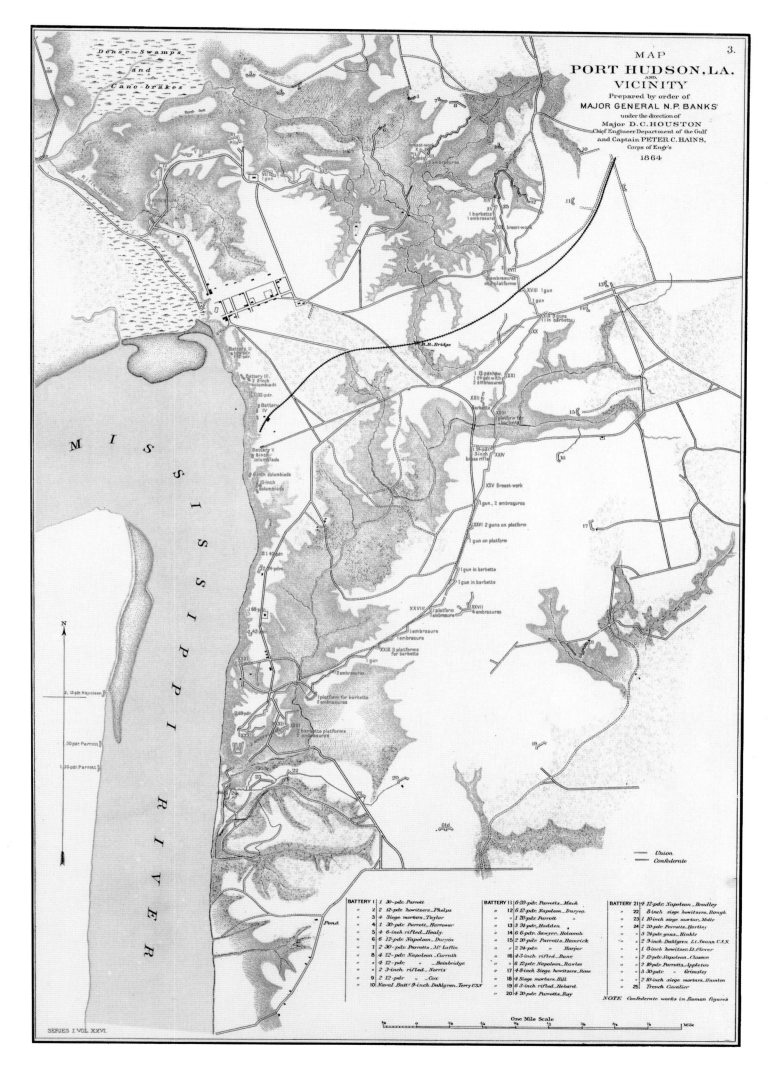

3.

MAP
PORT HUDSON, LA.
AND
VICINITY
Prepared by order of
MAJOR GENERAL N. P. BANKS
under the direction of
Major D. C. HOUSTON
Chief Engineer Department of the Gulf
and Captain PETER C. HAINS,
Corps of Eng'rs
1864

M I S S I S S I P P I   R I V E R

Dense Swamps
and
Cane-brakes

—— Union.
—— Confederate

One Mile Scale

BATTERY 1	1	30-pdr. Parrott
"	2	2 12-pdr. howitzers_Phelps
"	3	4 Siege mortars_Taylor
"	4	1 30-pdr. Parrott_Harrower
"	5	4 6-inch rifled_Healy.
"	6	6 12-pdr. Napoleon_Duryea
"	7	2 30-pdr. Parrotts_Mc.Laffin
"	8	4 12-pdr. Napoleon_Curnth
"	"	4 12-pdr. " _Bainbridge
"	"	2 3-inch rifled_Norris
"	9	2 12-pdr. " _Cox
"	10	Naval Batt.y 9-inch Dahlgren_Terry USN

BATTERY 11	6 20-pdr. Parrotts_Mack
"	12	6 12-pdr. Napoleon_Duryea.
"	"	1 20 pdr. Parrott
"	13	2 34 pdr. Hadden
"	14	6 6-pdr. Sawyer_Holcomb
"	15	2 20 pdr. Parrotts_Hamrick
"	"	2 24 pdr. " _Harper
"	16	4 3-inch rifled_Bane
"	"	6 12-pdr. Napoleon_Rawles
"	17	4 8-inch Siege howitzers_Rose
"	18	4 Siege mortars_Hill
"	19	6 3-inch rifled_Hebard.
"	20	4 20-pdr. Parrotts_Ray

BATTERY 21	4 12-pdr. Napoleon_Bradley
"	22	8-inch siege howitzers_Bough.
"	23	1 10-inch siege mortar_Molte
"	24	2 20-pdr. Parrotts_Hartley
"	"	3 24-pdr guns_Hinkle
"	"	2 9-inch Dahlgren Lt.Swann C.S.N.
"	"	1 8-inch howitzer_Lt.Oliver
"	"	2 12-pdr. Napoleon_Cloxton
"	"	2 10-pdr. Parrotts_Appleton
"	"	3 30-pdr. " _Grimsley
"	"	2 10-inch siege mortars_Hamten
"	25	Trench Cavalier

NOTE. Confederate works in Roman figures.

SERIES I VOL. XXVI.

wide river. The only route open to the Union forces under Grant was over the rough terrain to the east. This, however, was also dangerous as this route would position the Union forces squarely between the army under Vicksburg's commander, General John C. Pemberton, and units belonging to General Joseph Johnston, who had recovered from his wounds at Fair Oaks and was in command of troops in the region (even though the main concentration of his forces were near Jackson, Mississippi, about forty miles [64km] east of Vicksburg). Any move into this area between these two armies could have potentially disastrous consequences for Grant and his Union army.

Grant made four unsuccessful attempts in late 1862 and early 1863 to reach the dry ground east of Vicksburg, but was unable to achieve a favorable position. At one time, he ordered the digging of canals, but this was also a dramatic failure. All of his efforts were aimed at the goal of getting his brigades to the dry, high ground near Vicksburg without coming under the fire of the heavy guns of the city's defenders.

As the winter rains began to slow and the high water began to drop, Grant planned his early spring campaign. As he had done at forts Henry and Donelson the previous year, he

planned a combined operation against Vicksburg with the navy. Grant planned to move part of his force above Vicksburg to divert the attention of the defenders while the main body of his force marched through eastern Louisiana and down the west side of the Mississippi River, where the navy's transports would ferry them to the east bank. After gaining the eastern shore, Grant's men would march northeastward and prepare to attack the city. It was a bold and risky plan.

While General William T. Sherman led the diversionary attack north of Vicksburg, two of Grant's corps began to march south. On the night of April 16, the navy sent their gunboats and transports past Vicksburg's heavy guns, losing only one transport, and on April 30 the men were ferried across the river below Vicksburg.

In addition to Sherman's demonstration north of the city and the movement of infantry corps and the navy downstream, Grant ordered a bold diversionary raid to be launched into Confederate territory. Colonel Benjamin Grierson and his cavalry brigade rode out of La Grange, Tennessee, as the Federals began to move. By dividing his force, Grierson was able to confuse his pursuers as to his true objective and he destroyed railroads and Confederate military property as he tore through the region to the east of Vicksburg.

With all the movements of forces arrayed against him, General Pemberton remained confused in a situation in which he could do very little that was right. He had been ordered by Jefferson Davis to hold Vicksburg at all costs. Meanwhile, the other commander in the region, Joseph Johnston, knew that Vicksburg was a larger version of the trap Grant had sprung at Fort Donelson.

Once Sherman had reunited with the main body of the Union army, Grant gave orders to move against Johnston before turning west on Pemberton. Over the next eighteen days, Grant's army marched 200 miles (320km) with five days' rations, living off the land. Under these adverse conditions, Grant's men fought and won four battles before arriving on the high ground east of Vicksburg. Grant had defeated the only army in the area capable of any attempt to relieve Vicksburg once the planned siege began. More important to the Union's future in the area, Grant had demonstrated to Sherman that a large force could break contact with its base of operations as it conducted operations. This lesson would serve Sherman well in 1864, when he cut a swath of destruction through the South on his way to the sea.

Grant ordered a general assault on Vicksburg's defenses on May 19 and 22, but these were beaten back and the Union suffered severe casualties. As a result, the Union force

ABOVE: *The Confederates trapped inside Vicksburg began to strengthen their defenses as Grant's men began to prepare for a long siege. Heavy artillery (like this cannon, nicknamed "Whistling Dick," shown after its capture) prevented a direct assault on Vicksburg. Grant did not simply plan to starve the city into submission, but ordered a steady artillery bombardment. Little by little, Federal engineers pushed their trench lines closer to the doomed city's defenses. Vicksburg surrendered on July 4, 1863, after forty-seven days of constant siege—the same day Lee was withdrawing from Gettysburg.*

Vicksburg
May 18–July 4, 1863

Vicksburg was an ideal location for defense. High bluffs rose above the river, extending far to the north and south of the city. River delta and swamps blocked the approaches to Vicksburg from both north and south, respectively. The Confederates fortified the high ground (right)—especially the large bend in the river—with heavy artillery, making it nearly impossible to steam past the city's defenses. Grant realized he would not be able to attack Vicksburg from the river; the only reasonable approach lay in the high, dry ground east of the city.

Confederate defender General John C. Pemberton commanded thirty thousand troops in Vicksburg, and General Joseph Johnston, recovered from his wounds at Fair Oaks, commanded the rest of the Confederate forces in Mississippi from Jackson, forty miles (64km) away from Vicksburg to the east. Grant's plan was to cross the river south of the city and sweep to the north and east between Vicksburg and Jackson, taking care to prevent Johnston and Pemberton from uniting against the Union attackers.

In April 1863 Grant initiated a bold series of maneuvers. First, naval Flag Officer David D. Porter ferried corps under Grant to New Carthage. Then part of the army (under Sherman) conducted a diversion north of Vicksburg at Haynes' Bluff (along the Yazoo River) while the bulk of the army (under McPherson and McClernand) crossed to the western side of the Mississippi south of the city. Porter sailed downstream in the night, braving Vicksburg's defenses (and losing a transport in the process), to ferry McPherson and McClernand's corps across the river to Port Gibson, south of the fortress. There, they defeated Confederates under the command of Major General John S. Bowen. Grant (now reunited with Sherman, McPherson, and McClernand) broke away from his supply base and during the next eighteen days marched his men 200 miles (320km) around to the east, fighting the Confederates at Jackson and Champion Hill along the way, and ultimately trapping Pemberton inside Vicksburg. Forty-seven days later, on July 4, Pemberton surrendered.

settled in to conduct a full siege. Sherman held Johnston in check and Grant relieved politician-turned-general McClernand of his command for submitting a false report. The Federal trenches were extended slowly around the doomed city, and soon the population and defenders were reduced to near-starvation. By July 1, 1863, the Union brigades had completed their preparations for another assault, but the city's defenders were in bad condition and Pemberton asked for Grant's surrender terms. Pemberton surrendered on July 4, 1863, the day that General George Meade realized that he had won at Gettysburg in the east, a victory that conclusively demonstrated that the Union army had gained the initiative in the field.

The entire length of the Mississippi River came under the control of the Union on July 9, when General Nathaniel Banks accepted the surrender of Port Hudson. In losing control of the Mississippi River entirely, the Confederacy had been split in two. Grant meanwhile had repeated his success at Fort Donelson, neutralizing an entire Confederate army and their materials.

Another major strategic concern of Abraham Lincoln continued to be eastern Tennessee, home to a large number of Unionists as well as the site of major transportation routes, in particular a rail line linking Virginia with western Tennessee. In addition, the Tennessee River formed a natural route running north to south that could be used by the Confederate armies to invade Kentucky. Equally important, any Union advances aimed at Atlanta and the deep South would be facilitated if the river were under control of the Federals. Thus, eastern and central Tennessee were critical regions for both sides in the Civil War, and began to receive attention in mid-1863. Chattanooga was the key to the region.

General William S. Rosecrans marched his army out of Murfreesboro, Tennessee, a week before the surrender of Pemberton at Vicksburg. By September 4, his army was across the Tennessee River and well along the route to

UNION POSITIONS

De Soto Peninsula

Mississippi River

⸙ Vicksburg ⸙

ABOVE: *The bustling city (population 4,500) of Vicksburg, Mississippi, was home to contented citizens, many of whom had opposed secession in 1860. Unfortunately, the strategic location of the commercially active city turned it into a target for the Union, a target that would be defended at all costs by the Confederacy. Commanded by Pennsylvania-born Lieutenant General John Pemberton, Vicksburg's garrison repulsed assault after Union assault and was besieged by Grant's large army. Once the city's defenses were overwhelmed, the Union swiftly gained control of the entire length of the vital Mississippi River, effectively splitting the Confederacy into two sections. This detailed map and overhead view of Vicksburg by Lieutenant L.A. Wrotnowski (both the artist and lithographer) shows the formidable challenges faced by the Union forces in capturing the fortress city.*

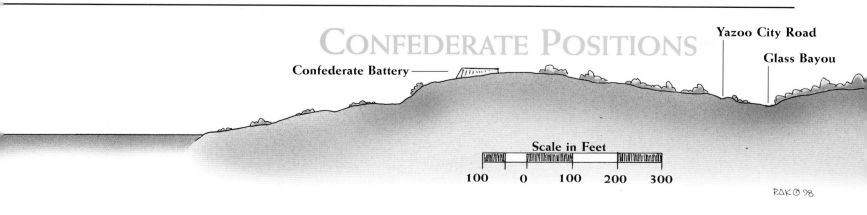

RIGHT: *Union General William S. Rosecrans, "Old Rosy" to his men, was a deeply religious man with a terrible temper. His early Civil War combat in western Virginia resulted in victories and an assignment in the western theater. Grant, however, felt Rosecrans was poor at coordinating with other officers. When Rosecrans came under Grant's command in 1864, Grant replaced him with General George Thomas.*

BELOW: *As Grant was trying to secure the Mississippi River, a sprawling conflict raged over control of Tennessee. The battle of Stones River was the culmination of the latter campaign, which began with a slow Union advance led by General Don Carlos Buell toward the Confederate rail junction at Chattanooga and a diversionary counterattack toward Kentucky led by General Edmund Kirby Smith that was eventually joined by General Braxton Bragg. Buell was forced to respond to Smith and Bragg's movements, and the armies of the North and South clashed violently at Perryville, Kentucky. The Confederates retreated south to Knoxville, where they were eventually pursued by the Federals, now under the command of General William Rosecrans. Once again the armies clashed, this time near Murfreesboro, on the banks of the Stones River in the closing days of 1862.*

At dawn on New Year's Eve, Bragg ordered a ferocious attack against the Federal right flank that pushed the Federal defenders back three miles (4.8km) to the Nashville Turnpike. Major General George H. Thomas, a Virginian, managed to form a new defensive line that held for the remainder of the day. Rosecrans, on overhearing Thomas say, "I know of no better place to die than right here," decided against another retreat, shifting his army along the front to counter the Confederates' attacks. Strangely, Bragg lost his nerve, delayed in continuing his successful onslaught, and was ultimately forced, himself, to retreat during the evening of January 2, 1863. The victory at Stones River secured Nashville as a base of operations for the North. This period map was drawn by C.S. Mergell, under the direction of Captain Nathaniel Michler.

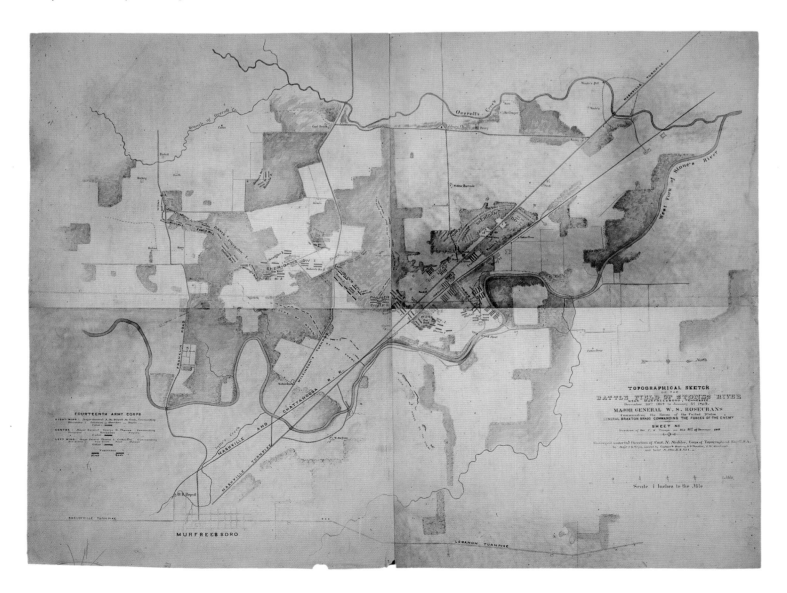

Chattanooga. Rosecrans had hoped to slip past Braxton Bragg's Confederates and trap him inside Chattanooga, but Bragg had anticipated this and withdrew to the south.

There were few good routes through the mountains in the region, and Rosecrans was forced by the lack of passes to disperse his columns over a forty-mile (64km) front to make any progress toward Bragg. At the same time, Bragg began to concentrate his forces in northern Georgia; and since his available force was larger than any single column under Rosecrans, Bragg hoped to be able to defeat each of Rosecrans' columns in turn.

By September 12, Rosecrans realized that Bragg was concentrating his forces in preparation for a fight. As a result, Rosecrans ordered his widely dispersed columns to unite. This required several days, during which time the Union army was extremely vulnerable. But Bragg delayed in ordering a general attack, instead deciding to wait for the arrival of reinforcements from Virginia.

Chickamauga

President Davis and General Lee had agreed to send reinforcements from the Army of Northern Virginia to support Braxton Bragg in Tennessee against the anticipated attack. Once the battle of Gettysburg was over, General James "Old Pete" Longstreet was sent west with a force of nearly fifteen thousand men.

It was a logistical feat simply to transport this large force across the dilapidated rail system serving the area. Since Burnside had managed to drive the defenders from the Cumberland Gap and Knoxville, Longstreet was forced to take a route other than the shortest. He and his corps covered 900 miles (1,440km), in trains with cars that were in poor condition, by way of Atlanta.

By September 17, Bragg was concentrating his forces just to the east of Chickamauga Creek, Georgia. As Longstreet's men began to arrive on the field on September 18, Bragg ordered a general attack. At first, the Union corps defending at the crossings fought so hard that only a few Confederate units were able to ford the creek, but most of Bragg's army was able to cross in the darkness that evening.

Rosecrans' last corps arrived on September 19, and the battle was fought in earnest in thick woods for the rest of that day. The remainder of Longstreet's corps arrived during the night and Rosecrans' men began to dig in to face the attacks that would come in the morning.

When Bragg ordered the attack to begin, one of Rosecrans' corps commanders, General George H. Thomas, was struck first. In the con-

fusion of battle, Rosecrans received a report that one of his units had been left unsupported, so he ordered another unit—one that was already on his line fighting the Confederates—to move to the support of the unit he thought was in trouble. When the relief unit in the line obeyed its orders and began to move, their withdrawal left a gap in Rosecrans' lines, an error that Longstreet quickly noticed. Longstreet ordered a direct attack into the gap created by Rosecrans' mistake, and the right flank of the Union army began to break into a general retreat in the direction of Chattanooga.

General Thomas, meanwhile, was able to hold a shaky defense together in the face of Rebel attacks, maintaining his positions until dark, when the fighting ended. Thomas, a native Virginian, won the nickname "The Rock of Chickamauga" for his brave stand against his fellow southerners.

Bragg had suffered 18,500 casualties (and Rosecrans 16,200) in the fighting at Chickamauga, and like many of his contemporaries, he allowed the enemy to withdraw to

BELOW: *The battle of Chickamauga (a Cherokee name that means "river of blood") was fought on steep hills covered with forest along the shores of the Chickamauga Creek. Six months after Stones River, Rosecrans stirred his army to pursue Bragg's army, stationed just thirty miles (48km) away. Bragg fell back to Chattanooga, which he then gave up almost without a fight. Falling back again, this time to Chickamauga Creek, Georgia, Bragg then shocked Rosecrans by fighting back and delivering a staggering blow to the northern army.*

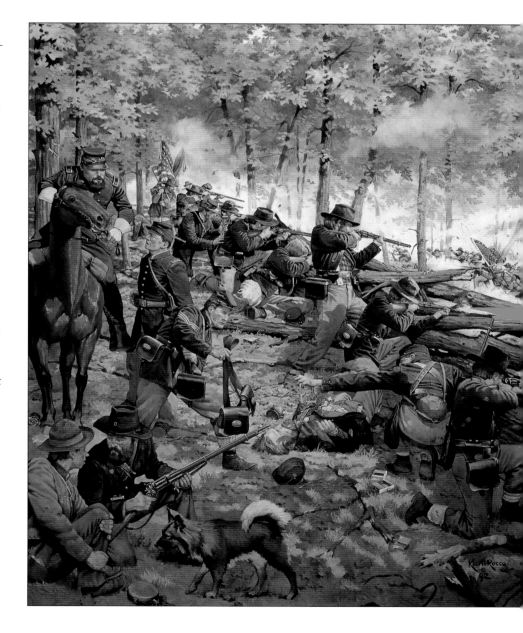

ABOVE: *Some of the unsung heroes of the Civil War were the civilian construction crews of the U.S. Military Railroad. They were able to repair destroyed rail lines nearly as fast as the Confederates were able to wreck them. It was their hard work in maintaining the railroads that permitted the Union army to move soldiers and supplies rapidly from one theater of operations to another. Here, following Grant's succor of the besieged troops at Chattanooga, U.S.M.R.R. crews prepare to work on the rail lines that would bring supplies to Sherman's army as it advanced on Atlanta.*

Chattanooga from his positions on the field without pursuing and destroying him. Despite Thomas' withdrawal, however, the Confederate army had managed to win a victory that they sorely needed at the time. And they had the remains of Rosecrans' army trapped in Chattanooga. The total of nearly 35,000 casualties was the highest over any two-day period of the war.

Chattanooga

Rosecrans moved into Chattanooga, sacrificing freedom of movement in exchange for a temporary respite after the bloody confrontation at Chickamauga. Soon the entire Union army was trapped. He had managed to lose his lines of communication because of a combination of factors: terrain, weather, and Confederate raiders. The few roads that were available to convoys were soon rutted with wagon tracks, making them impossible to traverse.

As supplies and rations began to run out, men and draft animals inside the city began to

go hungry. Eventually the animals began to die of starvation. Rosecrans looked for an opportunity to open a new route to the west, but his men were in insufficient numbers to force the Confederates from their positions on the steep ridges overlooking Chattanooga.

On September 23, the commanders in Washington began to take the situation in Chattanooga seriously. They had just cut the Confederacy in half along the Mississippi and won an epic battle at Gettysburg, but the Union was in danger of losing an entire army by capture. If Bragg were able to remove Rosecrans' army from the field, the Confederacy would recover the initiative in the area—politically, psychologically, and militarily—and the Union army might never be able to recover it. Something had to be done quickly if the dire situation the Federal government faced was to be salvaged.

Secretary of War Stanton had lost confidence in Rosecrans following the rout at Chickamauga. And as happened to many commanders who had lost battles during the war, Rosecrans was in danger of being replaced. Lincoln also had developed doubts about Rosecrans, and agreed to relieve him in the middle of October 1863.

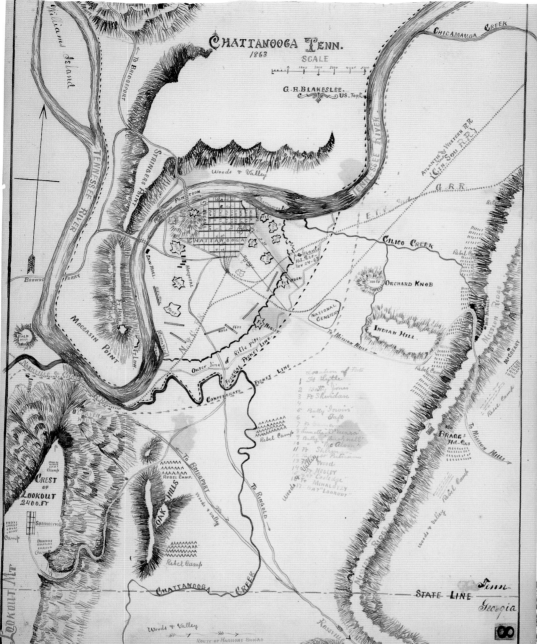

LEFT: *After being defeated at Chickamauga, Rosecrans withdrew his demoralized army into Chattanooga. Bragg followed immediately, having been reinforced by Longstreet and two of Lee's divisions. The Confederates occupied the high ground, primarily Missionary Ridge and Lookout Mountain. Once the primary supply routes into the city were closed, the Union army was forced to near-starvation as the narrow track available to them proved insufficient to permit the flow of supplies necessary to maintain the army. Grant, having completed the reduction of Vicksburg, and reinforced by two corps from the Army of the Potomac, broke Bragg's siege just in time. This battlefield map in pen and ink by G.H. Blakeslee of the U.S. topographical staff shows the disposition of the Union and Rebel troops.*

RIGHT: *The Tennessee River, seen here splitting around Williams Island from mountaintops to the west of Chattanooga, was to become a major supply line for Grant's army as river boats struggled to deliver six months' supply of food and ammunition to sustain a drive into Georgia.*

Missionary Ridge
November 25, 1863

Following the Union defeat at Chickamauga, Rosecrans retreated to Chattanooga, where he was besieged by the pursuing Bragg, whose Confederates took up positions along Missionary Ridge (right) and Lookout Mountain. Grant was placed in command of the situation, viewing the action with General Thomas from Orchard Knob (left), and he set about the task of clearing the Confederates from their strategic positions.

General William T. Sherman ordered his men across the Tennessee River and moved to positions along the north end of Missionary Ridge. On November 25, his attempts to drive the Confederates from their positions on the ridge toward the south stalled. As a result, Grant ordered the Army of the Cumberland to attack toward the base of Missionary Ridge to clear out Confederate skirmishers and draw some Confederate strength away from Sherman. The Army of the Cumberland cleared the first line of skirmishers, but soon came under fire from the next line of Confederate defenders. Feeling they had a score to settle with these particular Confederates, the Union attackers continued up the slopes without orders to do so, causing Grant to remark that "someone was going to sweat for it" if the charge failed.

The many Confederates Bragg had placed on the slopes began to rush toward the relative safety at the top of the ridge as the Army of the Cumberland continued their charge uphill. The defenders at the top were unable to fire for fear of hitting their own men, and soon, sixty Union regiments were on the summit. One of the attackers, an eighteen-year-old lieutenant, Arthur McArthur, retrieved his unit's flag after three color-bearers had fallen, an act that won him a Medal of Honor and would later serve to inspire his famous son, Douglas.

From their hard-won positions atop Missionary Ridge, the Union army witnessed the scattering of the Confederates. But their satisfaction was short-lived: Bragg was able to rally his men into new defensive positions and withdraw deep into Georgia.

Thomas, the Virginian who had held strong at Chickamauga, was given command of Rosecrans' army, but unity of command was attained by putting Grant in command of all the forces in the western theater.

The presence of a unified command, however, did not open lines of communication into Chattanooga and there were too few troops available to do it without outside support. At the time, Lee was recovering from the summer campaign that had culminated in defeat in Pennsylvania, and Meade's Army of the Potomac was relatively inactive. So General Joseph Hooker was ordered to move nearly twenty thousand men west by rail to Tennessee. The men began to board trains in Virginia on September 25 and their advance elements began to arrive within five days. At the same time, an additional seventeen thousand Federals under General William T. Sherman were shipped by steamboats from Mississippi. Soon, the Union army was in a position to break the siege at Chattanooga.

Their efforts were made easier by Bragg's mistakes. While the Union command structure was being unified under a single commander, Grant, the Confederate commander had split his force by sending Longstreet and his corps to attack Burnside at Knoxville.

Grant now had numerical superiority—nearly sixty thousand men as opposed to Bragg's forty thousand—and decided to go on the offensive with his entire force. Grant's plan was complex at a time when communications were limited, but he had able commanders whom he could trust to complete their assigned tasks successfully. Grant intended to hit both ends of Bragg's line at the same time as the trapped Federals in Chattanooga were ordered to move against the center of the Confederate line.

Joseph Hooker struck hard at the right side of Bragg's line and captured strategic Lookout Mountain on November 24. Sherman crossed the Tennessee River and surged forward to dislodge the Confederates on the left end of Bragg's

UNION POSITIONS

Orchard Knob

U.S. Grant's Headquarters

❧ Missionary Ridge ❧

LEFT: *This north-facing view along the crest of Missionary Ridge shows the advantage enjoyed by the defending Confederates. The determined Federal troops of the Army of the Cumberland were able to overtake the ridge (from the west, off to the left of this photograph) just the same.*

defenses, on Missionary Ridge. But Sherman's attack stalled on November 25 as he tried to push on to the south.

Grant ordered Thomas' Army of the Cumberland, once trapped by Bragg's army after being beaten at Chickamauga, to move against skirmisher rifle pits along the western slope of Missionary Ridge to assist Sherman. These veteran soldiers, having a score to settle, were ordered to capture just the first line of rifle pits; once they were fired at by the next line of skirmishers, however, they pushed on to capture that line as well. Thomas' soldiers struck onward until they captured the crest of Missionary Ridge. Satisfied, Grant watched them drive away their former antagonists.

The entire Confederate line fell apart at this point in the battle, and Bragg retreated into Georgia while Grant pursued him. One Confed-

erate division fought a rear-guard action to slow down the Union army, enabling Bragg to escape.

The rescue of the stranded army at Chattanooga was one of the clearest Union victories of the war. Eastern Tennessee, its Unionist citizens, and the great agricultural capacity of the region were lost to the Confederacy at a time when they were desperately needed. The transportation hub of Chattanooga fell into Union hands for the rest of the war and the Confederate's defensive line was broken. Grant had prepared a way to invade the last stronghold of the Confederacy. Soon, the deep South would feel the wrath of the Union armies.

In the east, the 1863 campaigns were being fought by officers and men who had gained a great deal of combat experience in two years of war. The incompetent officers had been weeded out—either by selection boards or by becoming

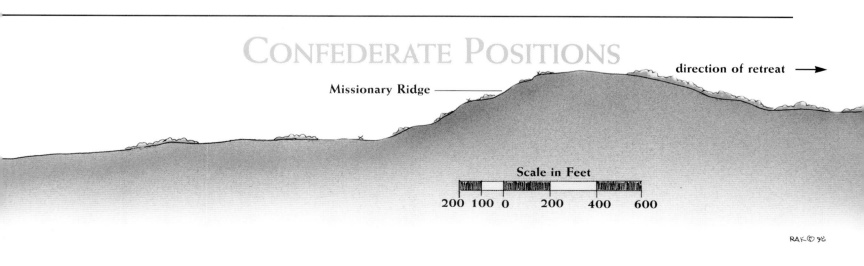

CONFEDERATE POSITIONS

direction of retreat →

Missionary Ridge ———————

Scale in Feet

200 100 0   200   400   600

RAK © 98

RIGHT: *Union General Joseph Hooker was in command of the Army of the Potomac at Chancellorsville. Overconfident, he had declared, "The Rebel army is now the legitimate property of the Army of the Potomac." Never more wrong than at this moment, Hooker lost his nerve during the terrible battle of Chancellorsville.*

OPPOSITE: *During the night of May 1, 1863, Lee met with Jackson and his cavalry commander, General J.E.B. Stuart, near the crossroads village of Chancellorsville, Virginia, to plan what was to become Lee's greatest victory. Lee decided to take a bold gamble by splitting his force—in the face of a numerically superior enemy—by sending Jackson on a forced march to attack Joseph Hooker's exposed flank. Jackson would receive a mortal wound while scouting between the lines at the end of the day. This night conference would be their last.*

RIGHT: *Confederate cavalry commander General J.E.B. Stuart had been with Lee when John Brown and his raiders were subdued at Harper's Ferry in 1859. He continued to serve Lee as his cavalry commander. At Chancellorsville, Stuart discovered Hooker's exposed flank—a vulnerability soon to be exploited by Jackson.*

BELOW: *The Union army, under its new commander, Joseph Hooker, prepared for the 1863 spring campaign in Virginia; in Falmouth, the army's photographer, Andrew J. Russell, had some of them pose. The unit in Russell's photograph, the 110th Pennsylvania Volunteer Infantry, was blissfully unaware that Stonewall Jackson would obliterate them, nearly to the man, in only a few short weeks in the dark forests of Chancellorsville.*

casualties—and skilled, experienced officers had taken their places.

At the end of the 1862 campaign that had culminated in the battle of Fredericksburg, the Army of the Potomac had gone into its winter quarters at Falmouth, Virginia, on the northern bank of the Rappahannock River. Meanwhile, the Army of Northern Virginia had remained between the Union army and Richmond. In late January 1863, Burnside was replaced by General Joseph Hooker, a professional soldier who soon brought discipline, training, and increased morale back to the army. While in winter camps, Hooker developed innovations still in practice in the modern army. Among other things, he developed insignia for the corps under his command and concentrated his cavalry units into a single cavalry corps that would receive wide-ranging combat assignments.

BELOW: *General Jubal Early's subordinates General John B. Gordon and cartographer Jed Hotchkiss hiked along a railroad lying along the base of the Shenandoah's Massanutten Mountain, where they changed into civilian clothing before entering a cornfield. The two Confederate officers posed as field laborers engaged in cutting corn as they collected information to be used in Early's battle plan at Cedar Creek. The Confederate attack on October 19, 1864, one month after their defeat at Winchester, initially drove the Union army from the battlefield. Sheridan arrived in the afternoon from Winchester, rallying routed Federal units as he rode forward, and inflicted a major defeat on Early in a massive Union counterattack. This illustration shows the undercover cartographers at work.*

ABOVE: *Jedediah Hotchkiss, a schoolteacher from New York, had moved to Virginia's Shenandoah Valley before the war. He served as a staff officer and cartographer for Jackson, supplying him with a constant source of accurate maps that were instrumental in "Stonewall's" impressive string of successful operations. Hotchkiss survived the Civil War to become involved in the development of natural resources inside the mountainous region of West Virginia.*

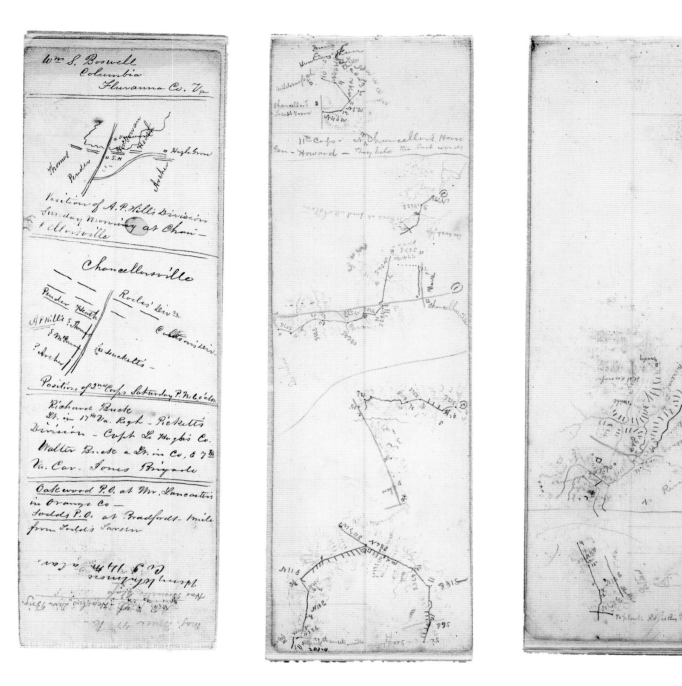

ABOVE: *Cartographers of the Civil War developed careful field notes and detailed sketch maps that were later converted into finished map sheets. Using just a compass, a pocket aneroid barometer, and a chain for taking measurements, these cartographers nonetheless proved themselves capable of creating very useful, accurate maps.*

Of the Civil War cartographers, Jedediah Hotchkiss was one of the best, if not the best. Ordered to Jackson's headquarters on March 26, 1862, Hotchkiss was told by Jackson: "I want you to make me a map of the Valley, from Harper's Ferry to Lexington, showing all points of offence and defence in those places." The map subsequently prepared by Hotchkiss proved to be invaluable in Jackson's classic 1862 Valley Campaign. Pictured above are three map sketches drawn by Hotchkiss of the battle of Chancellorsville, where Stonewall Jackson lost his life. The Library of Congress purchased Hotchkiss' collection of maps and papers in 1948; it is one of the most important and informative subcollections of the venerable archive.

Chancellorsville

As the weather began to warm, Hooker began to plan his spring campaign of 1863. He was determined not to make the errors made by his predecessor, General Burnside, by ordering frontal attacks against Fredericksburg's heights. His Army of the Potomac, numbering 134,000 men, was more than twice the size of Lee's army, and Hooker planned to strike both of Lee's flanks simultaneously as his cavalry corps raided deeply into the rear of the Confederate defenses. He ordered two corps under General John Sedgwick to cross the Rappahannock River and attack across the old battlefield at Fredericksburg while an additional two full corps were held in reserve. The Army of the Potomac was simply a colossus at this point in the Civil War and fully capable of winning its battles.

By the end of April 1863, Hooker's corps commanders had reached the scrub timber and thick brush of an area known as the Wilderness and were in the vicinity of Chancellorsville. Sedgwick had successfully crossed the Rappahannock at Fredericksburg, and a full cavalry division had ridden out to distract Lee. Everything was going according to Hooker's plan.

Unfortunately for Hooker, Lee was aware of the numbers arrayed against him because General J.E.B. Stuart, Lee's cavalry commander, was serving the Confederacy brilliantly. A single Confederate cavalry brigade watched over the Union cavalry division's movements and the rest of Stuart's cavalry kept Hooker's army under close observation. Lee knew that he was threatened by a superior force that was marching on both of his flanks as a third force drove toward his center at Fredericksburg.

Most commanders would have withdrawn from these multiple threats, trading both space and time to escape what seemed to be certain defeat, but Lee was different from most commanders. Instead of retreating the Confederate general chose to compensate for his lack of strength with a surprise offensive. He left a sufficiently strong force at Fredericksburg to oppose Sedgwick as the main body of the Army of Northern Virginia marched westward toward Chancellorsville.

As Lee moved toward the Army of the Potomac, "Fighting Joe" Hooker failed to live up to his nickname, instead losing his nerve. He ordered his men to withdraw to build defensive positions, including strong breastworks, anchoring their line in the east on the banks of the Rappahannock River, where they were safe from a flanking attack by Lee. It was an entirely different story in the west, though, where Hooker's right flank was unsupported and open to attack.

Again, J.E.B. Stuart's cavalry was able to spot the weakness in Hooker's battle plan: scouts located the exposed right flank and informed Lee. Leaving only a small portion of his force at Fredericksburg to protect the position this time, Lee sent troops under Richard Anderson and then Jackson to the west, to meet the Union forces at Chancellorsville. In the evening of May 1, Lee met with Jackson outside Chancellorsville and made the audacious decision to divide his outnumbered army—in the face of superior force—and attack Hooker in a bold pincer movement around the Union right flank. A violation

TOP: *At the battle of Fredericksburg, the high rock wall at Marye's heights had sheltered the Confederates, who had mercilessly mown down the attacking Federals (some 12,500 Union men were killed or wounded on that day). During the Chancellorsville campaign, however, the wall proved insufficient to repel the assault of General John Sedgwick, who had been ordered by General Hooker on the morning of May 3, 1863, to press the Confederate right flank and sweep westward to join the main Federal army at Chancellorsville via the Old Orange Turnpike. Sedgwick's VI Corps took Marye's Heights from Jubal Early's men (defending the wall in this illustration) in a bloody confrontation. Sedgwick then proceeded along the Old Orange Turnpike to Salem Church, where he was stopped by Confederate Lafayette McLaw's division. The next day, Lee ordered a three-prong attack to annihilate Sedgwick, but the wily Union commander escaped the trap that evening, crossing the Rappahannock at Scott's Ford. By May 5, the Union army was in full flight.*

BOTTOM: *Photographer Andrew J. Russell arrived with the Union army thirty minutes after the Confederates had abandoned their positions behind the stone wall at Marye's Heights and captured the aftermath of the hasty departure.*

OPPOSITE: *Much of the war in the eastern theater raged through the state of Virginia, including the battle of Fredericksburg (top). This map—of Loudoun, Fauquier, Prince William, and Culpeper counties—was likely made for Jackson by Jedidiah Hotchkiss and shows towns, waterways, roads, and residents.*

of the military principles of the day, the plan was recommended by the fact that Hooker would never anticipate it. In the end, Lee kept about seventeen thousand men with him to hold Hooker's attention as Jackson took the larger part of the army, approximately twenty-six thousand soldiers, on a wide swing involving a fifteen-mile (24km) march to assault Hooker's exposed flank.

Jackson moved his men out at dawn on May 2 and they marched swiftly in a generally westerly direction, swinging around and above the Federal positions, reaching Orange Turnpike near Wilderness Tavern by the early afternoon.

By 5:00 P.M., Jackson's leading formations charged of the woods, cheering and screaming out their "rebel yell" as they drove deer in front of them and into the Union lines ahead. In the face of this ferocious and unexpected attack, the Federal corps holding that part of the line began to dissolve.

The frenzied attack left the Confederate units disorganized, and Jackson's assault stalled as night fell. During the night, Jackson rode out on a commander's reconnaissance to locate routes that would allow him to trap the rest of Hooker's army before they could escape across the nearby Rappahannock. In one of the great

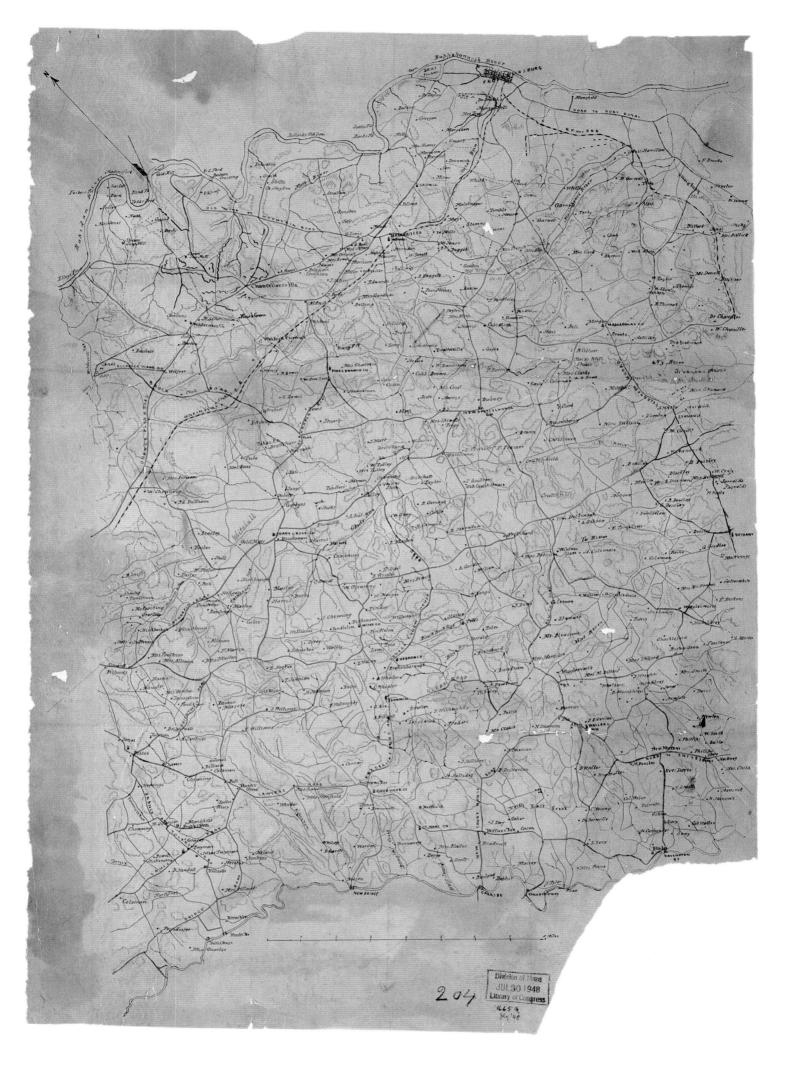

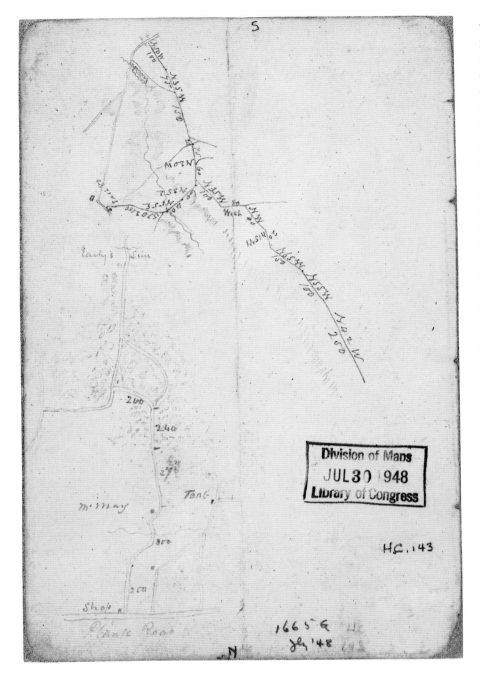

ABOVE: *Lee marched 21,000 men from Chancellorsville east to Salem Church, where he intended to destroy Sedgwick's force marching to the aid of Hooker. Sedgwick pulled back to pontoon bridges and asked for instructions from Hooker, who ordered his army and that of Sedgwick to cross to the relative safety of the north bank of the Rappahannock. Lincoln summed up this new disaster: "My God! My God! What will the country think?" This pencil sketch by Jedediah Hotchkiss contains notes on bearings and distances that would be used later to draw a finished map.*

OPPOSITE: *After the battle of Chancellorsville, Lee found himself in a familiar situation: the large Army of the Potomac had been defeated, and the way was clear for an invasion of the North. In early June 1863, Lee began to move his army away from Fredericksburg, using the Shenandoah Valley and shielding his movement from view by blocking the nearby mountain passes. As the operation got under way, General J.E.B. Stuart was surprised by Union cavalry at Brandy Station.*

Hooker learned of Lee's moves and ordered the Army of the Potomac into motion to protect Washington and Baltimore while attempting to destroy Lee's army as the Confederates began their long march into Pennsylvania. This map of the lower Shenandoah Valley, made by 1st Lieutenant S. Howell Brown of the Army of Northern Virginia in 1863, illustrates the terrain crossed as Lee's army marched north toward Gettysburg. The names of many local residents are included.

tragedies of the Civil War, he was shot as he rode into an ambush set by nervous North Carolina infantrymen. In little more than a week, Jackson would be dead of complications from the amputation of his left arm. Lee would remark about the loss that he had "lost his right arm." Lee appointed Major General Richard S. Ewell (a West Point graduate who had lost his leg at the second battle of Bull Run) as Jackson's replacement.

Meanwhile, Hooker ordered a few counterattacks that were initially successful, but the Union commander once more lost his ability to manage the battle plan. He ordered a general withdrawal all along his front, a detail that was not missed by Stuart. Just as Hooker was pulling back, the Confederate commander ordered an attack.

Hooker was unable to recover the initiative—in spite of his numerical superiority—and he was temporarily knocked unconscious by a cannon shot that struck a pillar on the porch of the Chancellor house as he was leaning against it. Even in the face of his injury, he didn't relinquish command to a more fit officer, and his medical director refused to declare him unfit for command. As a result, the mighty Army of the Potomac was effectively leaderless for the rest of the battle.

To the east, Sedgwick had managed to attack and capture the strategic Marye's Heights at Fredericksburg, but his success was to be short-lived. Lee took advantage of Hooker's inactivity to put into action another bold stroke. He split his army once again, leaving Stuart in place to occupy Hooker. Then Lee personally led twenty-one thousand men toward Fredericksburg on May 4 and fought a battle at Salem Church that resulted in a Federal retreat to the north and across the Rappahannock.

Lee turned once more to concentrate his army for a general attack on Hooker, who was in the worst possible position. His now-weakened army had its back against the Rappahannock River as Lee prepared to attack its front. In order to save the Union army, there was only one decision that could be made. Hooker ordered a general retreat over the river on May 6.

Although Lee had won his finest victory, the result was nonetheless a general stalemate between the Army of Northern Virginia and the Army of the Potomac. Lee had lost thirteen thousand men while Hooker had suffered seventeen thousand casualties. This great battle, for all of its maneuvering and terrible fighting, ended inconclusively. The next campaign would have different results.

After the victory at Chancellorsville, the Confederates regained their confidence. Lee had shown that skilled generals and brave soldiers were entirely capable of defeating superior numbers. Lee, after all, had bested an army that was more than twice the size of his own. And in the

MAP
OF THE
LOWER VALLEY

ABOVE: *Robert E. Lee ordered his three corps at Fredericksburg to begin their march on June 7, 1863. General Richard Ewell took the lead as the army marched northwest into Virginia's Shenandoah Valley through Winchester and on northward into the rich farmland of Pennsylvania's Cumberland Valley. Three days later, Hooker ordered the Army of the Potomac to march north—keeping itself between Lee's army and the large population centers of Washington and Baltimore.*

West Virginia's Confederate Brigadier General Albert Gallatin Jenkins' cavalry brigade penetrated to within four miles (6.4km) of Pennsylvania's capital, Harrisburg, before Lee ordered his army to concentrate—the Army of the Potomac had crossed the Potomac and was closing the distance between the two armies. This colorful map by Jedediah Hotchkiss shows the activities of the II Corps of the Army of Northern Virginia from June 4 to August 1, 1863. They went from Fredericksburg to Gettysburg and back to Orange Court House.

west, Grant had only just moved across the Mississippi—the city of Vicksburg was still intact. The Confederate army, political leaders, and population had good reason to be confident at this point in the Civil War.

But the northerners were becoming wiser, too. Lincoln and his generals had matured as strategists and their view of the war changed. Where they had looked to the capture of Richmond as the decisive act that would result in victory, they had now come to realize that the real objective they needed to pursue was the destruction of the Army of Northern Virginia under Lee. The goal was simple to state—it was altogether something else to accomplish.

BELOW: *As it had for several Confederate campaigns, especially Jackson's in May 1862, the Shenandoah Valley provided Lee with shelter and supplies as well as concealed his movements in part from the enemy as he moved once again to invade the North. This 1863 invasion followed a Confederate victory, Lee's masterpiece at Chancellorsville, just as his previous invasion had followed the success at Second Bull Run. One thing would be different this time, however: the Union cavalry. Not long after Lee set out from Fredericksburg for Gettysburg, the Union cavalry under Alfred Pleasonton clashed with J.E.B. Stuart's Confederate horsemen at Brandy Station, not far from Culpeper Court House. The battle was the largest cavalry engagement of the war and it signaled the end of Confederate domination on horseback. This painting by Don Troiani shows the 35th Battalion (known as "Comanches" for their ferocious battle yells) under Confederate Lieutenant Elijah White charging the New York Light Artillery under Captain Joseph Martin during the battle of Brandy Station. The Confederates carried the day, but the Union cavalry gained newfound respect and self-confidence from the encounter.*

BELOW: *The quiet town of Gettysburg (pictured here) received undesired attention from the Confederate army on July 1, 1863, when General Henry Heth's Rebels marched there in search of shoes, which were rumored to be there in abundance. Heth's men ran into the tough cavalrymen of John Buford's division at dawn as they marched up the Chambersburg Pike, and began to fight. By that afternoon, reinforcements of both armies were marching along the twelve roads that led to Gettysburg, and a huge battle began to develop. Later in the afternoon, the Federals were pushed southward, where they took up defensive positions along the high ground of Cemetery and Culp's hills.*

Gettysburg

The 1863 fighting season was still young, and the thrill of the victory at Chancellorsville only a few days old, when Lee and his troops began marching north and west. Lee's aim was to bring the war to the North. By moving within the Shenandoah Valley and its extension in the north, the broad Cumberland Valley, Lee was able to partially shield his moves from Union observation while protecting the trains that carried supplies for the imminent second Confederate invasion into the North.

Not long after learning of Lee's movements to the west, Hooker got word that J.E.B. Stuart's cavalry was at Brandy Station. In a bold move, given the South's reputation as superior horsemen, Hooker ordered his cavalry, under General Alfred Pleasonton, to intercept Stuart at Brandy Station. Pleasonton surprised Stuart and his cavalry at Brandy Station and the largest cavalry battle to occur in North America ensued. In the end, the Confederates had only barely turned back the assault. It was a victory of significant symbolic importance for the Union's cavalry. Meanwhile, Hooker moved the Army of the Potomac in order to protect the city of Washington from attack.

Lee crossed the Potomac and was soon inside Pennsylvania, where he was forced by a general supply shortage to disperse his columns. Stuart, perhaps in an attempt to recover his mildly tarnished reputation after Brandy Station, rode off to strike out on his own, leaving Lee without the scouting reports that had served him so well at Chancellorsville. Lee, marching blindly without Stuart, was deprived of accurate information about Hooker's actions. Eventually it was one of

ABOVE: *Brigadier General John Buford's cavalrymen formed a thin line of resistance as Confederate General Henry Heth's division moved toward the small town of Gettysburg. Buford's efforts to delay the Confederate attackers gave the Army of the Potomac time to arrive on the field. Buford (seated) is surrounded by his staff officers, including Captain Myles Keogh (standing at left), an Irish immigrant who would remain in the army after the Civil War and die with General George A. Custer at the battle of Little Big Horn in 1876.*

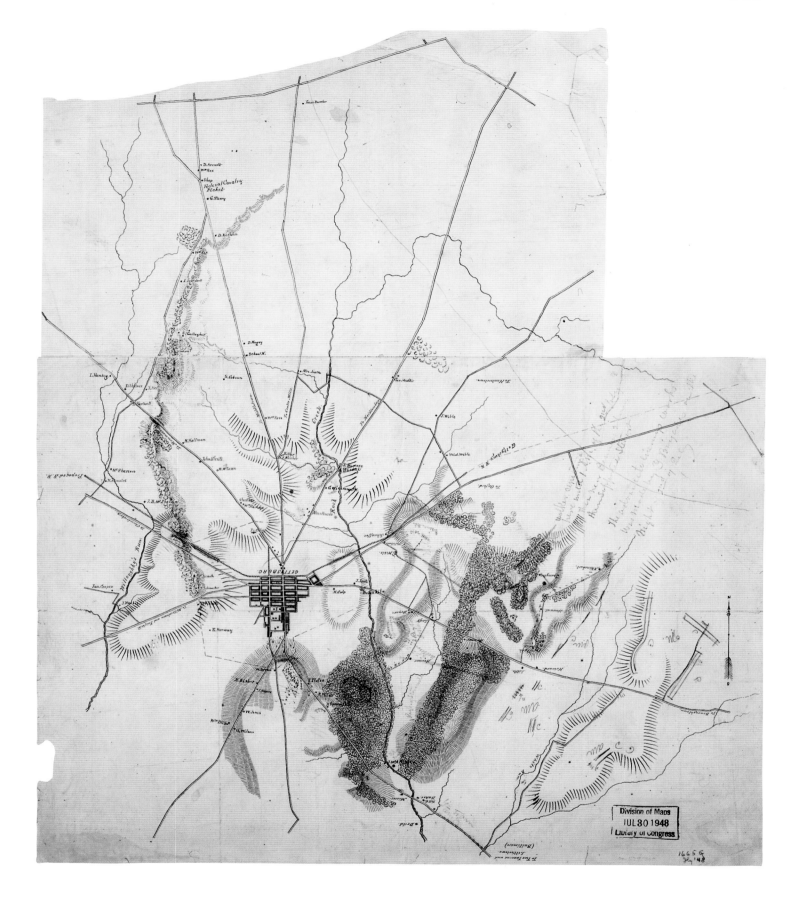

ABOVE: *Jackson's master cartographer Jed Hotchkiss was present with Ewell's II Corps at Gettysburg, where he prepared this excellent map. For good reason, the locations and terrain features on the right half of the map were labeled upside down. Ewell's area of operations was along the right side of the map, and approaching from the north, Ewell's commanders would have seen the locations in the perspective they were labeled. Hotchkiss had drawn a very effective map for the II Corps.*

ABOVE: *Following the daring victory at Chancellorsville, which had made it clear to Lee that a campaign of maneuver favored his outnumbered army, the Confederate general ordered just such an attack northward through the Shenandoah Valley. In June, various elements of the southern army began filing up the valley to join in the assault. To Lee's surprise, however, the Union reacted swiftly, and on June 29 the Confederate commander sent out urgent requests for reinforcements to support him at Gettysburg, Pennsylvania. Beginning on July 1 and lasting three grueling days, the battle of Gettysburg would prove the turning point of the war.*

This painting shows the men of the 2nd Wisconsin Volunteers (the Iron Brigade) loading their weapons on the run as they rush through McPherson's Woods to plug a gap in the Federal line on July 1 at the opening of the battle. This brigade of the I Corps, under General John Reynolds, was thrown into battle as soon as they arrived and so had almost no information about the enemy they were to face. And though they successfully defended the line for a while, by the end of the day they were forced to fall back through the town to Culp's Hill, where the roll call revealed that of the 302 men of the brigade who had begun the day, just forty-five had survived.

ABOVE: *During the battle of Gettysburg, Lee ordered his headquarters tent to be pitched across from this house, the home of the Widow Thompson. Mathew Brady took this photograph two weeks after the battle was over.*

BELOW: *Gettysburg was the first battle to clearly foreshadow the fate of the Confederacy. After the Union army successfully forced Robert E. Lee to withdraw from Pennsylvania, the Army of Northern Virginia was unable to fully resume offensive operations—except locally on a relatively small scale—for the remainder of the Civil War. Mathew Brady photographed some of the critical sections of the battlefield in and around Gettysburg: Big Round Top (right) and Little Round Top (left), where tired Confederates charged up the steep slopes. Brady is leaning against the tree at the left of the photograph.*

ABOVE: *Union General John Reynolds met with John Buford and realized the danger the scattered Union army had entered. He was ordering his men into positions within McPherson's Woods, when as he turned in his saddle a musket ball struck him behind his right ear, killing him instantly. Often sharing the dangers of the battlefield with his soldiers, Reynolds had become one of the most popular generals in the Union army.*

ABOVE: *Located at the far end of Meade's defensive line, two hills were recognized as keys to the entire battle. Big Round Top and Little Round Top were high enough to permit Confederate artillery to fire along the entire length of the Union line if captured by the Confederates. Both terrain features were soon under heavy attack from the troops of Longsheet's corps. Between the two hills was a rugged area later given the name "Slaughter Pen" because of the intense fighting that occurred here. This photograph, taken on July 6, shows bodies still strewn across the rocky landscape—the busy burial teams had not been able to reach this area before the photographers arrived.*

CONFEDERATE POSITIONS

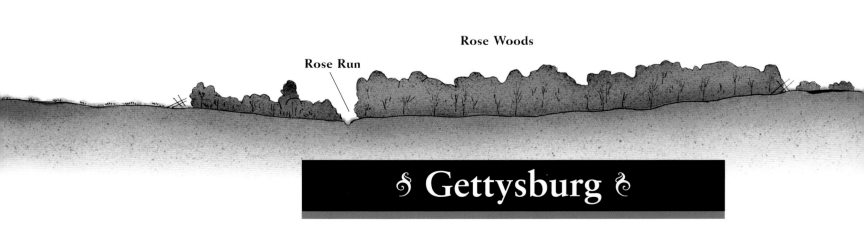

Rose Woods

Rose Run

§ Gettysburg ⸙

Longstreet's spies who brought the news that the Army of the Potomac had crossed the Potomac River, barely giving Lee enough time to concentrate his forces for the battle that was surely to come.

The Army of the Potomac had numbers on its side, with twice the number of Lee's Army of Northern Virginia (111,000 to Lee's seventy-six thousand men), but the structure of command was delivered a crippling blow. Their commander, Joseph Hooker—who had lost his nerve at Chancellorsville, but was a good tactician nonetheless—argued with General-in-Chief Henry Halleck and asked to be relieved of command. General George G. Meade was selected from the corps commanders on June 28 and placed in command as Hooker's army marched into battle against an army that had outmaneuvered and outfought the Army of the Potomac on so many previous occasions. Meade decided to prepare for a defensive battle in Maryland, but his plans—as well as those formulated by Lee—were to be overcome by events beyond the control of either man.

As the dispersed elements of both armies began to concentrate, troops began to come into contact with one another near the small town of Gettysburg, Pennsylvania, on June 30, 1863. The epic battle began to the northwest of the town on July 1 as Federal cavalry under General John Buford fought as dismounted infantry against General A.P. Hill's entire corps. The Union cavalrymen were soon joined by a full corps of the Army of the Potomac, its XI Corps, while Confederate General Richard Ewell, Jackson's successor, moved his corps to support Hill.

Ewell's brigades were able to break through the defensive positions of the XI Corps and the Federal soldiers were soon retreating through Gettysburg. These men moved into good defensive positions to the rear of the Army of the Potomac's artillery, located to the south of the town on two strategic heights, Cemetery and Culp's hills. It was at this point in the battle that Ewell failed to capture the Federal positions on

Gettysburg
Little Round Top, July 2, 1863

The first phase of attacks on the Round Top hills took place in Plum Run Valley, where the Confederates encountered little resistance as they took Big Round Top. Pushing on toward Little Round Top, however, the Rebels under Evander Law and Jerome Robertson encountered stiff resistance from defenders atop the hill. Meanwhile, Confederates under "Tige" Anderson and Henry Lewis Benning attempted to sweep in from the west to flank the hill, but met resistance in the rocky confines of the Devil's Den. Just the same, the Federals slowly began to lose ground, making it important for the Union soldiers to hold Little Round Top, a critical line of defense for their entire left flank.

Ordered to help hold the position, Colonel Joshua Chamberlain, the commander of the 20th Maine, moved his men into defensive positions on Little Round Top, but as soon as they arrived, Colonel William Oates and his 15th Alabama also appeared. Fire from the Federal troops forced the Confederate line backward, but Oates' men soon reformed to renew their attack. Chamberlain wrote of the fighting: "My regiment held the extreme left of the Union lines at Gettysburg. The enemy was shelling the crest heavily, and moving a large force to seize this commanding height, while we were rushing up to get to the position ourselves.... As it was a sort of echelon attack, the enemy was constantly coming up on my left, and outflanking me. The losses in my regiment were very heavy. In the center of the apex of the angle, made by throwing back the left wing, the color-guard was shot away, and the color-company and that next to it lost nearly half their number, and more than a third of my regiment was disabled.... I saw a heavy force that had just come up over the opposite slopes of Great Round Top, coming to envelop our left. They were close to us, advancing rapidly, and firing as they came. We expended our last cartridges.... every round was gone. Knowing the supreme importance of holding this ground, which covered the flank of Hazlett's Battery on the summit.... I saw no other way to save it, or even ourselves, but to charge with the bayonet. The charge was successful beyond all my hopes."

As the Confederates were rallying for another charge at the Union soldiers, who had exhausted their ammunition, Chamberlain ordered his 20th Maine forward in a bayonet charge that entered the pages of history. Oates' 15th Alabama bravely prepared to received Chamberlain's bayonet charge, but at the same moment the Confederates began to receive fire from Berdan's Sharpshooters, whom the 15th Alabama had fought earlier in the day and who had since climbed the slopes of Big Round Top behind the Confederate brigade. Oates had no other alternative than to order a retreat.

The position was saved, and the left flank of the Union army at Gettysburg held, but at a price: of the 386 men of the 20th Maine who had climbed Little Round Top earlier in the day, 130 had been killed.

UNION POSITIONS

Little Round Top

Devil's Den

Plum Run

Scale in Feet

100   0   100   200   300

P.A.Keene © 98

Cemetery Hill, as had been suggested by Lee. As a result, Meade's army was able to take advantage of their shorter interior lines to move men to important positions all along the high ground. By daybreak on July 2, Meade had completed all of his preparations for the second day of fighting.

Meade's lines were strong, but there were two positions where the Confederates could press their army into an effective breakthrough: Little Round Top was one of the critical points in the line, which should have guarded Meade's southern flank. As it was, Little Round Top was left undefended as the battle began in earnest. Meade's chief engineer, General Gouverneur Warren, made the discovery that there were no infantrymen positioned there and he persuaded the corps commander at the southern end of the

Federal line to send two small brigades to the hill. They arrived just as the Confederates arrived in force. The actions of Colonel Joshua Chamberlain and his 20th Maine Volunteer Infantry, which met the 15th Alabama Infantry, would enter into the history of the nation. Chamberlain was able to hold his position and forced the Confederates back onto the slopes of the hill, barely holding Little Round Top as the rest of the second day's battle raged nearby.

The second weak position in Meade's line was created as General Daniel Sickles moved his III Corps forward to what he thought was a better position. What had really happened when the politician-turned-general ordered his men forward beyond the main line was this: an outward bulge in the Federal defensive line developed,

LEFT: *The struggle for possession of Little Round Top on July 2, 1863, is considered to be one of the most famous small-unit actions in American military history. Many elements of both armies were involved in the struggle to control this critical height overlooking the Gettysburg battlefield. Among the Confederate attackers who took part in the attempt on Little Round Top were the men of the Texas brigade under Brigadier General Jerome Robertson. The 5th Texas Infantry, a group of battle-hardened veterans under the command of Colonel R.M. Powell, in particular distinguished themselves in the assault. They spent the day in hard fighting among the boulders of Devil's Den as they repeatedly attacked the Federals near the summit. Victory ultimately went to the Union that day, but the brave Texans were recognized for their actions nonetheless. This painting by Don Troiani shows the 5th Texas Infantry as they struggle under fire to scale the steep boulder- and brush-strewn hill.*

dangerously exposing the men along the bulge to Confederate attack, which they would have to endure without support. The attack came when Longstreet's men hit Sickles and his III Corps hard at the Peach Orchard, forcing the Union line back as far as Cemetery Ridge before Federal reserves were able to contain them. On the north end of the line, Ewell attacked late in the afternoon, but the Union soldiers held their positions at Culp's Hill. At the end of the day, Meade's line still held fast. Lee had struck at both of Meade's flanks on the second day and had failed to defeat the Army of the Potomac. He would try another approach on the third day.

The generals of the Civil War had been trained at the same school, West Point, from the same texts, and they had gained experience

ABOVE: *Little Round Top was considered to be the key to holding Meade's left flank. Union troops were ordered to the critical terrain feature just before Colonel Oates' 15th Alabama Regiment arrived to attack them. Oates reluctantly left Big Round Top, the highest elevation in the region, convinced the higher hill was the more critical piece of terrain. Oates strongly felt that fire from a few Confederate artillery pieces atop Big Round Top would permit the Confederates to shell Meade's line from one end to the other.*

The men of the 20th Maine and their commander, Colonel Joshua Chamberlain, had been told, "This is the left of the Union line....You are to hold this ground at all costs." Attacked again and again by the men of the 15th Alabama, who were charging their positions, the 20th Maine held, eventually advancing on the 15th Alabama with their bayonets fixed once their ammunition ran out. The nearly exhausted Confederates, surprised by the ferocity of the Union defenders, fell back, only to be struck by fire from behind.

1 MILE

through service in the same prewar army. They were so much alike that they were often able to anticipate each other in battle; this is exactly what occurred on the third day at Gettysburg. Meade knew that Lee had attacked both of his flanks on July 2, and reasoned that the attacks on July 3 would come at his center. The afternoon would prove him right.

Lee ordered a massive artillery bombardment of Meade's center that began at 1:00 P.M. on July 3, the greatest shelling that had occurred to that point in the war. The shells passed over the heads of the Union soldiers lying in their positions along their line, doing little actual damage in the two-hour barrage. The Union artillery, numbering approximately eighty pieces, stopped its return fire to conserve ammunition. The Confederate commanders made the erroneous assumption that the Federal artillery pieces were damaged and out of action.

Forty-seven Confederate regiments (the majority of which were under the command of General George Pickett) emerged from the woods that sheltered them, dressed their lines as if they were on parade, and began a seventeen-minute march across open ground toward the Union lines. Union artillery then opened up on the Confederate lines, which suffered heavy casualties as they approached the Union lines and broke into a run. The heavy fire from Federal cannon was joined by rifles. As the Confederates closed with the Union line, the cannon began to fire canister, producing shotgunlike blasts that cut broad swathes through the ranks of the attackers. A few of the men who had survived the crossing of the field broke through the lines opposing them, but they were quickly killed or

ABOVE: *The battle of Gettysburg (town at center) reversed the normal positions of the two armies engaged there (south is at the top of this map). Lee's forces had been operating deep within Pennsylvania as the Army of the Potomac began to approach from the south. Lacking the services of Stuart's cavalry to learn of the intentions of the Union army, Lee permitted his opponents to position themselves across his route of withdrawal. In the afternoon of July 1, Lee's divisions began to push Hooker's replacement, General George G. Meade, and his corps southward. The Federal XI Corps and I Corps withdrew through the streets of Gettysburg, where they took up new positions on Cemetery Hill, Culp's Hill, and Cemetery Ridge (above and to the left of Gettysburg), where heavy fighting was renewed on July 2, mostly in the region of the Round Tops (at the top of the map). This interesting relief map was made by Ambrose Lehman of Philadelphia in 1886 and shows the varied terrain over which the battle of Gettysburg was fought.*

OPPOSITE: *Lee had ordered assaults on Meade's right and left wings, and on July 3, after the heaviest artillery bombardment up to that time on the North American continent, he ordered an attack against Meade's center. The Federal artillery stopped firing to conserve ammunition, and their silence seemed to beckon the Confederate infantry into a suicidal frontal attack. Fifteen thousand Confederates in forty-seven regiments emerged from the woods on Seminary Ridge, and began to walk across open fields toward the Union lines at Cemetery Ridge. Union artillery opened fire and began to decimate the Confederate ranks, but the left of the Confederate line actually penetrated the Federal line—only to be killed or captured. The battle at Gettysburg cost both sides a total of more than 51,000 casualties before it was over.*

This map illustrates the battlefield, looking toward the south, and showing the town, fields, farm buildings, forests, streams, roads, and lands as they were at the time of the battle. It was drawn by Jedediah Hotchkiss and includes the names of the Confederate divisions and corps, but not the Federal.

RIGHT: *This photograph shows the Trostle House, where General Sickles set up his headquarters and not far from which he lost his leg in battle. Strewn about the house are the corpses of horses of the 9th Massachusetts Battery, a testament to the ferocity of the battle.*

BELOW: *The victors at Gettysburg posed for a photograph after Lee had withdrawn to Virginia. Lincoln expected Meade (sitting, center, with his legs crossed) to quickly pursue Lee's damaged army, but Meade's own army had suffered terribly in the three days of bitter fighting at Gettysburg. The Union commander may have lost an opportunity to win the war in 1863—much like the opportunity lost by McClellan following the brutal battle at Antietam. Gettysburg was the last important battle in the eastern theater in 1863; the damaged Army of Northern Virginia was seldom able to conduct offensive operations for the remainder of the Civil War.*

ABOVE: *His army severely battered by Lee's attacks at Gettysburg, Meade was slow to develop a pursuit of the retreating Confederate army (depicted here). Furious at the prospect of Lee's escape, Lincoln rapidly sent orders from Washington to prod Meade into action, but it was too late. Lee's rear guard bought enough additional time for the entire Confederate army to cross the Potomac River to safety.*

OPPOSITE: *This wonderful map accompanied the official Union report on the outcome of the battle of Gettysburg. It shows the ground covered by both armies in the course of the conflict. Lee's quartermaster ordered warehouses in the vicinity of Falling Waters to be torn down to provide materials for the construction of boats to support an expedient pontoon bridge across the broad Potomac River. Federal cavalry discovered the attempted crossing early in the morning of July 14, but an attack was delayed until midmorning. Lee's rear guard held back both Buford's and Kilpatrick's cavalry as Lee's Army of Northern Virginia escaped.*

captured. Lee had too few reserves and too great a distance to cover to be able to exploit this small breakthrough. The Federal reserves nearby were ordered to move swiftly to contain the small Confederate incursion (led by Brigadier General Lewis Armistead, the sole surviving commander under Pickett) ironically called the "high water mark of the Confederacy, the deepest penetration of Lee's army into the North."

The survivors of Pickett's charge withdrew and the battle was effectively over. General Judson Kilpatrick ordered a final—and suicidal—cavalry charge by Elon Farnsworth that was easily handled by Longstreet's hardened veterans.

The human toll of Gettysburg was terrible on both sides: Meade lost 3,155 killed, 14,529 wounded, and 5,365 missing and captured. Lee had also suffered severely, losing 3,903 killed, 18,735 wounded, and 5,425 missing and captured.

Lee's second invasion of the North had failed. The proud general withdrew toward the Potomac fords, where high water prevented any large-scale crossings. Because Meade's casualties were also high, the general was reluctant to press the issue. On July 13, Lee was able to cross over the river to safety in Virginia—effectively ending the campaign in the east for the remainder of the year. This battle would prove a turning point in the war for the fortunes of both sides.

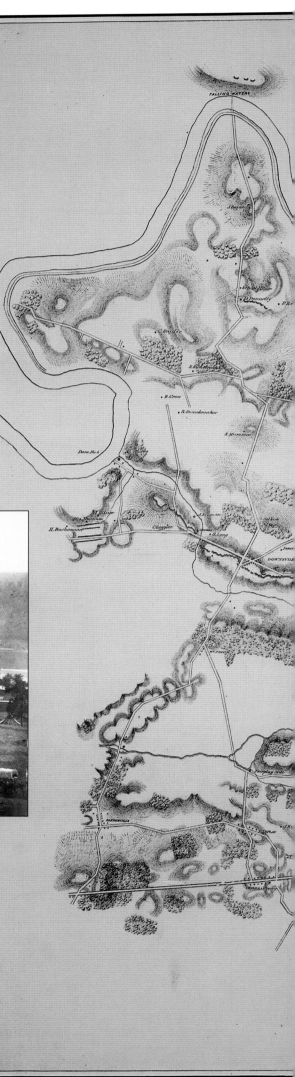

ABOVE: *The military initiative shifted over to the Federal side in July 1863: Grant had taken Vicksburg and Meade had won at Gettysburg, sending Lee's Army of Northern Virginia (which had lost 38,000 men, roughly 40 percent of the total) south. Lincoln urged Meade to pursue Lee, believing the Confederates could be destroyed if Meade were aggressive enough. Following Gettysburg, however, both the Army of Northern Virginia and the Army of the Potomac were badly battered, and neither was eager to add to the casualty list. As a result, Meade backed Lee up against the Potomac, but the Confederate commander was firmly entrenched and therefore dangerous. Meade hesitated to attack his foe, and Lee and his army were able to cross the Potomac to the relative safety of Virginia long before Meade could effectively act to prevent it.*

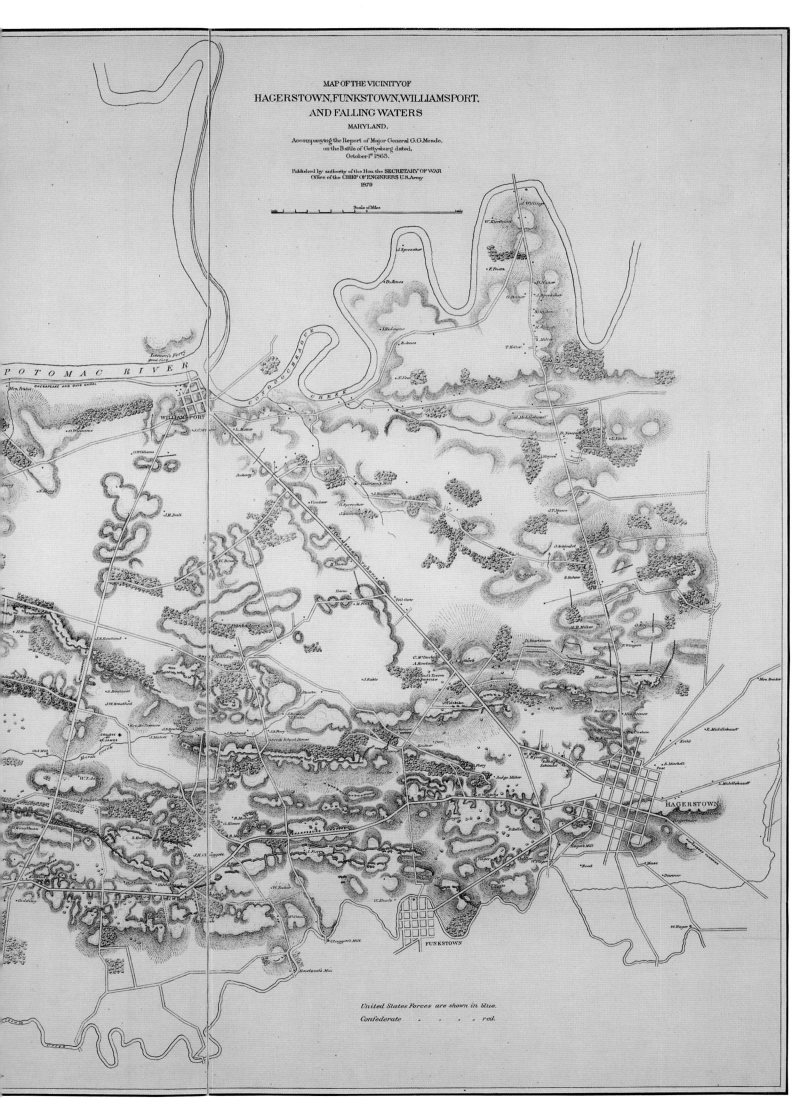

MAP OF THE VICINITY OF
HAGERSTOWN, FUNKSTOWN, WILLIAMSPORT,
AND FALLING WATERS
MARYLAND.

Accompanying the Report of Major General G.G.Meade,
on the Battle of Gettysburg dated,
October 1st 1863.

Published by authority of the Hon. the SECRETARY OF WAR
Office of the CHIEF OF ENGINEERS U.S.Army
1879

Scale of Miles

United States Forces are shown in blue.

Confederate " " " red.

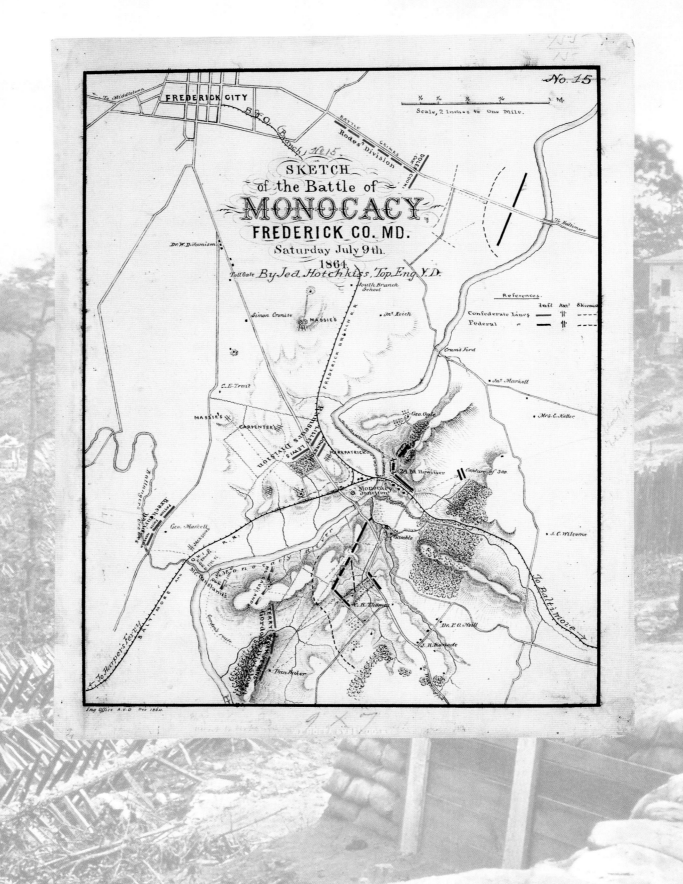

No. 15

FREDERICK CITY

To Middletown

B.&O. R.R.

Branch, No 15

Rodes' Division

BATTLE CRIMES

DOLES COMM

Scale, 2 Inches to One Mile.

SKETCH
of the Battle of
MONOCACY,
FREDERICK CO. MD.
Saturday July 9th.
1864.
By Jed. Hotchkiss, Top. Eng. V.D.

To Baltimore

Dr. W. Dikanison

Tollgate

South Branch
School

References:

Infl   Ax'l   Skirmish

Confederate Lines
Federal

Simon Cronise

MASSIE'S

Jn'o Keich

Crum's Ford

C.E.Truit

Geo. Ogle

Jn'o Markell

Mrs. E. Keller

MASSIE'S

CARPENTER'S

HOLTSMAN'S DIVISION

SIMLEY

KIRKPATRICK

24 M. Brewster

Cantur of 300.

Monocacy
Junction

Geo. Markell

H. Wilson

O & W. R.R.

Ramble

J. C. Wilson

To Baltimore

Monocacy River

Baltimore and Harper's Ferry

McClaslands

Gambel route

C. K. Thomas

Dr. T. O. Neill

J. H. Barnode

To Harper's Ferry

Dan Baker

Eng Office A.V.D. Dec 1864.

CHAPTER FOUR

The Civil War in 1864

The military strategy of both sides in the Civil War evolved as battles were won and lost during the first three years of combat. The Confederacy continued to wage a defensive war, though on occasion they had resorted to an offensive strategy (usually hoping to achieve a political result) by invading the territory of the Union. Lee had led major incursions into both Maryland and Pennsylvania, where he hoped to draw the Army of the Potomac into a decisive battle. And large Confederate forces had moved into border states in efforts to tie down large numbers of Federal defenders. The generally defensive strategy had served the Confederacy well to this point in the Civil War: the soldiers, officers as well as ordinary personnel, fought best when defending their home territory.

Cast in the role of the aggressor, the large armies of the North marched into border and southern states with the goal of bringing them back into the Union by force of arms. The process was made more difficult by the Federal government's tendency to replace generals as they lost battles while retaining the services of such former politicians as McClernand, Sigel, and Sickles— just to name a few—who had political constituencies but few military skills. There were few actual efforts toward creating a unity of command outside the general-in-chief's office, and the diversity of tactics used in the war gave it the appearance of several wars fought simultaneously by different armies. This had plagued the Union army at first, but as the North's leaders, especially Abraham Lincoln, gained experience in the management of large campaigns, they began to develop a modern strategic approach to warfare.

Lincoln in particular had demonstrated an evolution in his strategic views. During the early phases of

the war, he had viewed the capture of Richmond as the strategic goal toward which his armies should strive, but by 1864 he had identified the destruction of the Army of Northern Virginia and the other armies of the Confederacy as the goal to pursue. Lincoln also had come to the realization that he had to find a general who could carry out the new strategy.

At the time, there was an exchange of letters regarding Union strategy taking place between Lincoln and Grant. Lincoln, unable to find a general with any sort of strategic vision, had been acting as senior strategist for the Federal forces since he had relieved George B. McClellan in 1862. In this capacity, the president was actively soliciting new ideas from Grant. After a few theater-specific proposals from Grant, Lincoln requested that his commander in the west develop proposals for the grand offensive he hoped to launch when the 1864 spring campaign season opened. Impressed with the fighting qualities and the obvious intelligence of Grant, Lincoln soon acknowledged the skills of his new commander by elevating him to the post of general-in-chief of the entire army.

When Grant became commander of all the Federal armies, on March 12, 1864, his plans were complex and had a single objective: to destroy the Confederacy's armies by mobilizing the Union's armies as if they were just one army. Grant had a quality that others (for instance, Hooker) lacked, in that he could visualize and predict the complex movements of a great many troops. Technological developments were also available to him that made the task of managing widely spread forces much easier. He could easily telegraph orders and receive reports from all over the country as he developed plans for coordinated moves. Instead of removing Henry Halleck, the officer he replaced, Grant retained Halleck in Washington, D.C., to manage the administrative requirements of the entire Union army, freeing Grant to move with the primary force, the Army of the Potomac, as it prepared to confront Lee and his Army of Northern Virginia.

By April 1864, Grant was ready to move, with the balance of power clearly on his side. He had a two-to-one advantage in combat troops, with 300,000 men preparing to move against the 150,000 soldiers available to the entire Confederacy. The factories and railroads supporting the Union army's operations were getting better at making and delivering supplies at a time when the Confederacy's capacity to manufacture and deliver military goods was becoming severely compromised, both by increased demand and by the pressure of the attacking armies. Grant also

had the advantage of expert assistance from Henry Halleck in managing the administrative burdens of the army: Halleck made sure that the men were fed, paid, and hospitalized (when necessary) as they moved around the country—all details that would have distracted the new general-in-chief from his responsibilities of fighting and destroying the Confederacy's armies.

Four large Union armies were preparing to embark upon their spring campaigns. The Army of the Potomac, with Grant's headquarters in the field, were to move south in early May to engage Lee in the area of Fredericksburg. Meanwhile, General Benjamin Butler's Army of the James was to move from the vicinity of Fort Monroe toward Richmond, destroying the railroads near Petersburg, if possible, and drawing men from Lee's force in front of Grant. The third army, in the Shenandoah Valley under General Franz

Sigel, was to move south through the strategic valley (previously used as an invasion route by Lee) to destroy the critical rail and manufacturing center at Lynchburg, Virginia, afterward gaining the rear of Lee's defensive perimeter surrounding Richmond and Petersburg. Another full army, under General William T. Sherman, was assigned the task of invading the deep South and capturing Atlanta. Sherman and his men were to march through the broken Confederate defenses in eastern Tennessee and enter Georgia with the twin goals of destroying the large army under Joseph E. Johnston and laying waste to the resources in the South's heartland. The final, but smaller operation would be in the deep South, where General Nathaniel Banks was to cooperate with the Union navy to make an amphibious landing at Mobile, Alabama, drawing both Confederate resources and attention away from Sherman.

When Grant was given his command, a revolution occurred in the way the Civil War was fought. Whereas his predecessors had formulated their military strategy on the model of Jomini, in which maneuver was as important as actual combat, Grant understood that the destruction of the enemy's economic and material resources was as important as the destruction of its armies. This was a modern (and admittedly ruthless) approach to war. Whether this change resulted from Grant's common sense or the large numbers in the Union army of former German officers familiar with the teachings of Clausewitz (the forefather of modern military strategy) remains unknown. What is known is that the model developed by Jomini was to meet the model developed by Clausewitz in 1864, when the Union forces under Grant went on the offensive against the weakened armies of the South.

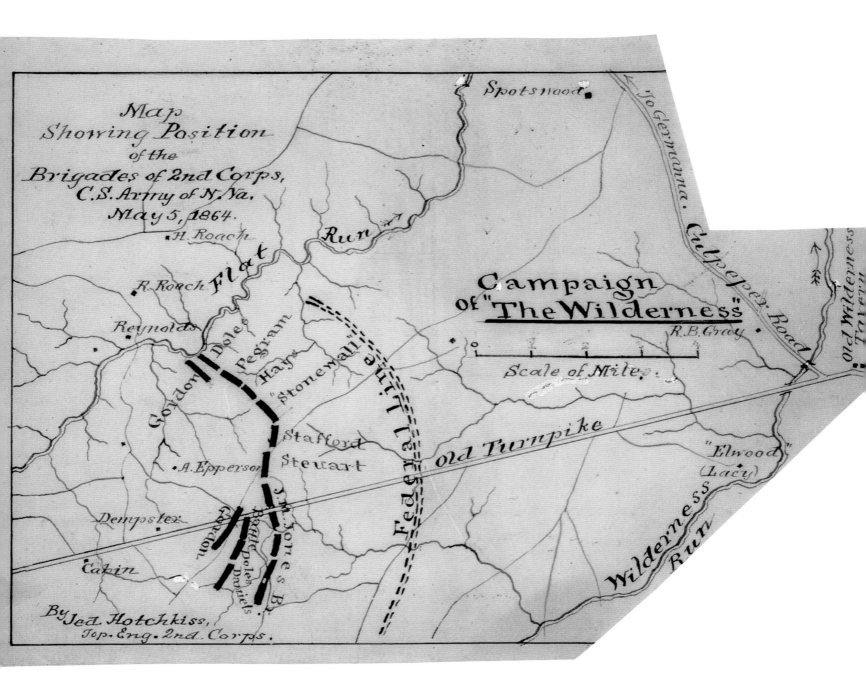

The Battle of the Wilderness

In northern Virginia on May 4, 1864, Grant ordered Meade's Army of the Potomac to cross the Rapidan River, beginning the campaign that would spell doom for the Confederacy. Knowing that his enormous army would require a tremendous logistics effort to keep the men supplied, Grant dispensed with his lines of communication as he moved south. The use of railroads as a supply system would put the Union army at the mercy of John S. Mosby and other Confederate cavalry commanders and require the use of large numbers of soldiers to guard the rail lines. The Army of the Potomac would also require tremendous numbers of mules and horses to pull wagons from rail heads to front line depots from

ABOVE: *This sketch by Jed Hotchkiss, who was with Ewell's II Corps, shows the fighting on the second day of the campaign in the Wilderness, May 5, 1864. The fighting began in Sander's Field, where a Union division under Charles Griffin attacked a division under Edward Johnson, of Ewell's corps. After battling back and forth through the undergrowth and dense woodlands south of the turnpike, neither side made significant advances. To the south of the area shown in this map, fighting developed between Heth's Confederate division and Richard Getty's division, which was pushed back initially and then supported with the arrival of Hancock's II Corps. The day ended in a standoff.*

OPPOSITE: *This map shows the area over which much of the action during the Wilderness campaign occurred, from May 4 to 6, 1864: on May 4, Grant's army crossed in two columns, at Germanna and Ely's fords, the forward (western) column (including the corps of Burnside, Sedgwick, and Warren) moving south over Germanna Plank Road while the other column (with corps under Hancock) swung to the east and south; Ewell, A.P. Hill, and Longstreet swept in from the west, along the Orange Turnpike, Orange-Plank Road, and Catharpin Road, respectively; beginning on May 5, fighting developed mainly along, as well as in the tree and undergrowth-choked terrain in between, Orange Turnpike and Orange-Plank Road. This map was surveyed and drawn by Major J.E. Weyss, under the direction of Nathaniel Michler; the lithograph itself was produced later by the N.Y. Lithographing, Engraving & Printing Co.*

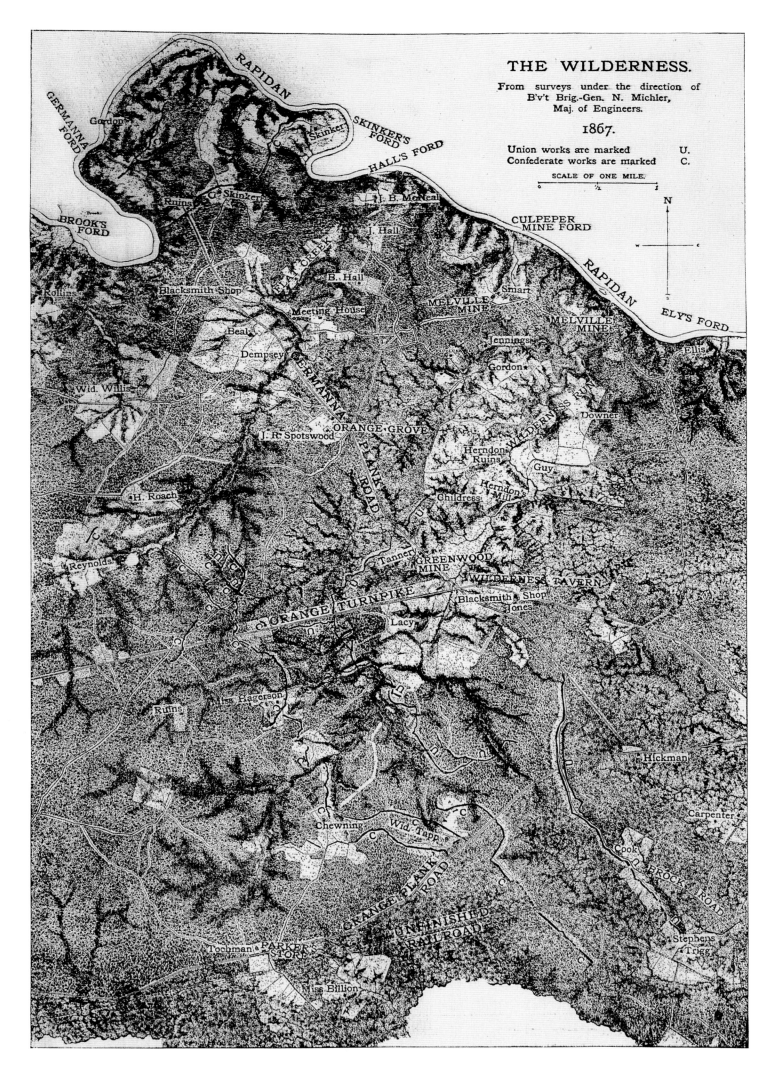

THE WILDERNESS.

From surveys under the direction of
B'v't Brig.-Gen. N. Michler,
Maj. of Engineers.

1867.

Union works are marked   U.
Confederate works are marked   C.

SCALE OF ONE MILE.

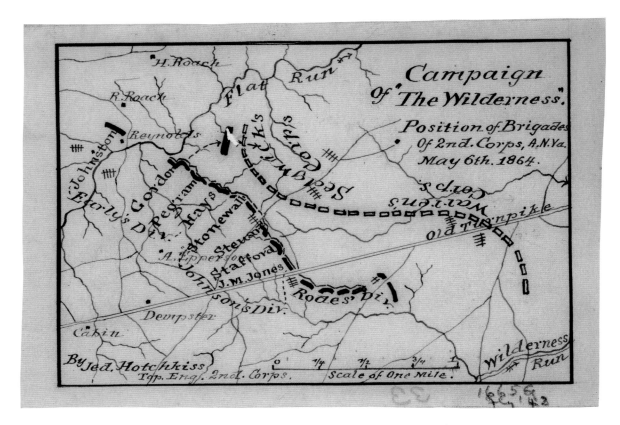

ABOVE: *This sketch from Hotchkiss' Wilderness series shows the position of the II Corps during the final day of fighting around Wilderness Run. Late in the afternoon, the brigades of Early's division (shown here) launched a surprise attack against the brigades of Sedgwick's VI Corps that drove the Union forces back, but then petered out with nightfall. The main fighting on this day actually occurred to the south of the area shown in this map, where elements of Union General Hancock's II Corps had battered A.P. Hill's line, only to be staggered themselves by Confederate reinforcements under General Longstreet. Ultimately the Union line was also reinforced, by Burnside, and the fighting ended in a draw. Notably, Longstreet was wounded by friendly fire during the engagement. Grant lost nearly 18,000 men to Lee's 7,500.*

which supplies were distributed. Grant decided to free himself from all of these transportation burdens by attacking toward Lee's right flank by placing himself squarely between Lee's army and the coastal waters of Virginia, where the navy could supply the land forces from safe havens along the Chesapeake Bay. There was risk involved in crossing Lee's front to strike each time at the right side of his defensive line, but the two-to-one numerical superiority enjoyed by Grant considerably lessened the risk faced by the Army of the Potomac.

Soon after crossing the Rapidan River, Grant moved into the Wilderness, where Hooker nearly had been destroyed the previous year. The army halted to allow their supply train to cross the Rapidan, and on May 5 Lee struck hard at Meade's right flank. Savage combat ensued in the thick, tangled brush and woods, described as "bushwhacking on a grand scale," and casualties mounted on each side. The fighting developed into a nightmare as dry forest litter caught fire and wounded men were burned to death in the flames. Longstreet's corps arrive on the battlefield on May 6, pushing Grant's army backward as the epic battle continued. Longstreet received a severe neck wound, and in the heat of the battle, with the outcome still in doubt, Lee prepared to personally lead an attack. The men in the Texas brigade began to cry, "Lee to the rear!"

and promised the greatly loved army commander that they would accomplish his tactical objectives while he managed the entire battle. The next day saw no major fighting, but it did see Grant make a bold decision.

The bloody battle of the Wilderness had not been decisive, though Grant had suffered greater losses than Lee. At other times in the war, Union commanders who had suffered such reverses as this simply retired to the nearby safety north of the Rappahannock River while they rested and repaired the battle damage they had sustained. Grant, however, was a different breed from the army commanders who had gone before him.

Grant calmly ordered his commanders to move south, passing Lee's army and positioning the Union forces between Lee and Richmond. In response, Lee and the Army of Northern Virginia moved on a course parallel to that taken by Grant, racing to gain a strategic crossroads at Spotsylvania before Grant's army could get there. The southerners hoped to construct breastworks and entrenchments there from which they would be able to defend the approaches to Richmond.

The race between the two armies featured a dazzling display by Grant's cavalry arm. On the way to Spotsylvania, Grant's army was delayed by Confederate cavalry. At first, Philip Sheridan, Grant's cavalry commander, was unable to react to the movements of J.E.B. Stuart, Lee's cavalry leader, because General Meade had ordered the majority of the Federal cavalry to guard the supply wagons. Sheridan objected to this practice, and Grant supported him, giving Sheridan the

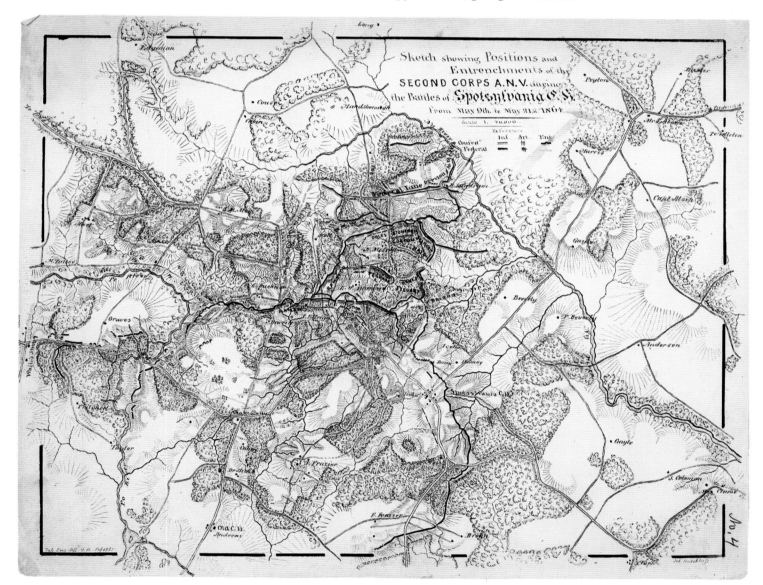

ABOVE: *Another of Jedediah Hotchkiss' excellent maps from his postwar collection of thirty-eight maps detailing the movements of the II Corps of the Army of Northern Virginia ("Report of the camps, marches, and entrenchments..."), this shows the area around Spotsylvania Court House where bloody fighting raged over the period from May 9 to May 21, 1864, as Grant pursued his ruthless campaign to bring Lee's army to heel. Really a fully developed map, this was probably colored and perfected sometime in 1892.*

latitude to lead all of his cavalry out on an expedition to locate and destroy the Confederate's cavalry.

"Litttle Phil" Sheridan and his cavalry corps, twelve thousand strong, departed on a sixteen-day raid. At Yellow Tavern, near Richmond, the Confederate cavalry was overrun and the gallant Stuart received a mortal wound during the fighting. Lee's fearsome cavalry would never again achieve the same strength or inspire the same sort of awe it once had.

Spotsylvania

Grant ordered attacks against Lee's fortifications at Spotsylvania on May 9, and in fighting that lasted for days, the Union army was able to penetrate Lee's lines on two occasions.

BELOW: *This map of Spotyslvania County by Jedediah Hotchkiss was probably extremely useful to Lee in planning his defense of the region. On the map roads are shown in red and drainage in blue; also included are the names of some of the residents of the region.*

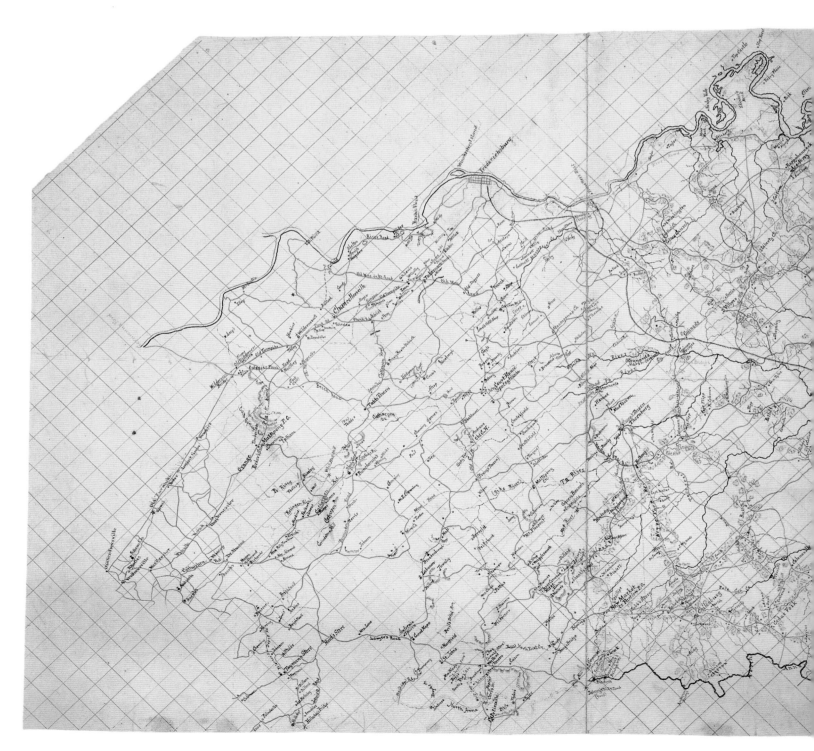

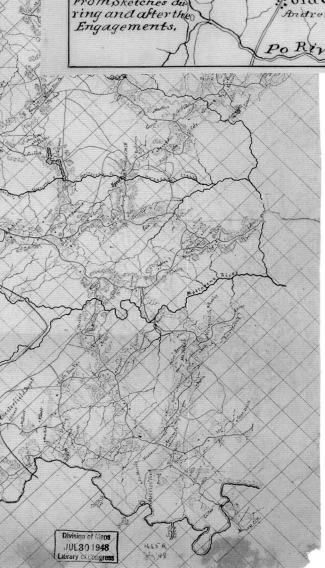

ABOVE: *Some of the bloodiest combat of the Civil War developed as the Union army fought to break through Lee's defensive line and divide his army. Twice they broke through, but Federal reinforcements were unable to get into position to capitalize on their success before Confederate counterattacks pushed them out and closed the gaps in Lee's line. Grant wrote, "We propose to fight it out on this line if it takes all summer," but he soon realized Lee's positions were too strong to overcome and he began to work his way south—once again looking for an opportunity to locate Lee's right flank. This finished sketch by Jedediah Hotchkiss showing the battles in the immediate vicinity of Spotsylvania Court House was completed after the engagement from the cartographer's battlefield notes. It was also included in Hotchkiss' postwar collection, "Report of the camps, marches and entrenchments...."*

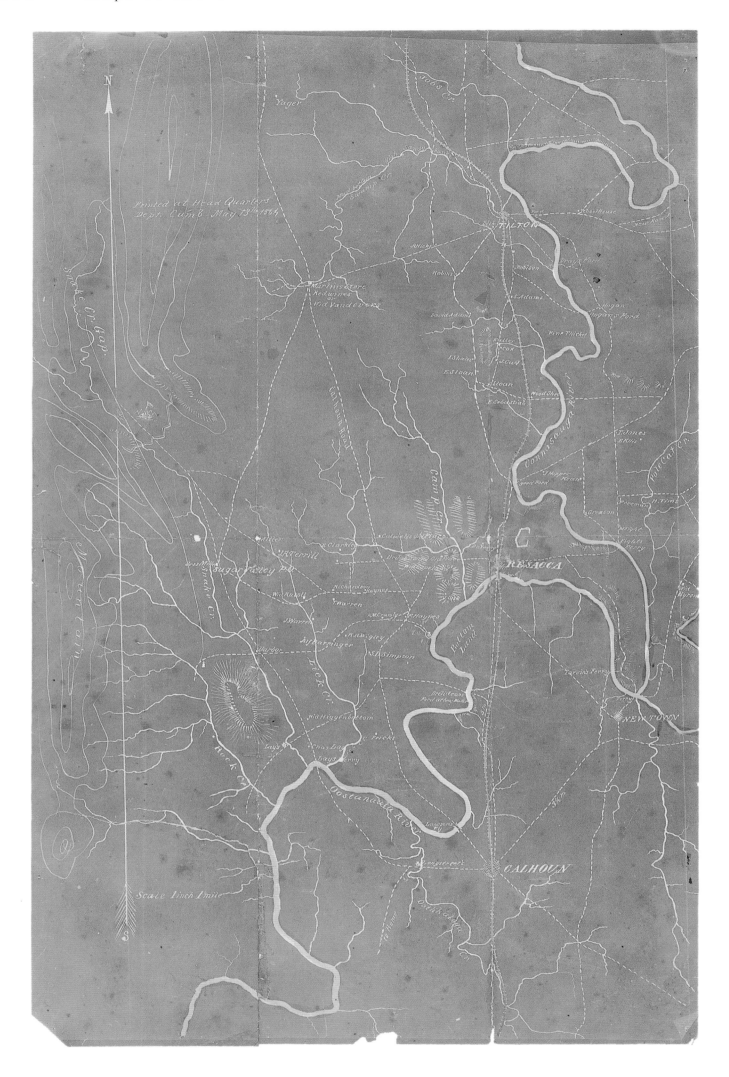

Unfortunately, they were unable to exploit these breakthroughs. It was at this point in the war that Grant's tenacity was most clearly demonstrated. He wrote to Washington that he "proposed to fight it out on this line if it takes all summer." After realizing that Lee's positions on the road to Richmond were too strong for the Army of the Potomac to capture, Grant ordered his commanders to move south, placing his army between Lee's army and the Union supply depots on the Chesapeake Bay that were regularly being replenished by the Union navy.

Cold Harbor

Lee withdrew to new fortified positions south of the North Anna River, but Grant continued to press him. Then Grant swung south, bypassing the Confederates, in order to hit Lee's left flank. Lee, in turn, also moved south to protect the approach to Richmond, building breastworks at Cold Harbor and establishing a defensive line that stretched eight miles (12.8km). On June 3, Grant assaulted the center of Lee's line, but the Union men were beaten back—it was one of the few times Grant made an error in the execution of his battle plan. After being repulsed, the Union army dug in not far from the Confederate forces and the bitter fighting continued. By June 12, Grant's forces, which had been attacking Lee's army for exactly one month, had suffered enormous losses: the Union casualties over that period totaled fifty-five thousand. Lee had lost roughly thirty-two thousand.

OPPOSITE: *Sherman pushed his three armies southward along the Western & Atlantic Railroad. Rather than attempting to fight Johnston in the narrow mountain passes, Sherman made several attempts to locate and turn Johnston's right flank. Each time, the Confederate commander shifted his forces to meet the new threat, and a battle was fought near Resaca, Georgia, on May 8, 1864. This map showing the position of the Army of Tennessee near Resaca was produced on May 13, 1864, at the headquarters of the Army of the Cumberland and is an early example of a photoreproductive process invented by Captain William Margedant, a Union topographical engineer.*

Grant's next move followed the pattern he had established early in the campaign as he continued on southward, pressing to turn Lee's right flank. Grant's forces crossed the broad James River on the longest pontoon bridge ever constructed up to that time, set up a supply base at City Point, Virginia, and moved into entrenched positions in front of Petersburg, Virginia, where they remained for most of the remainder of the war. This phase of the Civil War closely resembled the trench warfare of World War I: cannonades from the heavy guns, shells fired from mortars, and small arms fire were so severe that entrenched men dared not raise their heads for fear of being shot.

While Lee and Grant were fighting one another along Virginia's coastal area, the other armies in motion in the region were being countered by Lee's subordinate commanders. Butler was relatively easy to contain after he had moved up the peninsula toward Richmond. General Beauregard was able to block his progress by constructing fortifications at Bermuda Hundred. Butler, one of the Union's generals who owed his rank to the political process, was relieved for this failure.

Sigel also ran into problems as he started up the Shenandoah Valley. He was blocked effectively at the battle of New Market by General John C. Breckinridge, who was aided by the

BELOW: *Pontoon bridges—such as this structure across the North Anna River at Jericho Mill, where a part of Meade's army crossed—were hastily constructed by Federal engineers to replace structures burned by the retreating Confederates. Supply wagons, artillery, and additional bridging equipment were hauled across these temporary bridges as Grant pressed the Army of the Potomac toward Cold Harbor, Virginia. After the bloody repulse at Cold Harbor, Grant ordered the construction of a 2,100-foot (638.4m) pontoon bridge across the James River— the largest bridge of this type ever constructed—to position the Army of the Potomac for attacks against Virginia's large manufacturing and transportation center, Petersburg.*

cadets of Virginia's Military Institute. When Sigel was relieved of his command, he was replaced by General David Hunter, an aggressive commander who immediately regrouped Sigel's army to continue the advance toward Lynchburg as ordered by Grant. Encountering Confederate defenders near Staunton, Virginia, at the battle of Piedmont, Hunter defeated General "Grumble" Jones, who was killed, and cleared the way for an unobstructed march to the target, Lynchburg.

One lonely Confederate cavalry brigade, under Brigadier General "Tiger" John McCausland, harassed and delayed the march of Hunter's army for nearly two weeks, giving the Confederates time to reinforce Lynchburg: John C. Breckinridge arrived first and was followed by Jubal Early's entire corps. Hunter's men, short of rations as well as ammunition, were forced to retreat from the approaches to Lynchburg toward and through the mountains of West Virginia before reaching safety. For the Union, Hunter's march had the undesired effect of leaving the Shenandoah Valley clear of northern defenders. The route used twice already for an invasion of Union territory was once again open.

COLD HARBOR

From Surveys
under the direction of Bvt.Brig.Gen.N.MICHLER, Maj.of Engineers
and Bvt.Lieut.Col.P.S.MICHIE, Capt.of Engineers
By Command of
Bvt. Maj.Gen.l A.A.HUMPHREYS, Brig.Gen.l & Chief of Engineers
1867.
Scale of 3 inches to 1 Mile.

ABOVE: *The first month of Grant's 1864 offensive culminated in an attack on Lee's center at Cold Harbor. Lee had skillfully anchored his right flank on the Chickahominy River with his center spread across the old Gaines' Mill battlefield at Cold Harbor. On June 3, 1864, Grant ordered the attack at Cold Harbor, but he was beaten back, suffering heavy casualties. Grant later remarked that he regretted giving the order to attack. He soon ordered a continuation of the Union move south, and the Army of the Potomac crossed the James River on a huge pontoon bridge. This map was prepared under the direction of engineer Nathaniel Michler and shows Union and Confederate positions (marked "U" and "C" respectively) from June 1 to 3, 1864. The map later accompanied an article in the June 1887 issue of* Century *magazine.*

OPPOSITE: *Young cadets from Virginia's Military Institute were ordered forward to fill a gap in the Confederate line at the battle of New Market. These were only students, and General Breckinridge said as he gave the orders, "Put the boys in and may God forgive me for the order." After closing the gap in the Confederate line, the cadets soon charged into an opening in the Union line, capturing a Federal cannon. In the process, ten of their number were killed and an additional forty-seven wounded. As Breckinridge suspected they might, the cadets paid a high price for the Confederate cause at New Market.*

ABOVE: *The soldiers of the Army of the Potomac were able to enjoy a few days of rest before the opening of Grant's 1864 spring offensive against Lee's Army of Northern Virginia. These soldiers of the 170th New York Infantry Regiment, some of whom are shown here relaxing prior to mobilization, lost 336 men—killed, wounded, or missing— in the first month of combat.*

ABOVE: *The Wilderness Campaign was launched in the spring of 1864 by Grant, who hoped to grind Lee's forces down with vastly superior numbers of both men and matériel. The culmination of the campaign, the battle of Cold Harbor, made clear the fact that victory in this bitter war would not come easily—whatever numerical advantages the North enjoyed. The battle of Cold Harbor developed as Grant marched his army south toward Richmond; Lee responded by entrenching his men around the strategic junction at Cold Harbor. The attackers had been trying to break through Lee's lines for three days, when on June 3 Grant ordered an all-out assault against the entire Confederate line. General Francis C. Barlow's division, on Lee's extreme right flank, was able to break through initially, but was finally repulsed. The entire Union army settled down within one hundred yards (91.2m) of the Confederate line and a period of bitter trench warfare began. By June 12, the attack was over, the Union army having been soundly whipped. The lethal attack against Lee was the only battle of the Civil War that the Union commander openly regretted. This picture shows the XVIII Corps driving Longstreet's men before them during the battle.*

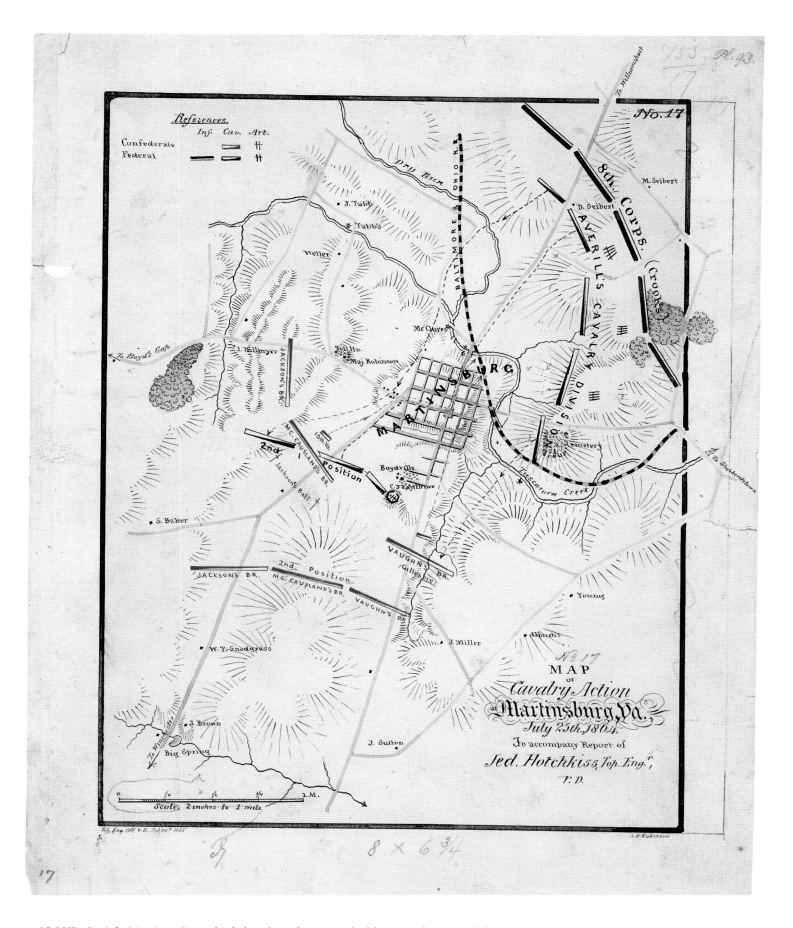

ABOVE: *On July 24, 1864, General Jubal Early—who in May had been sent by Lee to defend the Shenandoah Valley from the depradations of David "Black Dave" Hunter and who had gone on to nearly invade Washington, D.C.—seemed to be retreating from General George Crook's army, only to turn and strike Crook's force at Kernstown, Virginia. On July 25, Early sent his cavalry northward to destroy the recently repaired railroad tracks at Martinsburg, where it encountered the Union cavalry under William Averell. (Although Martinsburg was a small town in Virginia, the presence of the Baltimore and Ohio Railroad made it a target for the Confederates.) Despite these Confederate advances, however, by October, Early had been defeated at Cedar Creek and the strategic valley was firmly in the hands of the Union. This map, drawn by Jedediah Hotchkiss, was one of the thirty-eight maps in his "Report on the camps, marches and engagements…."*

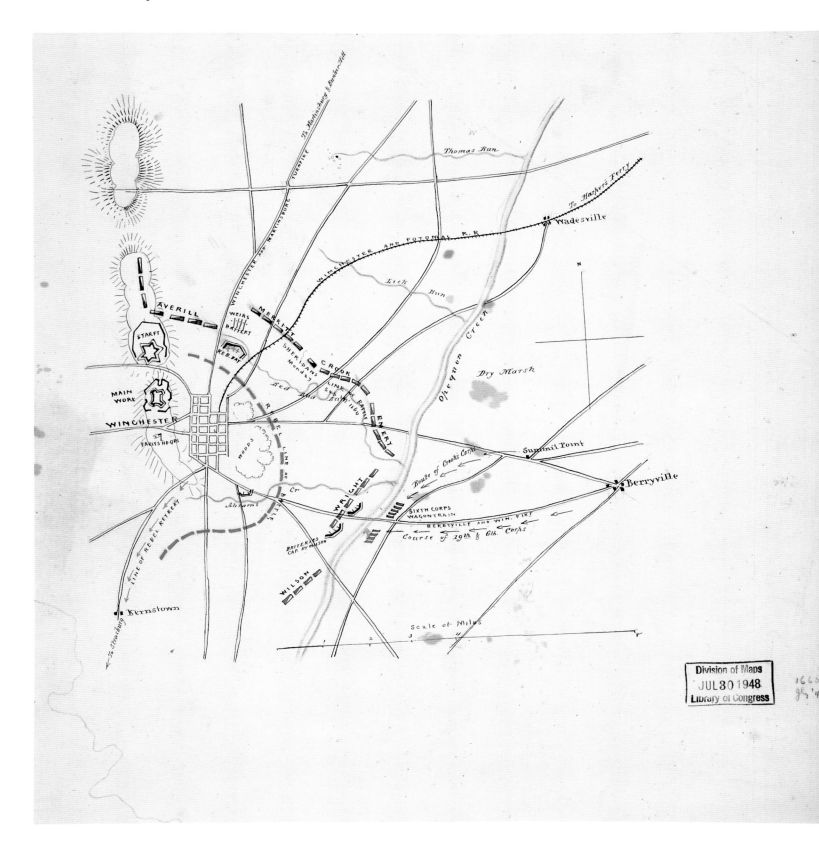

ABOVE: *Grant abolished the four separate military departments responsible for defending the vicinity of Washington and unified this region under a single commander, General Philip Sheridan. In August 1864, Sheridan was placed in command and ordered to follow Early "to the death." After a delay of over a month, as Sheridan attempted to determine Early's strength, a Federal spy in Winchester, Rebecca Wright, sent him a note—carried inside the mouth of a slave courier—to advise of a draw-down in Early's strength. Sheridan ordered an attack on Winchester, Early's headquarters, on September 19, 1864, soundly defeating the Confederate defenders. Soon the Federal army struck Early once again at Fisher's Hill, and nearly eliminated Early's entire army in October at Cedar Creek. Simultaneous attacks by Union cavalry toward Star Fort (left, center) and along the road from Berryville (right, center) were sufficient to overcome the Confederate defenders. Although this map is part of the Hotchkiss collection, it is thought to be a Federal map because it refers to the Confederates as "Rebels" and shows Union positions in detail.*

LEFT: *Harper's Ferry, Virginia (which became part of the thirty-fifth state, West Virginia) had changed hands several times throughout the war, beginning in 1861. Located deep within a river valley and surrounded by mountains, Harper's Ferry was nearly impossible to defend. Jackson described it best when he said he would rather "take the place forty times than undertake to defend it once." The small town was captured by the Confederate army under Jubal Early in July 1864 as the small Rebel army marched to attack Washington, D.C., in one of the most daring attacks of the Civil War.*

BELOW: *This extremely detailed terrain map of Harper's Ferry illustrates why the position was so difficult to defend. The map was surveyed and drawn by J.E.Weyss for Nathaniel Michler of the engineering corps in 1863. It was later published as seen here by the N.Y. Lithographing, Engraving & Printing Co. in 1867.*

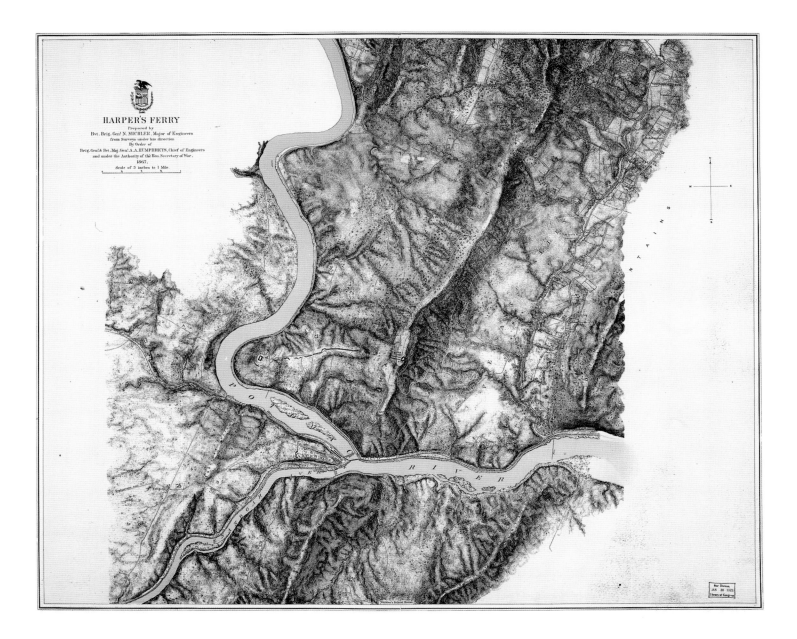

ABOVE: *At several points before and during the Civil War, Harper's Ferry was fired upon or destroyed by different factions as the strategic little transportation hub received lots of unwanted attention. This photograph shows the town after it has been leveled in one such attack, probably Early's 1864 bombardment (used to divert forces from the defense of Washington, D.C.). Note that the railroad tracks have been decimated and that many of the buildings of the town are merely bombed-out shells.*

Loudoun Heights

Bolivar Heights

Harper's Ferry

§ Harper's Ferry ?

Potomac River

Moving swiftly, Early was able to cross the Potomac River and enter Maryland, but on July 9, 1864, he was delayed in the battle of Monocacy by Union General Lew Wallace (later the author of *Ben Hur*). The short delay allowed reinforcements sent by Grant from City Point, the entire VI Corps, to come to the defense of Washington, D.C. Early, often underestimated by historians, had conducted a masterful campaign in the face of superior numbers, even managing at one point to extract his army from a trap he had willingly entered as Union forces, including Hunter's army, reentered the eastern theater by crossing West Virginia on the Baltimore and Ohio Railroad.

Sensing that Early's successes had resulted from the lack of a unified command in the Washington, D.C., area, Grant ordered the four military departments forged into one. He placed General Philip Sheridan, the pugnacious cavalry commander, in charge, with orders to destroy Early, whose stronghold was at Winchester. This was easier said than done: Sheridan lacked reliable information about Early's strength and intentions. Reacting to this need for data, Sheridan was able to recruit the services of a young woman inside Winchester, Rebecca Wright, who soon reported the march of a full division of infantry and a battalion of artillery back to Lee at Petersburg. Realizing his advantage, Sheridan attacked Early at Winchester on September 19 and drove the Confederates from the town. Early was forced from Fisher's Hill later in the month, and in October, Sheridan was able to defeat Early's army at Cedar Creek after a morning that saw a near rout of his own army. It was at this point in the war that the civilian population of Virginia began to feel the heavy hand of war: as part of the modern way of wag-

Harper's Ferry

Harper's Ferry became the site of a national armory in 1796, and with the completion of the Chesapeake and Ohio Canal, the Baltimore and Ohio Railroad, and the Winchester and Potomac Railroad, the small Virginia town became a strategic target just prior to and during the Civil War.

Sometimes described as the "bottom of a well," the small town was nearly impossible to hold against any determined attacker if the surrounding hills were lost to the defenders. When the original decision was made to develop a national arsenal here, strategists felt the deep valleys and steep mountain slopes would allow them to hold off any attacks made by an enemy, but its military history proved its location to be a weakness. Before the war, John Brown captured the armory easily with only a few men; in 1861 a small garrison of Federal defenders chose to burn the arms manufacturing facility as Virginia troops approached.

Located at the right are Loudoun Heights, and at the left, Maryland Heights. Once Maryland Heights was captured by Jackson in 1862, the twelve-thousand-man federal garrison was forced to surrender. In 1864, Jubal Early chose to bypass Maryland Heights, instead ordering several attacks to hold the garrison in place as he fought the battle of Monocacy and marched onward to attack Washington, D.C. The town that had little actual military value managed to gain a great deal of military attention during the Civil War.

Damaged both by warfare and floods, the small town never recovered its previous importance after the Civil War, and became a ghost town until tourism revived the area's economy.

Maryland Heights

Scale in Feet

200 100 0   300   600   900

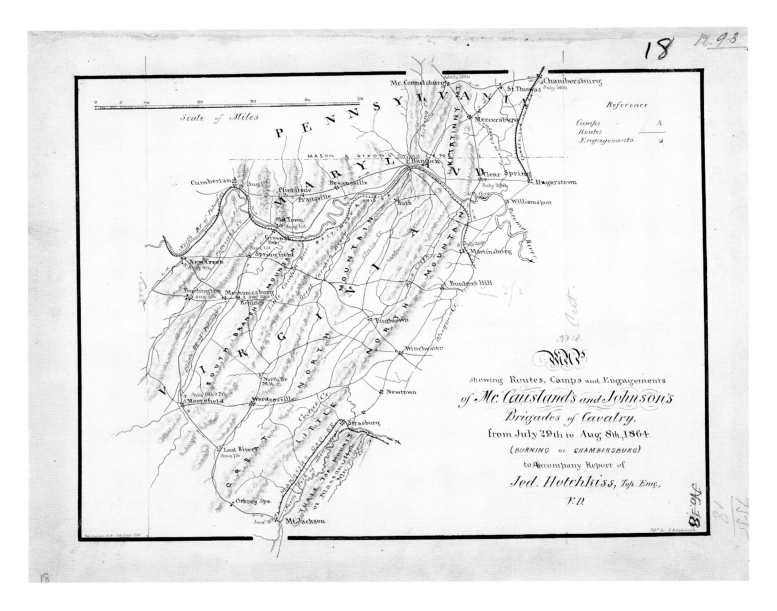

ABOVE: *Shortly after the battle of Monocacy, Early levied a ransom on the nearby town of Frederick, Maryland, apparently intending to pay for damage done to private property when the Shenandoah Valley was occupied by the Union's General David Hunter. Early sent one of his aggressive cavalry commanders, Brigadier General John McCausland, to Hagerstown, Maryland (upper right), to collect an additional ransom of $200,000. Claiming to have misunderstood Early's verbal orders, McCausland returned with $20,000, but Early next sent him into Pennsylvania. As McClausland rode into Chambersburg (top, right), he carried unmistakable written orders to collect a ransom or the town was to be burned. When the city fathers refused to pay—or were unable to—he ordered the small town put to the torch on July 30, 1864. The Confederates then withdrew to Cumberland (upper left) before continuing on to Moorefield (lower left), where they were routed in a surprise attack by the Union cavalry under William Averell. This map was drawn by Jedediah Hotchkiss and was one of the series of thirty-eight in "Report of the camps, marches and engagements...."*

OPPOSITE: *Fisher's Hill became a critical point in the Shenandoah Valley. While Early's Confederate army was small, it was composed of battle-hardened veterans, whom Sheridan treated with respect. He took over a month to fully measure Early's ability before he attacked at Winchester, Virginia, on September 19. Once Sheridan managed to get his full army onto the field, Early was beaten severely and forced to retreat south, up the Shenandoah Valley. Three days later, Sheridan struck Early again at Fisher's Hill, defeated him, and forced the Confederate army onward. Thinking Early to be in full retreat, Sheridan ordered his cavalry patrols to begin to devastate the entire valley. But Early had only fallen back, first to Port Republic, then to Kernstown. In the meantime, Lee sent Joseph Kershaw's division, a cavalry brigade, and an artillery battalion, to support Early. Surprising the Federals in bed, the vengeful Confederates swept through the Union camps along Cedar Creek on October 1. Falling back north to Middletown, Virginia, the shaken Federals rallied under Sheridan, who ordered a counterattack in the afternoon. The Rebels crumbled under sheer weight of numbers and left the field in what amounted to a rout. The strategic valley was now solidly under Union control. Part of the Hotchkiss collection, this map of Fisher's Hill was drawn by Lieutenant J. Innes Randolph for Major A.H. Campbell.*

Map of Vicinity of
Fisher's Hill

STRASBURG

LITTLE NORTH MT

SHENANDOAH RIVER

MASSANUTTEN MTS

TUMBLING RUN

TOM'S BROOK

MULBERRY RUN

Scale 1/40,000

4 Miles

ing war, Sheridan had been ordered to destroy the crops of the Shenandoah Valley, the source of much of the food supplying Lee's army at Petersburg. This, however, wasn't the only destruction of civilian property that was being carried out: Sherman was on the march in the deep South and he was sweeping everything before him.

The Atlanta Campaign

Sherman had marched out of his base area at Chattanooga on May 4, 1864, the same day Grant crossed the Rapidan, a simultaneous movement of two major Union armies that began to occupy the minds of Confederate defenders and politicians. Facing Sherman was Joseph Johnston, who was badly outnumbered and soon forced to conduct purely defensive operations. Throughout the campaign, Johnston defended his positions masterfully—despite his numerical advantage, Sherman was only able to cover 100 miles (160km) in seventy-four days. There were several major fights along the way, but Johnston always withdrew before losing in a major confrontation. Sherman ordered a costly attack on June 27 against Confederate positions at Kennesaw Mountain, where he suffered severe losses before returning to a war of marching and maneuvering that forced Johnston back into the defenses of Atlanta.

Although he had delayed an army of superior numbers, fighting an excellent series of defensive battles, Johnston was soon replaced by General John B. Hood. Johnston and Jefferson Davis seldom had kind words for one another, and once Braxton Bragg, Davis' special advisor, entered the military equation at Atlanta, Johnston was out and the aggressive Hood was in. Hood attacked from the Confederate defenses on July 20 at Peachtree Creek, where Sherman inflicted heavy losses on Hood's men, who were fighting in the open. Hood soon attacked a second time, again in vain. By August 31, Sherman began to extend his lines south to cut the railroads to Atlanta, and Hood, realizing the futility of defending Atlanta and lacking the strength to attack Sherman, withdrew into northern Alabama, where his weakened presence was generally ignored by the Union forces.

The successes of Sherman at Atlanta and of Sheridan at Cedar Creek generally ensured Lincoln's reelection against George B. McClellan in the fall elections. One of the hopes of the beleaguered Confederacy was that the prospect of an endless war would prove so discouraging to the northern population that it would embrace McClellan, the peace candidate in the presidential elections. Union losses at Monocacy, Winchester, Atlanta, or Cedar Creek may have been enough at that late date to spell the end of Abraham Lincoln's tenure as leader of the nation. As it turned out, Federal victories laid the groundwork for another term for Lincoln.

Sherman split his army, sending thirty thousand men back to the vicinity of Nashville to

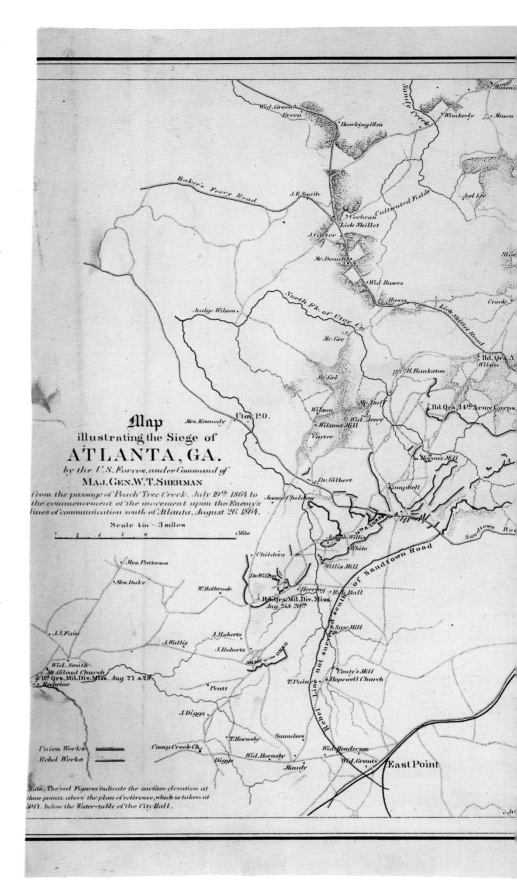

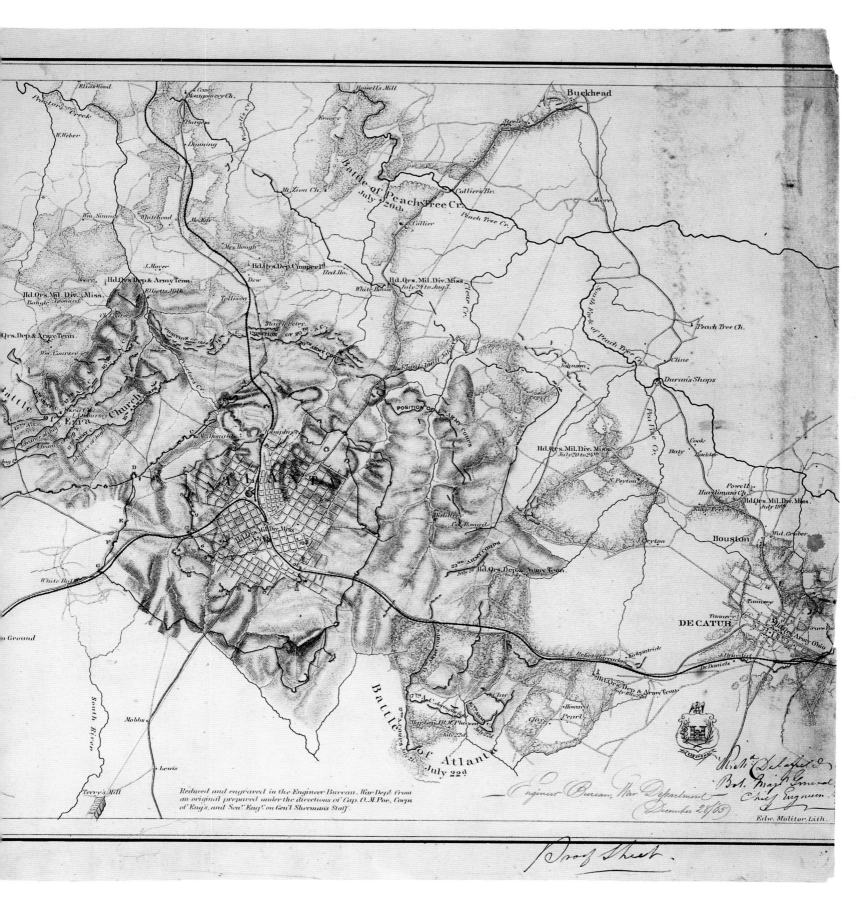

ABOVE: *Only Richmond had a greater industrial capacity than Atlanta, and General William T. Sherman began his campaign to capture the strategic city in Georgia on May 4, 1864. His force of 100,000 men sought to destroy General Joseph Johnston's 65,000 Confederate defenders. Johnston conducted a masterful defensive campaign, delaying Sherman in battle after battle. Mistaking Johnston's defensive operations for timidity, Jefferson Davis replaced him with General John B. Hood, a younger and far more aggressive commander, in July. On July 20, Hood foolishly ordered his army to attack Sherman. With his striking power greatly reduced by the resulting casualties, Hood abandoned Atlanta. Sherman occupied the city on September 1 and 2, 1864. Part of the Sherman collection at the Library of Congress, this map was prepared under the direction of Captain Orlando Poe and shows the Federal positions during the siege of Atlanta.*

RIGHT: *On July 20, 1864, as Sherman was conducting a general movement of his army along the northwest side of Atlanta, John B. Hood ordered his men from their fortifications to attack. Sherman was able to contain Hood's attack at Peachtree Creek. On July 22, as Sherman was preparing siege operations, Hood struck him a second time, to the east of Atlanta at Decatur. Elements of the Army of the Tennessee under McPherson were stationed at Decatur and barely turned the attackers back. This rough sketch was handed by McPherson to Sherman moments before the former was killed.*

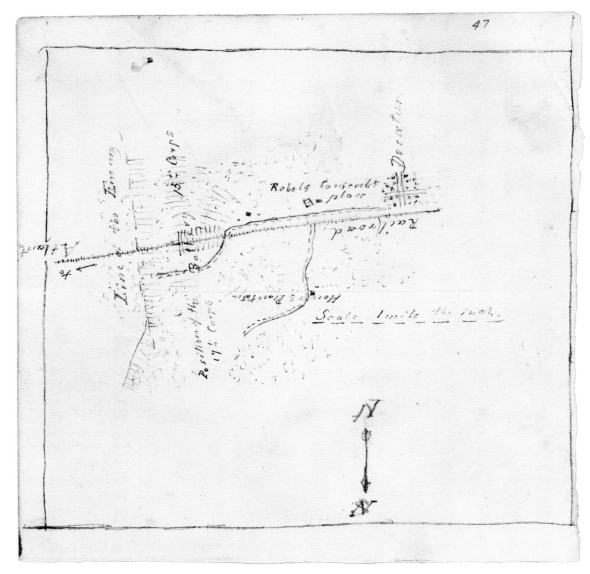

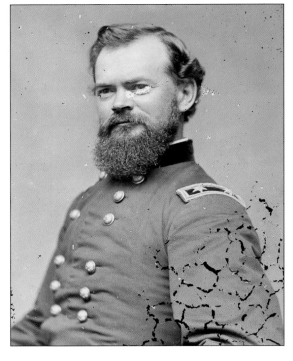

ABOVE: *The Civil War cost the nation the services of some if its most talented citizens. General James B. McPherson was the highest ranking Union officer to die in the Civil War, and he lost his life during the battle of Atlanta.*

ABOVE: *The commander of the Union's Army of the Tennessee, General James B. McPherson, rode between his divisions, but encountered a Confederate company whose commander ordered him to surrender. After raising his hat politely, McPherson attempted to escape by turning and riding swiftly away, but he was struck by a single bullet, which wounded him mortally. Seen here, the scene of the killing of the greatly admired combat commander was later photographed.*

LEFT: *Grant's close friend General William T. Sherman was assigned the critical task of leading half of the Union army—all of Grant's western forces—against the Confederate army under General Joseph Johnston. Sherman later said, "Grant stood by me when I was crazy and I stood by him when he was drunk; now we stand by each other, always." Sherman had a great challenge in front of him—attacking into the Confederate heartland with each mile being contested by the South's best defensive general.*

BELOW: *Atlanta's defenses included a twelve-mile (19.2km) ring of formidable fortifications that had been built up nearly a year before Sherman's arrival. Forts, trenches, and rifle pits were protected by sandbagged redoubts, which were in turn effectively shielded by rows of "chevaux-de-frise" (barriers of sharpened stakes affixed to long logs, visible in this photograph). Although considered nearly impregnable, Atlanta finally fell to Sherman's army, which had successfully repulsed Hood's attacks and compromised the rail lines to the south that brought supplies into the city.*

BELOW: *A huge column of Union troops began to march into Atlanta on September 2, 1864. The most important city in the Confederate west was soon in ruins as materials that might be useful to the southern army were destroyed. This photograph—showing the remains of Atlanta's railroad round-house, locomotives, and rolling stock—demonstrates the thoroughness of the destruction.*

defend Tennessee in case Hood moved north. Meanwhile, Sherman, with the main body of the army, broke free from his lines of communications—just as Grant had done at the onset of the Vicksburg campaign—to live off of the Georgia countryside while destroying all property in his path. His plan was simple: capture ports, where he could replenish his army's supplies from the Union navy, while swinging northward through South Carolina and North Carolina and coming up in the rear of Lee's army in Virginia.

Sherman broke away from his lines of communication on November 12, and like Sheridan in the Shenandoah Valley, began burning and destroying what the Union forces were unable to use to support themselves. In this fashion, his army managed to move across Georgia over a sixty-mile (96km) front until it concentrated at Savannah on December 10. The Confederate defenders evacuated the city on December 21, and Sherman gave it to the Union as a Christmas present. His men then collected supplies delivered by ship before turning north to go after Lee.

The Army of Tennessee under John B. Hood would soon be back in action. He had been forced out of Atlanta, but the aggressive commander was expected to remain in action until his entire force was eliminated. Sherman had detached two of his corps under General John Schofield to block any northward movement by Hood toward the Union base at Nashville. Pushing North, Hood nearly trapped Schofield at Spring Hill, Tennessee, on

November 29, but Schofield escaped the trap by making a dramatic night march.

Hood, however, was able to catch up with Schofield the following day at Franklin, Tennessee. Schofield was strongly entrenched, but Hood ordered his eighteen thousand soldiers to attack in a furious charge that recalled that of Pickett at Gettysburg. When the day was over, Hood had lost more than six thousand men and thirteen generals. The battle of Franklin accomplished little except the loss of many southern lives. The victorious Schofield was able to move his men to the defenses at Nashville to await another attack by Hood, who followed. But there was little Hood could do other than observe the actions of one of Schofield's commanders, George Thomas, the hero from the battle of Chickamauga.

On December 15, Thomas struck Hood and successfully held Hood's right flank in place as fast-moving Union troops enveloped the Confederate left. Hood's lines failed to hold and the Confederates were forced to withdraw two miles (3.2km) to new defensive positions. On the following day, December 16, Thomas repeated his maneuvers of the previous day, and swept the field. The once-proud Army of Tennessee disintegrated, retreating to Tupelo, Mississippi, and were saved from the pursuing Union cavalrymen by rear-guard actions by General Nathan Bedford Forrest. Hood's army ceased to exist as a fighting force after the battle of Nashville.

BELOW: *Union tents fill the background of this photograph of a Confederate gun position. Taken after the capture of Atlanta, this photograph illustrates the efforts made by Confederate engineers to strengthen their defenses against Sherman's attackers. This twelve-pounder cannon is aimed through an opening in the defenses that have been reinforced with filled sandbags to protect the gunners from Federal counterbattery fire. These strong defenses, manned by resolute defenders, would have been very difficult to overcome. Sherman was able to occupy Atlanta in early September 1864, after Hood had dissipated the strength of his army in two large but futile attacks on Sherman's army.*

ABOVE: *Railroads that carried critical supplies throughout the Confederacy were relentlessly destroyed by Union wrecking crews. Ingenious tools and methods for rapid destruction of railways were developed. For instance, saboteurs would lift the rails from the wooden ties, heat the rails to soften them, and twist the heated rails around trees. The twisted rails were called "Sherman neckties" by Union troops. Here a wrecking crew is seen destroying a railroad switch, a critical piece of equipment that was hard to replace in the war-ravaged Confederacy.*

LEFT: *As Grant prepared to move against Lee in the eastern theater of war, Sherman prepared to move against General Joseph Johnston's Confederate army defending the approaches to Atlanta. Several of Sherman's officers assigned to the Army of the Cumberland posed for this photograph, including (seated in the foreground, left to right) General Jefferson C. Davis (far left, no relation to the Confederate president), John Brannan, Richard W. Johnson (at the table), and William D. Whipple.*

CHAPTER FIVE

The Civil War in 1865

It was at this point in the Civil War that Grant was able to demonstrate his ability as a master tactician. His plans were simple and commonsense: Meade's Army of the Potomac would continue to press Lee along the Petersburg line while Sherman would continue his invasion of the Carolinas until he managed to link up with Meade and Grant in southern Virginia. At the same time, they would bring additional troops from central Tennessee, where they were no longer needed.

Within days, Schofield left Nashville and was moving by rail, riverboat, and ship to the eastern theater. The decision by Grant to rely on supplies delivered by Union navy ships along the Chesapeake Bay was to prove very useful at this stage of the war. Having a developed, centralized delivery system—complete with its own railroad—made it possible to feed and clothe the large army assembling in Lee's front yard.

In February 1865 Sherman captured Wilmington, North Carolina, the last port of the Confederacy, while Joseph Johnston, recently returned to command, tried unsuccessfully to halt him. Union forces were concentrating in the east—the end was near for Lee and the Confederacy.

Meanwhile, Early's forces had been eliminated at Waynesboro by Sheridan, who swiftly moved his large, experienced cavalry force and the entire VI Corps to unite with Grant in the lines at Petersburg. Sheridan's arrival gave Grant and Meade numerical superiority: 101,000 infantry, fourteen thousand cavalry, and nine thousand artillery compared to Lee's forty-six thousand infantry, six thousand cavalry, and five thousand artillery. There was little that Lee could do in the face of these odds, but he continued to fight on as long as the least glimmer of hope remained.

The key to victory against the South, at least so far as Lee's Army of Northern Virginia was concerned, was Petersburg. With four vital rail lines connecting the Confederate capital of Richmond and its industrial resources (the Tredegar Arms Works especially) with the armies in the south, Petersburg was a critical transportation hub. This heavily protected city was literally the Confederate lifeline and Grant knew it.

Although Grant had suffered terribly at Cold Harbor and despite the fact that the fighting in the Wilderness had been slow and costly in lives lost, the forward momentum of the Federal forces was inexorable. Grant understood that there was really no way the South could turn back the numbers he was able to muster. Finally backing Lee into Petersburg, Grant settled into a long and exhausting siege that eventually drove Lee out in search of food for his starving, ill-clad troops. Simultaneously with the abandonment of Petersburg, Lee ordered the forces at Richmond (located twenty-three miles [37km] to the south) to give up the city and destroy any matériel that might be of use to the Federals. This abandonment of the Confederate capital clearly signaled the imminence of defeat.

Meanwhile, on the off-chance that they might hook up with Joseph Johnston's force, the desperate Army of Northern Virginia headed in a westerly direction. But Grant was not about to let victory slip through his fingers, and pursued Lee at every step, effectively preventing the southern general from joining Johnston or prolonging the Confederate cause by reequipping and feeding his beleaguered army. Lee surrendered to Grant on April 9, 1865, a week after being driven from Petersburg.

PAGE 146: *Sheridan's cavalry struck hard at George Picketts' Confederates, who were entrenched at Five Forks on April 1, 1865. The swiftness of the Federal cavalry attack provided the Confederates no time to shift their artillery into more advantageous firing positions. Shortly after the attack was ordered, General George A. Custer's men were able to gain the rear of the Confederate positions. Unfortunately for the Confederates, Pickett and his senior commanders were away from their posts as the Union attack developed—instead of tending to their duties, they were enjoying a shad-bake at Rosser's headquarters at nearby Hatcher's Run.*

RIGHT: *Wilmer McLean had previously resided in northern Virginia, near the small town of Manassas. In July 1861 he was able to get a close view of the battle of Bull Run as it was fought across his farm. His house being used as a Confederate headquarters, his kitchen was struck by a cannonball. He moved his family to a safer area in March 1862, to the small community of Appomattox Court House. On April 9, 1865, his home was once again caught up in a Civil War drama. It became the scene of the meeting between Robert E. Lee and Ulysses S. Grant that brought an end to the Civil War.*

Five Forks

On March 29, 1865, Grant began his move against Lee. The cavalry, under Sheridan, rode out to the intersection of the Southside and Danville railroads, the source of most of the supplies for the Army of Northern Virginia. At the same time, Grant sent troops to turn Lee's right flank. General A.P. Hill struck hard at Grant's left flank and pushed them back near White Oak Road, but Union counterattacks on March 31 pressed Hill and his men back into their former positions.

On April 1, Sheridan moved forward to Five Forks, a strategic road junction located southwest of Petersburg. Here, General George Pickett attacked, driving Sheridan and the cavalry to Dinwiddie Court House.

At this point, Pickett made a serious error. Instead of pulling back to his original position and establishing contact with A.P. Hill's corps, he remained in place and left a gap in the Confederate defensive line. It was only the slowness of General Gouverneur Warren to respond to Sheridan's orders to attack Pickett's exposed rear that saved the Confederate commander from destruction. The next day, Sheridan struck at Pickett as Grant ordered a renewal of the attack against Lee's right. As a result, the Confederate line cracked. Lee withdrew from the Petersburg defenses and gave the orders to abandon Richmond as well. The beleaguered Confederate commander led the struggling Army of Northern Virginia westward in an attempt to escape the Union pursuers.

Lee had little to gain in prolonging the war at this point, but he pushed west in an attempt to reach Lynchburg or Danville and reunite with Johnston before moving into North Carolina. The retreat from Richmond was a moving battle that progressed slowly from April 2 to April 7. The end was near for the proud army: Ewell's entire corps was cut off and captured at the fighting at Sayler's Creek. Sheridan raced his cavalry to get into position in front of what little remained of Lee's retreating army.

Appomattox

Once the Union cavalry reached Appomattox Court House, Lee knew that the escape route of his army had been blocked and that the only sensible option remaining was to surrender. Lee met

ABOVE: *Appomattox Court House was the location of Lee's surrender to Grant. This pen and ink sketch map was drawn to show the place of Lee's surrender. Annotations include "house at which Gen'l Lee received Gen'l Sheridan afterwards Grant, —when agreement was signed," and "Appomattox C.H.", "Custar's (3rd) Cav. Div.," "Reserve cavalry brigade in advance on extreme right," "Lee's army massed," and "wagons retiring." This anonymous map was sent to the Library of Congress in an envelope marked: "Map of Lee's surrender. Found in one of the back closets of one of the old Scrimshaw Pavement Co.'s desks, 16 Court St. Fged."*

LEFT: *The Confederate defenders of Petersburg built row after row of log-walled trenches to shield themelves from Grant's bombardments and attacks. Within the relative safety of the trenches, Confederate soldiers were in excellent defensive positions from which they could repulse attacks by numerically superior Union troops. After the lesson Grant had learned at Cold Harbor, he relied on the use of a siege—much like the one he had coordinated at Vicksburg—and of heavy artillery, in particular mortars firing huge shells high into the air so their trajectory would carry them downward onto the Confederate defenders.*

RIGHT: *The Union mortar "Dictator" was used during the siege operations at Petersburg. The weapon weighed more than 17,000 pounds (7,700kg), so heavy that it had to be transported on a specially reinforced railroad car. Its shell weighed two hundred pounds (91kg) and contained twenty pounds (9kg) of gun powder. It could reach two and a half miles (4km) from the point it was fired and blow a deep crater into the fortifications where the huge shell exploded.*

LEFT: *Union mortars, firing a shell thirteen inches (33cm) in diameter, were so heavy that they had to be transported into firing positions by locomotives. The two-hundred-pound (91kg) shells were fired high into the air, arcing back into the Confederate defensive works, where their explosions produced large numbers of casualties and widespread destruction. These mortars were terrible weapons against which the Confederates had few, if any, real defenses. When the defenders came under fire from their devastating shells, they could only dig deeper into the earth and strengthen the roofs of their "bomb-proofs."*

BELOW: *With the Civil War drawing to a close, Union troops continued to attack Confederate defenders at Petersburg, Virginia, ultimately laying siege to the town. The siege sapped Lee's Army of Northern Virginia of its remaining strength. Once a breakthrough had developed to the west of the strategic town, Lee was forced to evacuate his defensive positions. Union troops entered Petersburg on April 3, 1865, and continued to press Lee's battered army westward toward Appomattox. This map sketch, prepared by the Engineer Office, 10th Army Corps, shows the northern approach to Petersburg and two of the vital railroad lines that passed through the town.*

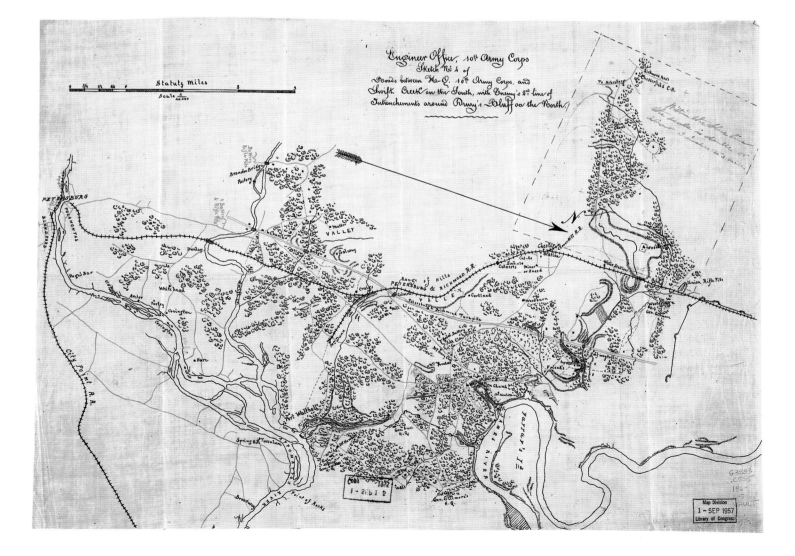

BELOW: *The Tredegar Arms Works were purchased by Joseph R. Anderson in 1848, and by 1861 it was one of the largest iron-manufacturing facilities in the entire country. During the Civil War, it provided the Confederacy with cannon, gun carriages, munitions, and armor plates for its ironclad vessels. Anderson kept the Tredegar Battalion in Richmond to protect the factory from looters as the city was captured by the Union army.*

ABOVE: *Though Joseph R. Anderson graduated fourth in his West Point class in 1836, he remained in the army for only fifteen months. Once the Civil War began, he volunteered for a field command and fought in the Seven Days' battles near Richmond until he was struck in the head by a spent ball. His resignation was accepted soon afterward, and he returned immediately to manage his factory, the Tredegar Arms Works.*

LEFT: *The Virginia State House, located in the top center of this photograph taken across the broad James River, survived the burning of Richmond with only minor damage. The nearby business center of the Confederate capital, however, was nearly destroyed by the fires that consumed much of the city.*

BELOW: *During the night of April 2, 1865, the Confederate government evacuated Richmond, heading for Danville, Virginia, where they hoped to be able to set up a new seat of government. Orders were given to set fire to Richmond's warehouses to keep their contents from falling into the hands of the Union army. Soon magazines filled with munitions were exploding to spread their burning contents throughout the former Confederate capital.*

BACKGROUND: *Union soldiers moving in to occupy Richmond beheld a surreal scene. As the government evacuated, looters and mobs had caused a great deal of destruction, and the unchecked fires had consumed large sections of the city. There were too few policemen to control the unruly mobs and firefighters were hopelessly unprepared to fight the extensive fires burning freely throughout Richmond. Little help was available from the Union army—many of its soldiers felt a purification by fire was the fitting destiny for the rebellious city that had been the capital of the Confederacy.*

BELOW: *After one of Sheridan's scouts, disguised in a Confederate uniform, led Lee's supply trains to be captured by Custer, Sheridan pushed his men toward Appomattox to block Lee's route to Lynchburg. Confederate John B. Gordon, with the assistance of Lee's cavalry, attacked Sheridan's positions on April 8, but Union reinforcements compelled Lee to withdraw to Appomattox. Simultaneously, Longstreet, commanding Lee's rear guard, turned suddenly to engage the pursuers at New Hope Church. These positions were held until the surrender on the following day, April 9, 1865.*

with Grant, who accepted his surrender on April 9, 1865. The Union commander was generous in victory: the 28,356 paroled Confederates were permitted to retain horses or mules, officers were allowed to keep their personal sidearms, and rations were provided for the prisoners. Additionally, Grant would not allow any of the victorious soldiers in the Army of the Potomac to cheer or fire salutes to celebrate the victory.

General Joseph Johnston surrendered to Sherman in North Carolina on April 26 and General Kirby Smith surrendered the last Confederate force west of the Mississippi on May 26, 1865. The long Civil War was over at last.

Epilogue

It was not to be a peaceful return to unification. Five days after Grant accepted Lee's surrender, President Lincoln—able to relax for the first time in four years—went to Ford's Theater in

Washington with his wife and two friends on April 14, 1865. During the performance, he was shot in the back of his head by a bullet fired from a small derringer wielded by an actor and southern sympathizer, John Wilkes Booth. Abraham Lincoln joined approximately 600,000 other Americans who died in the Civil War, to date the most costly war (in terms of lives lost) in the history of the United States.

The Civil War loomed large in American history for a long time. The Government paid veterans and cared for the many widows and orphans beginning soon after the war was over and continuing for the lifetime of the veterans. While the Civil War ended in 1865, the United States Congress passed special legislation as late as 1958—nearly at the centennial of the beginning of the war—permitting surviving Confederate soldiers and more than five hundred Southern widows to draw Federal pensions. To this day, the Civil War and the many batttlefields on which it was fought influence the lives of Americans—because of the effects that it had, and its great cost, and because of the tumultuous events that led to it.

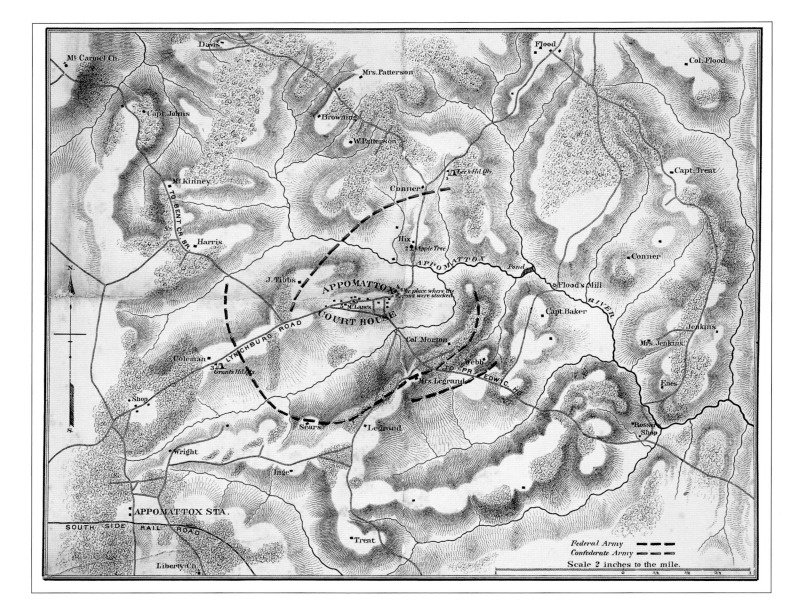

LEFT: *A complete study in contrasts met in Wilmer McLean's parlor on April 9, 1865. Lee wore his best uniform, was tall and dignified, and looked every inch the aristocratic officer under any set of circumstances. Grant, on the other hand, wore an ordinary uniform coat, spattered with mud, and had a pair of field glasses slung across his shoulder instead of his officer's sword. Yet he matched chivalry with chivalry, allowing Confederate officers to retain their personal weapons, horses, and baggage. On Lee's request, Grant permitted individual soldiers to retain the horses they owned. Unlike the Union army, the Confederates brought their personal horses with them into the army. Lee summed the terms up by saying, "This will have the best possible effect on the men."*

ABOVE: *Soon after the end of the war the Union army conducted an enormous victory parade in Washington, D.C. The "Grand Review" was intended to symbolize the end of the terrible Civil War. Two separate armies were present at the event, the eastern army responsible for the defeat of Lee and the western army under Sherman, which had recently devastated the deep South. The rivalry between the two armies required two separate parades, on May 23 and 24. The "East" marched first.*

Bibliography

Barnard, George N. *Photographic Views of Sherman's Campaign*. New York: Dover Publications, 1977.

Beyer, W.F., and O.F. Keydel, eds. *Deeds of Valor*, 2 vols. Detroit: The Perrin-Keydel Company, 1906.

Bradford, Ned, ed. *Battles and Leaders of the Civil War*. New York: Meridian, 1989.

Catton, Bruce. *American Heritage New History of the Civil War*. New York: Viking, 1996.

Cowles, Capt. Calvin D., et al. *Official Military Atlas of the Civil War*. New York: Fairfax Press, 1983.

Dowdney, Clifford. *The Wartime Papers of Robert E. Lee*. New York: De Capo Press, 1961.

Gardner, Alexander. *Gardner's Photographic Sketch Book of the Civil War*. New York: Dover Publications, 1959.

Gordon, John B. *Reminiscences of the Civil War*. New York: Charles Scribner's Sons, 1903.

Guensey, Alfred H., and Henry M. Alden. *Harper's Pictorial History of the Great Rebellion*. Chicago: McDonnell Brothers, 1866.

La Bree, Ben, ed. *The Confederatre Soldier in the Civil War*. Paterson, N.J.: Rae Publishing Company, 1959.

Leslie, Frank. *Leslie's Illustrated Civil War*. Introduction by John Stanchak. Jackson, Miss.: University Press of Mississippi, 1992.

Macdonald, John. *Great Battles of the Civil War*. New York: Macmillian, 1992.

McDonald, Archie P. *Make Me a Map of the Valley*. Dallas: Southern Methodist University Press, 1973.

McPherson, James M. *Battle Cry of Freedom: The Civil War Era*. New York: Oxford University Press, 1988.

Miller, William J. *Mapping for Stonewall: The Civil War Service of Jed Hotchkiss*. Washington, D.C.: Elliott & Clark Publishing, 1993.

Phillips, David. *Crucial Land Battles*. New York: MetroBooks, 1996.

——. *Daring Raiders*. New York: MetroBooks, 1998.

Roper, Peter W. *Jedediah Hotchkiss: Rebel Mapmaker and Virginia Businessman*. Shippenburg, Pa.: White Mane Publishing, 1992.

Sheridan, Philip H. *Personal Memoirs of P.H. Sheridan*. New York: Charles L. Webster & Company, 1888.

Starr, Stephen Z. *The Union Cavalry in the Civil War*. Baton Rouge, La.: Louisiana State University Press, 1981.

Stephenson, Richard W., ed. *Civil War Maps: An Annotated List of Maps and Atlases in the Library of Congress*. Washington, D.C.: Library of Congress, 1989.

Taylor, James E. *The James E. Taylor Sketchbook: With Sheridan in the Shenandoah Valley in 1864*. Dayton: Morningside House, 1989.

Troiani, Don, and Brian C. Pohanka. *Don Troiani's Civil War*. Mechanicsburg, Pa.: Stackpole Books, 1995.

U.S. War Department. *The War of the Rebellion*. Official Records of the Union and Confederate Armies, 128 vols. Washington, D.C.: U.S. Government Printing Office, 1890–1901.

Various. *The Battle Atlas of the Civil War*. New York: Barnes & Noble Books, 1996. (Originally published under the title *Echoes of Glory* by Time-Life Books, 1991.)

Weigley, Russell F. *The American Way of War*. Bloomington, Ind.: Indiana State University Press, 1973.

Wideman, John C. *Naval Warfare: Courage and Combat on the Water*, from Civil War Chronicles. New York: MetroBooks, 1997.

Wiley, Bell Irvin. *They Who Fought Here*. New York: Bonanza Books, 1959.

Photography Credits

Index